ANCIENT ROME

ANCIENT ROME

City planning and administration

O. F. Robinson

London and New York

First published in 1992 by Routledge
First published in paperback in 1994
by Routledge
11 New Fetter Lane, London EC4P 4EE
Simultaneously published in the USA and Canada
by Routledge
29 West 35th Street, New York, NY 10001

© 1992, 1994 O. F. Robinson

Typeset in 10/12 Garamond by
Falcon Typographic Art Ltd., Edinburgh
Printed in Great Britain by
T J Press (Padstow) Ltd, Padstow, Cornwall

British Library Cataloguing in Publication Data
Robinson, O. F. (Olivia F.)
Ancient Rome: city planning and administration. – New edn
I. Title
307.12609376

Library of Congress Cataloging in Publication Data
Robinson, O. F.
Ancient Rome: city planning and administration/
O. F. Robinson.
p. cm.
Includes bibliographical references and index.
1. City planning – Rome. 2. Municipal government – Rome.
3. Municipal corporations (Roman law) I. Title.
HT169.R7R63 1992
307.1'26'09376 – dc20 91–16820
ISBN 0–415–10618–4

CONTENTS

PREFACE

This book has its origins in a simple question from my husband in 1974. He was then secretary of the Scottish Office Working Party on Civic Government (which led eventually to the Civic Government (Scotland) Act, 1982), and he came home one evening with some point which had been under discussion (I cannot now remember what) and asked how they had managed in Rome. Not knowing, I said I would look it up; to my amazement I was not able to do so. For some years I continued to think that there must somewhere be a book by a learned nineteenth-century German; but if there was, he never published it, daunted perhaps by the difficulties. I was and am daunted, but still feel that the task is worth attempting. Unlike central government, local government impinges on people, particularly city-dwellers, every day of their lives.

Because the book has been so long in gestation, I confess that I cannot remember everyone who has kindly criticised or commented on my ideas, made suggestions, enlightened my ignorance, shown me where to find out more. But I am grateful, especially to all those who have been my patient audience at the presentation of my many papers on the theme over the years, frequently at congresses of the Société Internationale pour l'Histoire des Droits de l'Antiquité. More particularly I should like to thank – alphabetically – Professor John Crook, Professor Bruce Frier, Professor Bill Gordon, Mr Paul Jeffreys-Powell, Dr Lawrence Keppie, Mr Andrew Lewis, Dr John Patterson, Dr Nicholas Purcell, Professor Michael Rainer, Professor Geoffrey Rickman, Dr Alan Rodger, Professor Simshäuser, Dr Boudewijn Sirks, Professor Roberto Viganò, and Professor Alan Watson, for the discussions I have had with them, and their comments on my work.

For their hospitality in allowing me to work in their institutes (sometimes on several occasions), as well as their comments, I want to thank Professor Henryk Kupiszewski and the others in the Institute of the History of Law at Warsaw University (and Warsaw and Glasgow Universities for arranging my visit), Professor Georg Wolf and the University of Freiburg, Professor Andreas Wacke at Cologne, Dr Flury and the Thesaurus Linguae Latinae, Professor Theo Mayer-Maly and his colleagues at Salzburg, Professor Diego Manfredini at Ferrara, and Professor Giuliano Crifò and the University of Perugia. The University of Glasgow gave me sabbatical leave in 1982; Professor Dieter Nörr gave me almost a second home at the Leopold-Wenger-Institut in Munich, where I spent three months supported by a grant from Deutscher Akademische Austauschdienst. A British Academy Small Grant then assisted me to spend three months in Rome at the Institute of Roman Law, thanks to the kindness of Professors Pugliese and Mario Talamanca; while there I also had the privilege of working in the American Academy. I hope they all know how grateful I am.

My deepest thanks, however, must go to Sebastian, who has read my drafts, corrected my Latin, improved my English, and cooked my dinners; to him I dedicate this book.

February 1991

INTRODUCTION

Limitations of space and time

Ancient Rome was a large city, even by modern standards; there was nowhere of comparable size in Europe until the Industrial Revolution. Its unique scale meant that a different level of organisation was needed, for example in the water supply, from that which would have been satisfactory in a smaller town. It meant that there could be closely-packed housing (for the majority) and yet urban sprawl. Life may have been uncomfortable – it was certainly short – for very many people, but it was tolerable for most; otherwise we would surely hear much more of riot and civil commotion. The law played a part in enabling people to live together, just as it did when cities began to re-emerge in the twelfth and thirteenth centuries.[1] So this book is a study of 'such provisions of the law as should govern the conduct of citizens living together . . . [and of] provisions regulating the behaviour of citizens towards each other (an area for which the Working Party has coined the term "good neighbourliness")'.[2]

My concern is with the law dealing with the local government of Rome: what ought to be done, and what arrangements were made and by whom so that these things should be done, to allow a population of perhaps a million, or even more, to live together.[3] (Admittedly, the City was a net consumer of people; high immigration was shakily balanced by a high death-rate, but how far the legal structures were successful is not central to the main theme.) I have therefore looked primarily at the areas of government rather than at the particular officials who carried out the governmental functions, and it is in this that my

1 Hyde (1973): 83.
2 Report of the Working Party on Civic Government, 1976, I.5.
3 On population, see ch. 1.

approach perhaps differs most from previous considerations of the City's legal functioning.[4]

This study of the administration of the City concentrates on the period from the last century BC through the third century AD. Until the late Republic it is not at all easy to distinguish between Rome, the city state (and nascent imperial power), and the City of Rome, and it is in the government of the City – a capital city, which poses its own problems – that I am interested. The granting of citizenship to all Italians south of the Po in 89 BC as a consequence of the Social War marks the point from which one can usefully look for a local government law applicable to the City.[5] This extension of the citizenship is what made possible the gradual municipalisation of the Roman magistracies. The Urban Prefect's acquisition under Constantine of general responsibility for nearly every aspect of running the City marks the end of this period of Rome's government[6]; the nature of developments in the third century, however, remains somewhat murky.

Rome was not only a huge city, she was a capital. The administration of a capital, more than of any other large town, is likely to be subject to intervention by central government,[7] both because of its very presence and because the capital is a show-case for the country, the likely centre of tourism, and (in most cases) the hub of business activity. A capital, too, is likely to require more effort to be spent on the maintenance of law and order, since it attracts the hopeful and the hopeless, the ambitious and the frustrated, the rich and those who live off them. So areas such as long-term planning and the provision of shows and spectacles were undertaken largely by the emperors. Nevertheless, they can be counted as local government, since they are related specifically to Rome, distinct from general imperial administration or the emperor's relations with provincial cities.

What are the problems of running a city, any city? First, there is the form of government, typically the election, or

4 Kühn (1864–5), though he uses civic *munera* as a framework, which is closer to my idea; Mommsen (1887) II: 1032–73; Hirschfeld (1905), who sees the administration from the imperial perspective; de Martino (1972–5), who never really considers the City as an entity.
5 A point made long ago by Hardy (1912): 137–8 and 140.
6 Chastagnol (1960).
7 Homo (1971): 127.

appointment, of a council or of a city manager. This is primarily a constitutional question, and we are concerned with administration. In Rome the composition of the Senate and the conduct of its business had been established well before the first century BC. But the creation of senatorial commissions – *curatelae* – in the early Principate was aimed at increased efficiency, moving towards professionalism. The Urban Prefect could, in due course, reasonably be described as a city manager.

An essential for running a city is knowing what the needs of the citizens are and are going to be, 'planning' in the broad sense. Linked with this are such matters as zoning and regulations on building and demolition.[8] Public buildings need supervision; there was in Rome a commission for this purpose – *cura aedium sacrarum et operum publicorum*. Traffic control and the maintenance of unobstructed roads and footpaths are also necessary.[9] Precautions against floods and the control of navigation are normally a responsibility of the authorities in a riparian city,[10] hence the *cura riparum et alvei Tiberis*.

The provision of a water supply – *cura aquarum* – and ensuring the provision of a food supply are necessary for urban living. Water, in particular, is closely linked with the promotion of public health and hygiene.[11] Licensing, i.e. controlling, services available to the public, is another field of civic administration; such services at Rome included markets,[12] places of refreshment and also trades and professions of various sorts.[13] Recreation and leisure make another area of public concern.[14] Precautions against fire – the *vigiles* – and any other likely disaster,[15] together with forces to preserve law and order, are also normally a responsibility of local government.[16]

---

8 Cf. Civic Government (Scotland) Act 1982 s.12 on buildings, s.15 on rights of way.
9 Cf. Civic Government (S) Act s.14: no litter or obstruction: storage of offensive substances: cleansing and rubbish removal.
10 Cf. Civic Government (S) Act s.16 on the seashore.
11 Cf. Civic Government (S) Act s.11 on baths and laundries; s.13 on sewers and drains; s.14 on public health and sanitation.
12 Cf. Civic Government (S) Act s.5 on markets.
13 Cf. Civic Government (S) Act s.2 on licensing.
14 Cf. Civic Government (S) Act s.10 on recreation and leisure.
15 Cf. Civic Government (S) Act s.9 on safety precautions against fire.
16 In the Civic Government (S) Act sections 3, 4 and 7 are on criminal offences, miscellaneous offences and public processions – matters of petty crime or disorderliness.

The provision of housing, or of public transport, was not something that the Romans understood as a public responsibility,[17] and education only came to be seen, and that in a limited way, as a matter of public provision towards the end of our period. Nevertheless, it is clear that, particularly at a time when the role of local government is being radically challenged, there may be something to be learned from another society's efforts to cope with comparable needs.

17 Nor were there equivalents to the Civic Government (S) Act s.6 on lost and found property, or s.8 on lighting (the absence of which will be considered under Streets).

1

THE PHYSICAL CITY

The city founded by Romulus lay conveniently on a permanently navigable river, not too far from the sea – some 24 kilometres in a direct line, more than 30 by water – and was easily fortified. In addition the site was well supplied with springs, and healthy because of the hill-top breezes. The founder might almost have had foreknowledge of the city's destiny, says Cicero.[1]

THE CITY'S BOUNDARIES

The City was properly the area within the *pomerium*. This was created when a furrow was solemnly ploughed round the site of a city, of which the earth made a wall – *murus* – on the inner side; within this was the *post-murum*, marked out with stones. It set limits for the taking of the auspices for the city.[2] Though the *pomerium* remained the limit of the City for religious functions, it had ceased to be so for administrative purposes even before the first century BC, when Sulla is said to have enlarged it.[3] His *pomerium* seems to have coincided with the Servian Wall (traditionally the city wall of the regal period, though what survives dates largely from the fourth century, after the Gallic sack; it was restored in 87 BC), except that the Aventine was excluded. It was further extended by Julius Caesar,[4] Claudius,[5] Vespasian,[6] and Aurelian.[7] (It seems reasonably certain that

1 Cicero *de re p.* 2.5.10–6.11.
2 Varro *LL* 5.143.
3 Seneca *de brev. vitae* 13.8; Gellius 13.14.
4 Gellius 13.14; Dio 43.50. This extension is probable, but not certain.
5 Tac. *Annals* 12.23–4; ILS 213 (= CIL VI 1231).
6 FIRA i 15 (p.154ff), *lex quae dicitur de imperio Vespasiani*, vv. 14–16; ILS 248 (= CIL VI 1232).
7 SHA *Aurelian* 21.9–11, which also says that so did Nero and Trajan; but, apart from this statement, there is no evidence. No *cippi* (marker stones)

Augustus did not extend it;[8] as Mommsen pointed out, he got what he wanted, and more flexibly, through the establishment of the Fourteen Regions.[9])

Claudius' motives may well have been partially fiscal;[10] if the *portoria*, the duties levied at the gates,[11] were charged at the *pomerium*, then to include the Emporium and Monte Testaccio areas and also the land between the via Flaminia and the Tiber within the official City boundary would bring in all the most commercially active districts; the Aventine proper and the Pincian were of less commercial importance but, being well-populated, they were better in than out. Claudius may well have had also a legal and antiquarian interest in bringing about a greater coincidence between the *pomerium* and the XIV regions (or indeed the built-up area) since technically so many matters of religion and of jurisdiction were confined to the City. Surviving *cippi* (marker stones) give some indication of the limits to which Claudius and Vespasian extended it, and Hadrian seems to have restored their work.[12] The *pomerium* probably never extended across the Tiber, and there remains uncertainty about the western side in general.[13] The Aurelian Wall was probably built simply to the demands of defensive tactics;[14] the built-up area of the City at the end of the Republic seems already to have stretched considerably beyond its future line, as much as 5 or even 10 kilometres from the city centre.[15] The wall seems to lie on the approximate line of Commodus' customs frontier for the City, which itself perhaps originated in Vespasian's censorship and extension of the *pomerium*[16] (also marked by *cippi*[17]).

have been found, but if Aurelian did extend it, his wall presumably marked the line.

8 Despite Tac. *Annals* 12.23 and Dio 55.6, who may both have been confused by the establishment of the XIV *regiones*. Seneca (*de brev. vitae* 13.8) was closer to the time than they and he made no mention of an extension and, surely conclusively, there is no reference to any such enlargement in the *Res Gestae*. See also Labrousse (1937).

9 See 'The divisions of the City', later in this chapter; Mommsen (1887): II, 1072–3.

10 Labrousse (1937).

11 de Laet (1949); Palmer (1980).

12 ILS 311 (= CIL VI 1233).

13 Platner and Ashby (1929): 392–6.

14 Richmond (1930): 8–9.

15 Quilici (1974): 428; he almost calls it a conurbation, ibid.: 436.

16 Pliny *NH* 3.5.66.

17 ILS 375 (= CIL VI 1016); VI 8594.

Defining the City and its boundaries was also necessary for legal purposes. A procurator was held to act for one who was present in Rome if his principal was in the gardens,[18] in the forum, in the city or in the built-up area.[19] When there was a legacy of 'the victuals which are at Rome', it was questioned whether this meant what was within the built-up area or only what was within the wall; while the boundary of most cities was their wall, at Rome it was the built-up area, and it was this which defined the City of Rome.[20] We find Gaius explaining that 'statutory courts are defined as being in the City of Rome or within one mile of the City'.[21] Here, 'in the City' might mean within the *pomerium* or the walls, and the mile must surely have been somewhat elastic since the built-up area is not static;[22] one may compare the definition of the jurisdiction of the Urban Prefect as exercisable within a hundred Roman miles.[23] The *mille passus* – or thousand yard – doctrine was certainly familiar to Gaius, but as early as the so-called *lex Julia municipalis* of Julius Caesar's time there are several such references.[24] The jurists, however, did not refer to the *pomerium*, and seem generally to have been concerned to minimise any anomalies: 'As Alfenus says, "the city" is Rome girdled with a wall' – one must remember that when the jurists were writing

18 Market gardens, which lay around Rome to supply her with foodstuffs, or pleasure gardens such as those which Julius Caesar left to the people – Dio 44.35 – or those which in the Empire covered the Esquiline. See further ch. 8.

19 D.3.3.5–6, Ulpian 7 *ad ed* and Paul 6 *ad ed*: 'qui in hortis est' and 'qui in foro et qui in urbe et in continentibus aedificiis'.

20 D.33.9.4.4, Paul 4 *ad Sab*: Si ita legetur 'penum quae Romae sit' utrum quae est intra continentia legata videtur an vero ea sola quae est intra murum? et quidem urbes fere omnes muro terminus finiri, Romam continentibus et urbem Romam aeque continentibus.

21 G.4.104: quae in urbe Roma vel intra primum urbis Romae miliarum accipiuntur.

22 E.g. D.50.16.154, Macer 1 *ad legem vicens*: Mille passus non a miliario urbis sed a continentibus aedificiis numerandi sunt.

23 D.1.12.1.4, Ulpian *de off. p. u.*

24 FIRA i 13 (p.140ff), *tabula Heracleensis*, vv. 20, 26, 50, 64, 67, 68, 69, and 77. This inscription was held by von Premerstein (1922) to be a record of Julius Caesar's legislative programme passed, indiscriminately, by Mark Antony after the assassination. This view still seems likely for the sections dealing with the City of Rome; see Frederiksen (1965). The non-identity of the *lex Julia* and the *tabula Heracleensis* is maintained by de Martino (1954): 225ff and again in (1972–5): III, 352–5. Brunt (1971): 519ff deals primarily with the earlier part of the *tabula*, which does not seem to be Caesarian.

7

Rome's walls were still Servian – '"Rome" is also the built-up area . . . by everyday usage'.[25] Paul said much the same and so did Terentius Clemens.[26]

POPULATION

Probably some three-quarters of a million people lived within this area at the end of the Republic.[27] Attempts have been made to estimate the population by using the figures given for the number of recipients of the grain dole,[28] or the information on the number of houses and apartment blocks listed topographically in the Regionaries.[29] In general the arguments of Brunt[30] seem convincing. The City was probably at its largest in the mid-second century, and the likeliest rough figure for its population then, taking into account the alleged Augustan base, is a million plus. Although figures given in the Regionaries[31] are undoubtedly corrupt and frequently inflated, as is clear from the seating alleged for the Colosseum (and it is hard to believe the numbers of *horrea*, for example, listed for the Palatine), nevertheless archaeology reveals facilities for a numerous resident population, even allowing for many visitors. An article by

25 D.50.16.87, Marcellus 12 *dig*: Ut Alfenus ait, 'urbs' est Roma quae muro cingeretur, 'Roma' est etiam qua continentia aedificia essent . . . ex consuetudine cotidiana . . . .
26 D.50.16.2pr, Paul 1 *ad ed*: 'Urbis' appellatio muris, 'Romae' autem continentibus aedificiis finitur, quod latius patet. In a further sentence of the passage already cited, D.33.9.4.5, Paul included the gardens adjoining the City, even as Ulpian had done in D.3.3.5. D.50.16.147, Terentius Clemens 2 *ad leg. Iul. et Pap*: Qui in continentibus urbis nati sunt, 'Romae' nati intelleguntur.
27 Beloch (1886) is still fundamental for discussion of the evidence on which an estimate may be made; see also Maier (1953–4): 321ff, where he lists various totals that have been reached.
28 See further in ch. 10. Oates (1934) produces a figure of a million and a quarter under Augustus, rising a little during the first century, and then shrinking. Hopkins (1978): 96–8 prefers to remain just under the million.
29 Hermansen (1978a) does not even venture a figure.
30 Brunt (1971) ch. 21, 'The urban population of Rome in the Republic', pp. 376–88; he reckons (p.116) 'at least half a million citizens' at the end of the Republic.
31 The Regionaries are two lists, the *Curiosum* and the *Notitia*, which seem to be different versions of a document which was probably designed in the early fourth century as a guide for visitors to the City; they give a description of Rome by *regio* – see Hermansen (1978a). They are probably most accessible in Jordan (1871–1907): 539–74.

Hermansen ends with a citation from Ammianus,[32] for whom the expulsion of teachers from the City in 383 was recent; the actors and dancing girls, however, had remained to pacify the populace. 'A city which absorbs 3,000 foreign chorus girls has a considerable population.'[33] It is agreed by all that Rome shrank considerably in the third century and that the foundation of Constantinople as a rival capital – New Rome – will also have drawn off considerable numbers, so the population in the time of Constantine and his sons is likely to have been under the half million. (Modern Glasgow is a city of comparable size, which has been over the million and has now shrunk.)

THE DIVISIONS OF THE CITY

The City and its population were subdivided. In the Republic there were four *regiones* within the *pomerium*, Suburana, Esquilina, Collina and Palatina,[34] the original basis of the four urban tribes; the Capitoline seems to have been excluded from the organisation, rather like Washington, DC. Their significance may have been primarily religious,[35] but there also may have been an administrative function; at any rate in the so-called Caesarian *lex Julia municipalis*[36] the two curule and the two plebeian aediles are 'to arrange between themselves, either by agreement or by lot, in which part of the City each of them shall see to the repairing and paving of the public roads within the City of Rome and within one mile of the City of Rome, and shall have the special charge of such business'. But the four *regiones* did not long survive this law.

In 7 BC Augustus created a new administrative order within the City, dividing it into fourteen *regiones*;[37] this was presumably linked with his division of Italy into new administrative regions.[38] The outline boundaries of these *regiones* are fairly

32 Ammianus 14.6.19.
33 Hermansen (1978a): 168.
34 Varro *LL* 5.45f; DH 4.14.1. Pailler (1985) argues that from 212 or 196 BC there were five *regiones*, hence the *quinqueviri cis uls Tiberim*.
35 Palmer (1970): 84–97, discusses them briefly in relation to the archaic itinerary of the Argei.
36 FIRA i 13 (p.140ff), *tabula Heracleensis*, vv. 25–8, here tr. Hardy (1912); I use the name to refer to the City sections.
37 Suet. *Aug*.30; Dio 55.8. Their siting was aligned along the main roads out of Rome.
38 Pliny *NH* 3.5.46.

generally agreed[39] (but there is room for doubt and argument in some details); they were presumably extended outwards as the City grew. Their outer boundaries do not seem to have coincided with the *pomerium* or with the Aurelian Wall; they included both the Capitol and the Aventine, and Trastevere became the Fourteenth Region. (The problem is the more awkward because the seven ecclesiastical and the twelve to fourteen medieval regions, which do not themselves coincide, are also different from the imperial wards.[40]) Augustus' Regions were originally known only by their numbers, but the Regionaries give them names.[41]

Under Augustus the supervision of each Region was entrusted to a praetor, a tribune of the people or an aedile.[42] Under Hadrian at the latest, and possibly earlier, we find that the Republican magistrates have been replaced by *curatores*;[43] there seem to have been *procuratores* earlier.[44] Clearly there was an office staff.[45] Elagabalus is said[46] to have suggested the appointment of fourteen urban prefects – the allegation is that he wanted more drinking companions – and a modified version of this proposal seems to have been put into effect by Severus Alexander, who created fourteen consular *curatores* 'audire negotia' with the Urban Prefect.[47] The Regions were also the geographical base for the stationing of the *vigiles*, the firefighters. From their beginnings each of the seven cohorts of the *vigiles* had two Regions in its charge with, eventually, a *statio* in one and an *excubitorium* in the other.[48] This helps to explain why we find the *praefectus vigilum* concerned in the early third

39 Platner and Ashby (1929): 444–8.
40 Graffunder (1914): 486; Platner and Ashby (1929): 394, fig.4.
41 Implied in Pliny NH 3.5.66–7; Frontinus *aq*.79; Tac. *Annals* 15.40; Suet. *Dom*.1; and the *cippi*.
42 Dio 55.8; ILS 3616; 3619; 3772 (= CIL VI 453; 451; 760) – praetors; ILS 3617; 3618; 3620 (= VI 449; 450; 452) – tribunes.
43 ILS 6073 (= CIL VI 975); 1216 (= X 3752). ILS 4914 (= VI 826), of Domitian's time, has a praetor still in charge of a region.
44 ILS 9017 (= CIL VIII 18909).
45 ILS 1908; 1917 (= CIL VI 1869; 32299); VI 4022; 8685.
46 SHA *Elag*.20: Voluit et per singulas urbis regiones praefectos urbi facere, et fecisset si vixisset, promoturos omnes turpissimos et ultimae professionis homines. This is Mommsen's reading; the codex Palatinus gives us 'urbes lenones' for 'urbis regiones' (Loeb, p.146).
47 SHA *Sev. Alex*.33; ILS 1209 (= CIL XIV 2078). The Regionaries, however, list two curators for each region, so they seem to have been doubled later.
48 See ch. 7.

century with the restoration of an *aedicula* by the *magistri* of
a *vicus*,[49] the sub-division of a Region and itself an ancient
grouping. It is possible that the *praefectus vigilum* had had to
oversee the existing *curatores* because they lacked adequate
authority, and that the introduction of consular curators was
designed to speed the administration of justice and to free the
praefectus vigilum for more specialist duties. The *regiones* seem
to have persisted at least until the imperial became the papal
city. They are the frame for the picture of fourth- or late third-
century Rome given to the tourist in the Regionary Catalogues,
and since the organisation was used in Constantinople, and
was flourishing under Justinian,[50] it presumably represented
a convenient area to administer. We hear of a few specific
dealings by *regio*, other than those already mentioned; for
example, Severus Alexander is said to have provided both baths
and *horrea* on such a basis,[51] and there is nothing intrinsically
unlikely in this.

The Regions were sub-divided into *vici*.[52] The *vici* had a
long Republican history as the base of some sort of collegiate
organisation for the worship of the *lares compitales* – crossroad
deities – and the supervision of the *ludi compitales*.[53] They had
also on occasion proved administratively convenient, for we
hear of the distribution of oil or cheap corn *vicatim* by the
aediles,[54] and I suspect that this means more than just street
by street.[55] Under Augustus' reorganisation there were 265
vici,[56] each with 4 *vicomagistri*; later there were 48 *vicomagistri*
in each Region, irrespective of the number of *vici*. It is likely that
Augustus' reorganisation increased the number of *vicomagistri*

49 ILS 3621 (= CIL VI 30960). The Scholiast to Juvenal 14.305 – cited in Mayor
   (1881): 344 – also represents the *vigiles* as caring for the *vici*.
50 Nov. J. 43.1.1; *Notitia Urbis Constantinopolitanae*, in Seeck (1876).
51 SHA *Sev. Alex*.39.
52 Suet. *Aug*.30.
53 DH 4.14.3–4; Asconius *in Pison*. (K S 6–7), OCT p.7: solebant autem
   magistri collegiorum ludos facere sicut magistri vicorum faciebant,
   Compitalicios praetextati, qui ludi sublatis collegiis discussi sunt. Cf.
   ILS 5395 (Ostia); 6375 (= CIL IV 60) (Pompeii); Waltzing (1895–1900): I,
   98–111; Wissowa (1912): 171–2.
54 Livy 25.2.8; 30.26.5–6.
55 Suet. *Julius* 41: recensum populi nec more nec loco solito sed vicatim
   per dominos insularum egit atque ex 320,000 accipientium frumentum
   e publico ad 150,000 retraxit.
56 Pliny *NH* 3.5.66.

in enlarging their role.[57] There is one huge surviving inscription on the *basis Capitolina*[58] which dates from AD 136; it gives 262 names of *magistri*, showing that the majority were freedmen. They had *fasti*[59] and employed *servi publici*,[60] specifically the slaves who had previously been employed as a fire brigade.[61] Later their number seems to have been reduced from 1060 to 672, probably under Constantine.[62] Their religious duties continued to be important,[63] and indeed this may be the reason why Constantine cut down on their numbers and why they fade from sight in the Later Empire. *Vicomagistri* were not confined to Rome,[64] but in the provinces too their most important function was their religious one.

They also had administrative functions,[65] on a parochial scale. The existence of an organisation down to this humble level, with magistrates[66] elected from within the community, must have facilitated the dissemination of information or instruction in many spheres – and one can here also recall the existence of the *Acta Diurna*. They also may have provided a channel through which grievances over the state of the paving stones or unmoved rubbish, etc., could pass to the appropriate authorities. The relationship of the *vici* to the *pagi* is not clear, as in the inscription from the Esquiline[67] (probably concerned with the burial ground there) in which they are recorded as having power to proceed *per pignoris capionem* (the ritualised taking of a pledge) against those who dump rubbish or hold unauthorised cremations, under the general charge of the plebeian aediles. It seems likely that the *pagi* ceased to exist after the creation of the XIV Regions.

Perhaps it was from the predecessors of the Augustan *vico-*

---

57 ILS 6074 (= CIL VI 2222) lists *magistri* who do not seem to have existed before 6 BC.
58 ILS 6073 (= CIL VI 975).
59 ILS 3617; 3620 (= CIL VI 449; 452).
60 ILS 3219 (= CIL VI 35); 3610–12 (= V 3257; X 1582; VI 446–7).
61 Dio 55.8.
62 Bleicken (1958).
63 Festus 416L *Statae Matris*; ILS 3309 (= CIL VI 766); 5615 (= VI 282).
64 E.g. ILS 4818 – Metz, 5404 (= CIL IX 5052) – Picenum, 6661–4 (= XI 417; 421; 419; 379) – Rimini.
65 To be deduced from Festus 113L *Magisterare*.
66 Livy 34.7.2–3 refers to them as having the *toga praetexta* – at least when presiding over the *ludi compitalicii*.
67 Festus 502L (= 371M); ILS 6082 (= CIL VI 3823).

magistri that the *quinqueviri uls cis Tiberim*[68] were drawn. They seem to be at about the same social and effective level. The *vicomagistri* seem to have had a rather higher social status to start with; Livy's comment about the *toga praetextata* could surely not have applied to a predominantly libertine class, even though he does say: 'hic Romae infimo generi'. It seems possible also that their numbers increased, and their status was thereby lowered, in consequence of Augustus' creation of the Regions.

68 Horace *Sat*.2.5.55; Livy 39.14.10; Mommsen (1887): II, 611, suggests that there were one each for the four Republican regions and one for Trastevere. Pomponius (D. 1.2.2.31 and 33, *enchiridion*) must be wrong in thinking that they had any connection with a senatorial career.

2

PLANNING: THE OVERALL VIEW

Planning in the modern world is principally the science – or art – of looking into the future and seeing what needs must be met during the coming year, the coming five years, the coming twenty years. Using its estimate of these needs, an authority – a city or a region or a country – plans its future development, its distribution of resources, its use of land or buildings, in a word, its priorities. Subsidiary to this are the planning controls which the authority imposes on the individual. These are governed by the authority's view of its own development, but they are more concerned with matters that arise from the initiative of the private person than with public works. The Romans recognised both these aspects of planning. Nevertheless, the structure of their society and, for their own City, their awareness that they were restricted by the past, their site being determined by necessity rather than free choice,[1] meant that planning was a less important sphere of governmental activity for the Romans than for us.

THE CONCEPT OF PLANNING

There can be no possible doubt that the Romans were aware of the concept of the planned city. For intellectual guidance there was the authority of Aristotle, while archaeology reveals the carefully-planned siting and layout of late Republican colonies.[2] There were professional *agrimensores* or land surveyors[3] and, in the Empire at least, professional architects.[4] From the start, a

1 Strabo 5.3.7.
2 Aristotle *Politics* 7.11.1330. See also Owens (1989).
3 Dilke (1971).
4 Vitruvius himself, and Vitruvius 1.1.

new town was provided with adequate defences, with essential
public buildings such as temple and forum, with a water supply
– without which a town could not be considered habitable[5]
– and its concomitant system of drains, with paved streets,
and with magistrates having jurisdiction over these things.[6]
Vitruvius wrote that the architect must have an understanding of a healthy environment, including the water supply, be
familiar with the law on such servitudes as the right to eaves-
drip, drains and light, and also building contracts,[7] as well as
possessing a knowledge of music, astronomy, mathematics, and
philosophy.[8]

A city's construction could be divided into two parts, public
works and private building. There were three areas of public
provision – that is, provision for the public, even if by private
patronage: defence, religion, and amenity. Of these, amenity
included 'the arrangement of public areas for communal use,
such as docks, forums, porticoes, baths, theatres, pedestrian
precincts, and other places made public for similar reasons'.[9]
Vitruvius wrote about the long term as well as the present
moment, and it has been remarked[10] that the actual layout of
Roman colonies, in that it did not use up all the available space
from the start but lent itself to further development, was in itself
almost a form of planning, if rather passive. Vitruvius, however,
gave more attention to the sphere of building regulations (the
subject of the next chapter) than to the priorities of future
development.

5 Philostratus *Vit. Soph.*551.
6 E.g. before 61 BC the *lex municipii Tarentini*, FIRA i 18 (p.166ff) vv.
   39–42; 43 BC, *lex Ursonensis*, FIRA i 21 (p.177ff) cc. 77–8; the Flavian
   lex Irnitana, JRS 76 (1986, p.147ff) Tab. IIIA <ch. 19> vv. 5–9. See also
   Salmon (1969): 26–8; 85–8.
7 E.g. Vitruvius 7.5.8, where he explains that unusually costly paints are
   excluded from the specification and charged direct to the client, not
   the builder.
8 Vitruvius 1.1.10.
9 Vitruvius 1.3.1: Publicorum autem distributiones sunt tres: e quibus
   est una defensionis, altera religionis, tertia opportunitatis. . . . [est]
   opportunitatis communium locorum ad usum publicum dispositio, uti
   portus, fora, porticus, balinea, theatra, inambulationes, ceteraque quae
   isdem rationibus in publicis locis designantur. He also held (5.2.1)
   that *aerarium, carcer* and *curia* should adjoin the forum, as should the
   basilica, and explained (1.7.1) the proper siting of temples as well as
   of the forum.
10 Ward-Perkins (1974): 30.

Livy regretted[11] that the opportunity was not taken after the Gallic sack of 390 BC to rebuild Rome on modern lines, but, as has frequently been pointed out, the grid plan was at that time not known to the Romans. It also seems likely that, although severely damaged, Rome was in fact not sufficiently destroyed on that occasion for building on the site to have a genuinely fresh start.[12] Further, once the decision had been taken not to migrate to Veii, sentiment or tradition would lead to reconstruction rather than new design.[13] (After the great fire of AD 64 we are told that the will of the gods did not allow that the plan of their temples be altered.)[14] There was no disaster in the later Republic comparable to the Gallic sack which might have offered an opportunity of large-scale reconstruction. But the fundamental reason why a city planned as an entity could not be considered in Republican Rome was the constitutional arrangement of annual magistracies; even the censors, who had in theory five years in which to exercise their office, normally laid it down after some eighteen months. Such civil servants as there were, even though they seem sufficiently organised to have had some sort of a career structure,[15] were too subordinate, too inferior to their political masters, the magistrates, to be in a position to formulate or sustain policies, even if they did act as guides through the daily routine.[16] Only Sulla, whose dictatorship foreshadowed the Empire, may perhaps have had both the ambition and the resources – 3,000 talents from the Mithridatic wars – to attempt not just single buildings, but a renewal of the heart of Rome, the Forum and Comitium, with the Tabularium as backcloth.[17] Julius Caesar was the first who certainly, and perhaps uniquely, had a vision of re-creating the City and adapting it to future needs.

11 Livy 5.55.
12 Ogilvie (1965): 751. Cf. Livy 5.50 & 53.
13 Cf. Cologne or Warsaw after the 1939–45 War.
14 Tac. *Hist*.4.53.
15 Jones (1949b).
16 E.g. Plut. *Cato minor* 16.
17 Van Deman (1922).

JULIUS CAESAR AND AUGUSTUS

Suetonius described Caesar as meditating urban redevelopment[18] in a list of projects which included, among other plans, the codification of the law and the draining of the Pomptine marshes. Within the City, Suetonius mentioned the intended new Forum which would act as a link between the old Forum area and the Campus Martius, as well as the temple of Mars, and the design for a huge theatre backing onto the Tarpeian cliff. We learn more from the horrified reactions of Cicero.[19] That Caesar should plan to divert the course of the Tiber, to build over the Campus Martius, and to extend the official area of the City does suggest that he had a wider sense of planning than the simple creation of a monumental centre, although this was not to be lacking. His breadth of vision is confirmed by the Roman sections of the *tabula Heracleensis*; these are not improperly called the *lex Julia municipalis* since this part of the inscription applies to Caesar's projected legislation, even if passed by Antony after the assassination.[20] The law is in itself an expression of the concept of planning.

The surviving fragments of this Julian Act as far as they concern Rome deal with street maintenance and cleansing, traffic, public spaces and porticoes, the safeguarding of the rights of contractors for public revenue or public services, and the use of public spaces for official purposes.[21] Particularly in the section on the streets, there is very little to distinguish the terms of this Roman law from those of a modern – or at least a nineteenth-century – one, taking drafting conventions into account. (The rest of what we find assembled in this inscription deals with the municipalities and with other periods, and is constitutional in character as much as administrative.)

Caesar's death checked his plans, partly because of the creeping outbreak of civil war, which lasted on and off for the next twelve years, and partly because of the cautious temperament of his successor. Caesar was a man for the new, the exciting, the grandiose, and it may have been his style as much as his

18 Suet. *Julius* 44: de ornanda instruendaque urbe.
19 Cicero *ad Att*.13.20; 13.33; cf. 13.35.
20 FIRA i 13 (p.140ff). Discussions of this inscription are listed in footnote 24 in ch.1.
21 *Tabula Heracleensis*, vv. 20–55; 56–67; 68–72; 73–6; 77–82. They will be discussed in ch. 5.

constitutional position that brought him to his death. Augustus was cooler. Where Caesar was blamed for tearing down dwellings and temples to clear the site for his theatre,[22] better known as the Theatre of Marcellus, Augustus deliberately restricted the size of his Forum for fear of being seen to dispossess those living nearby.[23] Augustus' concern was to restore 'normality', or the appearance of it, to erect a conservative façade behind which the new constitution could put down roots; his adoptive father's plans were too radical for the reassuring image which he wished to create. He was content to be able to make the famous boast that he had found the City brick and left it marble,[24] although finding it stone and leaving it brick would have been nearer the truth. His immense programme of public works, whether those for which he was directly responsible[25] or those of his son-in-law Agrippa,[26] as well as those which he encouraged in other great men[27] or which were provided by the Senate,[28] was all within the Republican tradition, if we take them one by one; it was the scale which was unprecedented.

However, Augustus' acceptance of the idea of urban redevelopment is not unlikely; he may have deliberately focused on the Campus Martius to free the area south of the Forum for dwellings. (He, or perhaps Caesar, seems to have zoned areas of Rome as proper to *domus* or *insulae*, or at least assigned some areas as suitable for the latter.[29]) He certainly took novel measures for the administration of the City in creating the new organisational structure of the XIV Regions,[30] a term

22 Dio 43.49.
23 Suet. *Aug.*56.2: non ausus extorquere possessoribus proximas domos.
24 Suet. *Aug.*28.
25 *Curia Julia*, temple of Apollo with its porticoes, *aedes Julii*, Octavian portico by Pompey's theatre, the *pulvinar* at the Circus Maximus, and ten other temples recorded as built – *RG 19*; Capitol and Pompey's theatre restored; *forum Julium*, basilica Julia, and eighty-two temples restored, as well as aqueducts and the *via Flaminia* – *RG 20*; temple of Mars the Avenger, *Forum Augusti*, Marcellus' theatre built – *RG 21*.
26 Aqueducts, Baths and the first Pantheon.
27 E.g. Statilius Taurus' amphitheatre, L. Marcius Philippus' portico with his restoration of the Temple of Hercules of the Muses, Asinius Pollio's magnificently restored *Atrium Libertatis*, L. Cornelius Balbus' theatre, L. Cornificius' rebuilding of the temple of Diana, Munatius Plancus' rebuilding of the temple of Saturn.
28 E.g. the *Ara Pacis*, but see Weinstock (1960).
29 Homo (1971): 498; Boethius (1956).
30 See ch. 1. Suet. *Aug.*30; cf. Pliny *NH* 3.5.66–7; Dio 55.8.

that soon came to be an official designation of the City. By using magistrates of the Roman people to head each Region, Augustus took another definite but unobtrusive step in the municipalisation of Rome.

THE PRINCIPATE AFTER AUGUSTUS

Julius Caesar and Augustus had both, in their notions for the re-creation of a monumental City, thought in terms of legal constraints. Thereafter these fade into the background; planning becomes a game for emperors. Tiberius did some building on the Palatine,[31] and he also made some attempt to deal with the problems caused by the Tiber's floods,[32] but in general he was too parsimonious, too cautious to be interested in urbanism; moreover, the later part of his reign he spent withdrawn from the City. If Tiberius was too mean, Caligula was too mad. Claudius had an interest in the City as an entity, as is apparent from his enlargement of the *pomerium*,[33] even though that was primarily symbolic of the extension of the Empire. Further, Claudius' views on citizenship and on the membership of the Senate[34] show that he could have seen Rome in the same municipalised light as had Caesar, and perhaps Augustus. He was certainly interested in major building projects; it is probable that his harbour at Portus should be viewed as planning for the City;[35] but it must remain obscure whether he can fairly be called a planner in the long-term sense or whether he was merely reacting, sensibly, to an immediately-felt need.

Nero seems to have been capable of visualising a renewal of Rome. Indeed, the accusations and hints found in our literary sources[36] suggest that he may also have had the will to take the necessary first steps, however drastic, in putting his vision into practice. But it seems equally probable that he saw Rome only as a frame for himself; his orientation of the Via Sacra and the

---

31 *Domus Tiberiana*, etc; Homo (1971): 311 has a list of the major imperial public works.
32 See ch. 6.
33 See ch. 1.
34 FIRA i 43 (p.281ff); Tac. *Annals* 11.23–5; cf. FIRA i 71 (p.417ff).
35 Pliny, *NH* 36.24.125. See ch.6 on the Tiber.
36 Tac. *Annals* 15.38–43; Suet. *Nero* 38; Dio 62.16–18. But see Hülsen (1909) on the outbreak being one day after the full moon, and so unlikely to have been deliberate.

rebuilding he carried out in the Forum were concerned with the approach to his *domus Aurea* or Golden House.[37] He did not live to complete the reconstruction of the City after the Great Fire,[38] and perhaps this would have been more radical if he had, but it is difficult to see through the veil of his egocentricity. We are told that frontages were regulated and aligned along broad streets, that building heights were restricted, and that colonnades were to protect the façades of the new buildings. The new layout of the City, about which Tacitus managed to complain, particularly when combined with the rudiments of a building code, does suggest a more than day-to-day approach to the problems of the City.[39] The verdict on Nero as planner rather than simply builder must be 'not proven'.

Much of the rebuilding of the City was in fact carried out under the supervision of the more conservative, or realistic, Flavians, who had also to repair the consequences of the civil wars of 69 where these had touched the City.[40] We are told as well that they gave the via Sacra district back to the people; the Golden House was pulled down and on part of its site the great amphitheatre, later nicknamed the Colosseum, erected. Vespasian took steps to house the homeless by allowing them to take over and build on unoccupied sites;[41] he also enlarged the *pomerium* slightly[42] and held a censorship,[43] which some have thought[44] provided the information on which the Marble Plan[45] was based. Titus was the emperor who had to react to the terrible fire of 80, as well as to other disasters such as the eruption of Vesuvius, but he did not have the time which might have shown whether he had any interest in urbanism. The catastrophe of 80 gave further scope to the third of the Flavians, Domitian, a monumental egoist but a competent administrator. He seems to have created an imperial Works Department, the

37 Van Deman (1925).
38 Boethius (1932).
39 Tac. *Annals* 15.43; Suet. *Nero* 16 & 38.
40 E.g. Tac. *Hist*.3.71 & 82–3.
41 Suet. *Vesp*.8: vacuas areas occupare et aedificare si possessores cessarent cuicumque permisit.
42 FIRA i 15 (p.154ff), *lex quae dicitur de imperio Vespasiani*, vv. 14–16. See ch. 1.
43 Pliny *NH* 3.5.66–7; Hülsen (1897).
44 E.g. Ashby (1923): 50.
45 The Marble Plan – *Forma Urbis* – is a ground-plan or street map of the City incised on marble, ed. Carettoni (1966); see also Dilke (1985): 103–6.

opera Caesaris,[46] but his interests were probably confined to monumental building, rather than urbanism proper. Trajan was an emperor who favoured improvements rather than novelties, as both Pliny the Younger and Frontinus witness.[47] His Market, however, was original. 'These streets, offices and shops were planned as integral parts of an urban redevelopment program',[48] renovating what was destroyed in the building of his Forum. It certainly seems to be evidence of his practical outlook, but again appears to be reaction rather than the result of a unified vision of the future.

Hadrian was addicted to building, was perhaps himself competent as an architect,[49] and left buildings all over the Empire, that is, when he had not the opportunity to found a city.[50] However, he may not have spent enough time in Rome to give thought to planning for, as opposed to building in, his capital. This view is not held in the recent work by Boatwright; she maintains that 'Hadrian's personal involvement with Rome was broad in its scope and an intense and continuing commitment',[51] and that 'he permanently changed the urban landscape and touched all segments of the population'.[52] He renewed the *cippi* which marked the *pomerium*, and had a programme of particular public works, both new building and restoration, on a considerable scale.[53] The arguments for a more comprehensive approach by him must be based on archaeology, since the literary evidence is sparse. 'Moreover, in every case where we can examine it, attention was paid to providing access to or through his complexes, and to ensuring good urban communication.'[54] Antoninus Pius and Marcus Aurelius do not seem to have thought at all of long-term urban reform; restoration was

---

46 CIL VI 9034, where one Onesimus appears as 'redemptor operum Caesar'; see also Anderson (1983).
47 Pliny *Pan*.51; Frontinus *aq*.93.
48 MacDonald (1965): 79.
49 SHA *Hadrian* 14.8; Dio 69.3–4; 'the art which Hadrian himself practised' – Rodenwaldt (1936): 796.
50 SHA *Hadrian* 19–20; *Ep. de Caes*.14.4–5; various Hadrianoples, and Antinoopolis in Egypt.
51 Boatwright (1987): 20.
52 ibid.: 236.
53 ILS 311 (= CIL VI 1233) on the *pomerium*; his Mausoleum (ILS 322 = VI 1112), known now as the Castel Sant' Angelo, and the Pantheon – see MacDonald (1965): 94–121; Boatwright (1987): 64–6.
54 Boatwright (1987): 237.

enough for Pius[55] and Marcus erected a few monuments,[56] but was mostly occupied on the frontiers.

THE SEVERANS AND AFTER

Another major fire, probably in 192, was suffered under Commodus.[57] It was left to Septimius Severus to oversee the rebuilding of the City. The Severans have been described as 'the last dynasty to be responsible for extensive changes on the face of the City . . . [but there was] no concentrated or organised building programme as there had been under Augustus',[58] although there was some new construction and much major restoration. Caracalla,[59] Elagabalus, and Severus Alexander[60] observed this policy but after that preoccupations of foreign and civil war absorbed the emperors' attentions. Then too, by the third century the immense weight of existing buildings, the huge legacy of the past, must have been an enormous and expensive albatross round the neck of the authorities – whether the emperor himself or, more frequently in practice, the *curatores operum publicorum* or the Urban Prefect.

The chief new aspect of the City in the half-century before Diocletian was the work of Aurelian, completed by Probus, the new Wall.[61] After some six hundred and fifty years, Rome had returned to being a walled city, a city whose name was not in itself enough protection. It is possible that Aurelian extended the *pomerium* to coincide with his Wall; on the other hand, the Wall did not include the whole area of the XIV Regions, for both *Regio* VII and *Regio* V in the north and *Regio* I in the south extended beyond it.[62] Aurelian's criterion was simply military; he viewed the City as a defensible area, which was a new vision of a sort. His reign did not last long enough for us to know if he would or could have done more.

55 Homo (1971): 313.
56 Besides, judging from his correspondence with Fronto, one wonders whether he was too fussy a man to have a wider vision; he seems to have been well-meaning but too concerned with details. Williams (1976) makes much the same point.
57 Dio 73.24; Herodian 1.14.
58 Benario (1958): 712.
59 His Baths were begun in his reign, and the Circus Maximus restored.
60 SHA *Sev. Alex.*24.3 – for what it's worth.
61 Richmond (1930).
62 Hülsen (1897).

Diocletian was a frontier emperor, and a soldier; we have an enactment of his giving priority to walls over *spectacula*.[63] He engaged in some public works at Rome, most notably his Baths. One suspects that, like Augustus but with desperation rather than hope, he was attempting a 'normalisation' of life, and at the same time trying to strengthen his own position by propaganda in bricks and mortar. Then came the foundation of Constantinople, New Rome, and, even apart from this, strategic considerations required that in the West the emperors should be based in more northerly cities, such as Milan, Trier or Ravenna; never again did they have their formal residence in Rome. The population of the City seems to have shrunk, perhaps slowly at first, and there can have been progressively less need for future developmental planning. The decline of Rome's importance enabled a true municipalisation; the Senate was on its way to being simply another town council, although it took the centuries of the Later Empire for the glory to fade completely. In the early medieval world there was a return almost to the city-state of the Republic.

OVERALL PLANNING: ADMINISTRATION

In discussing what evidence there is for any coherent, long-term planning in the City one must talk in terms of the emperors. In the Republic serious planning had only been possible for dictators – in the modern sense. In the Principate, while Rome continued to be a showcase, it was to display the emperors rather than the *res publica*.

Town planning in the sense defined at the start of this chapter was not an activity which could be left to subordinates, although here the position of the Senate was ambivalent. In many areas it was in theory the colleague of the emperor; the various commissions concerned with public works were senatorial posts, and often acted *ex senatusconsulto*. However, for much of the Principate not only did the emperors normally reside in Rome, as a modern head of state usually resides in the capital city, but also, as one of their fundamental bases of power, they held a magistracy whose operation was in theory confined to the City, the tribunate of the people. They also frequently held the consulship, which involved local duties within the City

63 CJ 11.42.1 – Diocletian & Maximian.

as well as command of the Roman armies. Thus they were to a certain extent themselves local magistrates and one can attempt to distinguish this aspect of their powers. The term *urbs sacra* for Rome became current under Hadrian and official from the time of Septimius Severus; this nomenclature, by using the word 'sacred' with its imperial associations, reinforced the connection between the City and the emperor. Another relevant factor is the extent to which central government must always have power to intervene in local government, on questions of policy if not matters of detail; long-term planning is perhaps the most political aspect of local government. But certainly it is possible to distinguish the emperors' plans for the *urbs* from those for the *orbis*.

The Urban Prefect was the only magistrate, or official, in the City with an overall task, not restricted to a particular jurisdiction.[64] Our sources show him taking initiatives in matters of detail, putting up statues,[65] restoring and repairing on his own authority,[66] and so on, but he was constrained by the existence of offices, inferior indeed but not subordinate to him, such as that of the *praefectus annonae*.[67] He seems to have been in a similar position with regard to the various *curatores*, who were, however, for the most part simply administrative commissioners, without apparent planning functions.

The powers of the Prefect of the City were preeminently jurisdictional and disciplinary; although the *cura urbis* was his,[68] it was in many ways residuary. The Prefecture presumably had, as well as the office staff,[69] a staff of experts in various fields (but it hardly seems likely, as is assumed by one modern architect,[70] that the professional architects were the prime movers in the creation of a New Town after 64 – although MacDonald does admit that it was necessary for them to have government support). The various books that have survived from ancient Rome on architecture, surveying and the like, make out a good case

---

64 Vitucci (1956).
65 SHA *Sept. Sev.*24.
66 E.g. CIL VI 1112.
67 CJ 1.28.1 – AD 368 – reflects the earlier situation; see ch. 10.
68 D.1.12.1.4, Ulpian *de off. p. u*: Initio eiusdem epistulae [of Severus] ita scriptum est: 'cum urbem nostram fidei tuae commiserimus'; quidquid igitur intra urbem admittitur, ad praefectum urbi videtur pertinere.
69 Discussed in ch. 12.
70 MacDonald (1965): 28.

for the necessary existence of a professional, as well as a clerical and executive, staff at the disposal of the authorities. The speed with which Nero[71] or Aurelian produced a response to crisis is some evidence of this; we know too that Pliny requested Trajan to second a surveyor to Bithynia.[72] But the regular task of the architects was surely the supervision of public works, not long-term planning.[73] Any advice in general terms, rather than in relation to a specific project, that they gave to emperor or prefect is likely to have been concerned with the subordinate sphere, with what can loosely be described as building regulations. Private building on a lavish scale went on throughout the Empire; the provision of public works in Rome by private individuals did not cease with the Republic, but it declined sharply.[74] At Rome the construction of public buildings became an imperial function, as did the care of those originally erected by private persons. Naturally, it was more and more for the emperors that the professionals worked.

We have seen traces of planning in the strict sense in some areas, for example, the *pomerium* and the walls. But was the fact that much of the City was surrounded by gardens the result of accident or design? Lacking outer suburbs – which follow from modern mass transit systems – ancient Rome can have had no need for a 'green belt', but nevertheless the City needed 'lungs'.[75] How far were the *horti Maecenatis* and the other public gardens created with public health in mind? Some of them provided a safe cover for the burial pits of the poor on the Esquiline.[76] It is possible that parks and gardens were created only because they were 'nicer' for the emperor and his circle, but Vitruvius' remarks on the need for a salubrious site make it clear that the authorities could have considered public health in addition to their own pleasures. Furthermore, work on building and public works in Rome has tended to confirm that the emperors probably wished to provide a fairly steady source of paid work for the labouring poor, in the interests of social

71 On Nero's men, Tac. *Annals* 15.42.
72 Pliny *Ep*.10.17b-18; see also FIRA i 72 (p.419ff); D. 10.1.8, Ulpian, 6 *opin.*
73 Brunt (1980): 82–3.
74 See ch. 4.
75 Seneca *Ep*.104.6.
76 See ch. 8.

stability.[77] It seems somewhat more probable than not that the emperors did take such factors into account.

The practical, pragmatic nature of Roman government makes it likely that public utility was combined with imperial pleasure, but the latter probably had priority. Certainly there was no large-scale programme of private housing for the poorer classes, no care for the interests of the dispossessed as the monumental centre of the City grew ever larger; we have to wait here for the eighteenth century. Random and intermittent account was taken of such issues, but Nero's grant of citizenship to a Latin who built a house[78] was aimed at those who built mansions, not tenements. Things had probably been worse in the Republic[79] when there was no clear authority to blame or implore. Was it only unpopularity, or actual hardship for the citizens, that Augustus wished to avoid when he restricted his preliminary demolition and thus his Forum? Housing is one vital area of modern concern, though not for the Romans; another is traffic. Traffic was a problem in Rome.[80] Were porticoes a deliberate attempt to separate pedestrians and vehicles? Or were they designed as monuments to personal glory with convenient side effects, such as providing shelter from the rain,[81] or furnishing somewhere for the display of works of art? We may be certain that there was no 'piano regolatore', but there does seem to have been deliberate action as well as mere reaction.

THE DISTINCTION BETWEEN PUBLIC AND PRIVATE

An essential step in the development of even the limited concept of planning that is detectable among the Romans was the distinction between public and private land, or, indeed, between sacred and other land. There were many purposes for which a record would need to be kept of such status.[82] To protect public rights, the commissioners for water and for the banks and bed of the Tiber had powers to exercise such delimitation (*terminatio*), and erected *cippi* to mark the boundary. Public land

77 Brunt (1980); Skydsgaard (1983); Thornton and Thornton (1983).
78 G.1.33.
79 Yavetz (1958).
80 See ch. 5.
81 Vitruvius 5.9.1, talking of colonnades beside theatres.
82 FIRA i 13 (p.140ff), *tabula Heracleensis*, v. 82 mentions the land set aside by the censors for *servi publici*; cf. Livy 27.11.16.

was on occasion sold, not merely leased, to private persons, as under Julius Caesar's agrarian law of 59 BC;[83] more commonly, private land was acquired for public use by compulsory purchase. Under Tiberius we even find a commission of *curatores locorum publicorum iudicandorum*.[84] Some modern Romanists have been unwilling to accept the existence of 'expropriation' in a society which they see as preeminently individualistic and patrimonial but, as de Robertis convincingly pointed out,[85] if the concept of the patrimony was strong, so too was that of *imperium*. Moreover, as a pointer to the complexity of Roman attitudes, the prohibition on demolishing one's own property is highly relevant.[86] Expropriation in the strictest sense, i.e. without compensation, seems unknown to Roman law – it is, indeed, inequitable – but compulsory purchase there most certainly was. And in a regime of compulsory purchase, the purchasing authority sooner or later tends to get its way.

We have evidence that moveables could be acquired for the public – a less emotive issue than the acquisition of land. A *scriba* in 181 BC found books, allegedly from Numa's reign, on his land; the praetor held that they were subversive and should be burned. The scribe appealed to the tribunes; they were clearly uncertain whether this was a suitable occasion for the exercise of their *intercessio*, for they referred the matter to the Senate. The Senate voted in favour of burning the books but said that compensation, to be agreed by the tribunes, should be paid; this, however, the scribe refused to take.[87] Much later, evidence is provided by Frontinus, who records the resolution of the Senate by which materials for the repair and maintenance of the aqueducts could be commandeered from privately owned land, with compensation to be paid at a level agreed by a man of good will – in other words, at a fair price.[88] A text of Ulpian is somewhat ambiguous: if you have stone quarries on your land, without your permission nobody, either in a private capacity or by public title, may cut stone unless he has a right to do this; where by custom there is freedom to quarry, the landlord is to

---

83 Dio 43.47.4.
84 ILS 5939 (= CIL VI 1266), 942 (= V 4348), 950 (= XIV 3602); CIL VI 1267; cf. e.g. ILS 5921 (= VI 31759). See also Mommsen (1887): II 993.
85 de Robertis (1936 and 1945–6); see also Ankum (1980); Jones (1929).
86 See ch. 3.
87 Livy 40.29.
88 Frontinus *aq*.125 & 128.

receive the usual indemnification, and to be inconvenienced as little as possible.[89] A public authority appears then not to have the right to take stone simply by virtue of public office; that would be *ultra vires*, but the right to take must be express, perhaps by the terms of a municipal charter or, in Rome, by senatusconsult. And the normal civil exercise required of a servitude would seem to be applicable when stone was taken by public authority, as well as a solatium being due. Under Constantine, we are told that when a slave has earned his freedom by performing some service for the state, the fisc will pay his price to the owner thus dispossessed.[90]

The procedure of which Livy gives an account may well have been that which was normally followed in the Republic. In this model, the magistrate who wanted to take the land or thing into the public domain – which could include its destruction – would state his intention to the possessor. Instead of a public inquiry being held, it was possible for the possessor to appeal to a tribune, who could satisfy himself concerning the balance between the public good and the private right; tribunes did have the right to summon witnesses. The tribune was then in a position to decide on using his *intercessio*,[91] whether to veto the magistrate's intended action or to bring about a temporary stay pending further investigation or discussion, as in the case of Numa's books.

When we turn to the compulsory acquisition of land, there is nothing so clearly described. From Livy again we hear of the occasion when M. Licinius Crassus blocked the building of a proposed aqueduct by refusing to allow it over his land.[92] Cicero's speech on the *lex agraria* contains the sentence: 'This good man has promised that he will not buy from the unwilling. As if we did not know that a forced sale is an affront to justice,

---

89 D.8.4.13.1, Ulpian 6 *opin*: Si constat in tuo agro lapidicinas esse, invito te nec privato nec publico nomine quisquam lapidem caedere potest, cui id faciendi ius non est; nisi talis consuetudo in illis lapidinicis consistat ut si quis voluerit ex his caedere, non aliter hoc faciat nisi prius solitum solacium pro hoc domino praestat; ita tamen lapides caedere debet, postquam satisfaciat domino, ut neque usus necessarii lapidis intercludatur neque commoditas rei iure domino adimatur.

90 CJ 7.13.2 – AD 321.

91 We do hear (Appian BC 1.1.12) of a tribunician veto used to stop dispossession under T. Gracchus' agrarian law.

92 Livy 40.51.

a voluntary sale an occasion of profit.'[93] I am convinced by the arguments of de Robertis[94] that the main target of Cicero's polemic was the extravagance of the proposal. (Obviously, much turns on the definition of 'unwilling'; for most people there will come eventually a price for which they are not unwilling.) Consider Cicero again on the preparations for the Forum Julii: 'We couldn't settle with the owners for a smaller sum';[95] we are told elsewhere[96] that the cost of the land was more than 100 million sesterces. Suetonius tells us that Julius Caesar did not assign contiguous lands to his veterans, to avoid the expulsion of those who possessed them;[97] but this implies that he could have and, in any case, it was reasonable to take land of which the title was potentially dubious.[98] As we have already seen, Augustus is said to have restricted the size of his Forum to avoid expropriations, and the same emperor, in the edict on the aqueduct at Venafrum, laid down that the water should not be brought through any private land against the will of the proprietor.[99] Similarly, Tiberius' first plans for controlling the Tiber were put aside after petitions from the municipalities which would have been affected by his flood control schemes.[100] These are the texts which can be used to deny expropriation, together with the saving clause common to the *lex municipii Tarentini*, the *lex Ursonensis* and the *lex Irnitana*,[101] which all say that public works should be done 'without injury to private interests'.

---

93 Cicero *de leg. ag.*1.5.14: Cavet enim vir optimus ne emat ab invito. Quasi vero non intellegamus ab invito emere iniuriosum esse, ab non invito quaestuosum. Cf. ibid. 2.27.72; 2.30.82.
94 de Robertis (1945–6).
95 Cicero *ad Att.*4.16.8: ut forum laxaremus et usque ad atrium libertatis explicaremus, contempsimus sescenties sestertium; cum privatis non poterat transigi minore pecunia.
96 Pliny *NH* 36.24.103; Suet. *Julius* 26.2.
97 Suet. *Julius* 38: adsignavit [veteranis] et agros, sed non continuos, ne quis possessorum expelleretur.
98 Cf. Pliny *Pan.*50.
99 FIRA i 67 (p.400ff) vv. 45–6: neve ea aqua per locum privatum invito eo cuius is locus erit ducatur.
100 Tac. *Annals* 1.79.
101 FIRA i 18 (p.166ff) vv. 39–42; i 21 (p.177ff) c.77; *JRS* 76 (1986, p.147ff) Tab.IXA <ch. 82> vv. 29–34. They all say, with only very minor variations: . . . vias fossas cloacas iv vir ii vir aedilisve eius municipii causa publice facere inmittere commutare aedificare munire volet intra eos fines qui eius municipii erunt, quod eius sine iniuria privatorum fiat, id ei facere liceto.

There is, however, no reason to suppose that in such matters politics played any less part in the Roman world than in the modern one. In the oligarchy of the Republic it is hardly surprising to find an influential, and very rich, senator able to block a proposal which displeased him.[102] Sulla took particular care that his army should not inflict damage on crops, fields, men or cities,[103] for political reasons. Augustus had a particular desire to calm fears of insecurity, and so may well have preferred not to expropriate the unwilling in Rome itself.[104] At Venafrum, the reference[105] is not to the line of the aqueduct outside the town but to the distribution within it; inside this small area the problems caused by unwilling landowners might not have been worth the trouble. It is also possible to argue *e contrario* and say that this prohibition on bringing water through private land against the will of the owner would not have been made explicit unless such an act was normally within the powers of the civic magistrates. In the municipal charters, *sine iniuria* is an ambivalent phrase; *iniuria* suggests wrongfulness as well as damage. There is no injustice if the situation is, for example, one covered by the interdict which forbade anything to be done in a public place, or that concerning drains. And it is to be borne in mind that in the clause of the *lex Ursonensis* on bringing in aqueducts to the town, we are specifically told that if the proposal has been submitted to a quorum of two-thirds of the town councillors and if the majority of these have agreed to the line proposed by the municipal magistrate, then the aqueduct can be brought across land, although not through buildings, and no one is to prevent the water being brought in.[106]

Laws were used for the distribution of land;[107] the Roman state had the power to acquire and to alienate. Some instances

102 I believe that there are some interesting kinks in British railway lines for just this sort of reason; my own great-grandfather only sold land to the railway company on condition that they build a bridge to preserve his access to the shore.
103 Velleius 7.25.1.
104 Suet. *Aug.*56.2.
105 FIRA i 67 (p.400ff), *edictum de aquaeductu Venafrano* vv. 45–6, cited above.
106 FIRA i 21 (p.177ff), *lex Ursonensis* c. 99: neve quis facito quo minus ita aqua ducatur. We hear from Tacitus of compensation being paid after a senator complained that his house had been undermined by the construction of a public road and aqueduct – Tac. *Annals* 1.75.
107 E.g. Cicero *ad Att.*2.16; 2.18; Velleius 2.44.4; Plut. *Pompey* 47; *Caesar* 14.

admittedly come from troubled times. Dio's account[108] of Caesar's land law of 59 BC records that he took first from those who were willing to sell, and then from those who were not willing, at the price of the valuation of their land for the assessment of taxes – a nice touch, in that it penalised those who had contrived to underpay their taxes. Why should Julius Caesar go to the trouble of compulsory purchase if there was land enough without? In 36 BC Augustus had taken public land at Capua, giving the Capuans in exchange land at Cnossos in Crete, and also an aqueduct,[109] and this suggests that he would have taken such measures even in Rome if there had been sufficient need. Augustus also boasted that he had paid cash to the Italian, and other, towns for the lands which he had assigned to his veterans in 30 and 14 BC, the only founder of a military colony so to do.[110] He made no mention of his settlements of veterans in 41–40 and in 36 BC, because these had involved the usual confiscations.[111] It is hard to see how else Aurelian could have built his walls, which not only took people's land but sometimes even smashed or cut through their houses and tombs.[112]

There are some juristic texts which have a bearing. Africanus seems to have accepted compulsory purchase for public works as a hazard akin to *vis maior* as far as sale or relations between landlord and tenant were concerned.[113] Ulpian referred both to the compulsory purchase of land for the settlement of veterans and to land for roads becoming public.[114] Paul too talked of land either sold off or granted to veterans by order of the emperor.[115] Since I adhere to the view of Jones[116] and others that there was true ownership, though not quiritary ownership, of provincial land, these texts seem to confirm that a form of compulsory purchase did exist. Moreover, on *a priori* grounds such an institution seems likely for any state where there are massive

---

108 Dio 38.1.
109 Dio 49.14.
110 *RG* 16.
111 Cf. the Praetorians in 25 BC – Dio 53.25.
112 Richmond (1930): footnote 58, and personal observation; SHA *Sev. Alex*.25 probably refers to compulsory purchase.
113 D.19.2.33, Africanus 8 *quaest*, discussed most recently by Ankum (1980): 169–75.
114 D.6.1.15.2, Ulpian 16 *ad ed*; 43.8.2.21, Ulpian 68 *ad ed*.
115 D.21.2.11pr, Paul 6 *resp*: ex praecepto principis partim distractas, partim veteranis in praemia adsignatas.
116 Jones (1941).

public works and a fairly dense population. What the procedure was under the Principate is difficult to discern; the safeguard of tribunician intercession had disappeared – for one could hardly rely on the emperor's impartiality in this context. I am inclined to guess that there was no form of general public hearing, merely an individual appeal; perhaps the level of compensation was fixed, as with the materials for the maintenance of the aqueducts, by some trustworthy person delegated to this end. The appointment of such an assessor would not be inappropriate as long as the legal regime of the formula lasted, with its *iudex* and *recuperatores*, nor would it be inconsistent with the classical concepts of *bona fides* and of the *bonus paterfamilias*.

The rather different problems of the prohibition on demolition in general and of the official order to pull down what the citizen has built unlawfully, even on his own land, will be considered, along with building regulations, in the next chapter. Planning for Rome did, then, exist, but intermittently, and on a very different scale from modern practice.

3

BUILDING CONTROLS

There were some general rules that applied for most of our period on the height of buildings; on ambit, that is the space to be left around a building; on materials that might be used; and also on relations with other buildings.[1] Much, however, seems to have been left unregulated, or at least unenforced. We do not find, for example, any evidence that planning permission, in the sense of prior consent to a proposed use of land, was required for ordinary private buildings, though there were clear restrictions on erecting public buildings.[2]

In the time of the Twelve Tables, the mid-fifth century BC, the law was concerned with the space to be left between properties (and with demolition, treated here in a separate section). The Twelve Tables were, however, dealing with farms and detached dwellings,[3] not a crowded metropolis. When Rome was a small city-state, public buildings, such as temples, probably predominated within the Servian Wall. Until the expansion in the later third century BC it is likely that all houses in Rome, unless mere hovels, were of the *atrium* type (a style which still predominated at Pompeii and Herculaneum at the time of their destruction in AD 79), although some may have shared an external wall with a neighbour.[4] But the growth of the City in the third century led to a literal upwards growth. An anecdote from Livy illustrates this tendency; in 218 BC an ox climbed of its own accord to a third storey – since this was in the Forum Boarium, one suspects

---

1 Such as the mention in Vitruvius – 1.1.10 – of praedial servitudes.
2 D.50.10.3, *Macer de off. praesidis.*
3 Cicero *Topica* 4.24, where, following Publius Scaevola, he restricts *ambitus* to the space covered by a roof put up to protect a party wall; Varro *LL* 5.22; D.10.1.13, Gaius 4 *ad XII T.*
4 Implied by Plautus, *Miles* 140–3.

that the beast was in a panic from the smell of blood – and then, terrified by the uproar of the occupants, threw itself down.[5]

BUILDING REGULATIONS

Vitruvius, who was essentially an architect of the Republican style, records that statute forbade a thickness of more than 1.5 feet for party walls; other walls were built of the same thickness to save space.[6] The standard sun-dried (as opposed to baked) brick was 1.5 feet by 1 foot and so, since such a wall could not be more than a brick thick, it could not sustain more than one storey.[7] Urban need was great, however, and so new materials came to be used, such as stone, kiln-dried bricks and concrete; with these, high buildings were put up, whose walls were tied in by the floor joists of the flats within, of which the upper floors enjoyed fine views to great advantage. Thus buildings of many storeys and great height multiplied, and the Roman people had outstanding dwellings without hindrance.[8] It is not clear why the Republican laws should have prohibited thicker walls, but the point is that there were laws, *leges publicae*, on the construction of houses quite early in the history of Rome's administration. Vitruvius tells us further that at Utica, a town he knew at first hand, no sun-dried bricks could be used for walls unless they had been certified by a magistrate as being five years old and completely dry; he himself held that sun-dried bricks should not be used until they were at least two years old.[9] This sounds like a reference to legislation, and indeed if there could be a regulation of this nature at Utica, a similar kind of rule is hardly impossible at Rome.

Another possible early law may have concerned roofing. Pliny tells us that until the war with Pyrrhus Rome had been roofed

5 Livy 21.62.3.
6 Vitruvius 2.8.17: Leges publicae non patiuntur maiores crassitudines quam sesquipedales constitui loco communi. ceteri autem parietes, ne spatia angustioria fierent, eadem crassitudine conlocantur; cf. Pliny *NH* 35.49.173.
7 And Vitruvius' remark (2.3.2) about the degradation of sun-dried brick emphasises this.
8 Vitruvius 2.8.17: altitudines extructae contignationibus crebris coaxatae cenaculorum ad summas utilitates perficiunt despectationes. ergo moenibus e contignationibus variis alto spatio multiplicatis populus romanus egregias habet sine impeditione habitationes.
9 Vitruvius 2.3.2.

with wooden shingles, but since then with tiles.[10] He made no mention of any law or any reason why Roman roofing styles should have changed, but it is reasonable to deduce that the motive was fire prevention, and that such a sudden and complete change from shingles to tiles was consequent upon a law.

We certainly hear of legislation limiting the height of buildings.[11] Strabo tells us that there was constant need in the City for timber and stone because of the multitude of collapses, fires, and the repeated sales which were often accompanied by demolition and rebuilding. With this in mind, Augustus put a limit of 70 feet on the height of new buildings erected on public streets.[12] (Augustus is also recorded as having read to the Senate from such books as Rutilius' *de modo aedificiorum*.[13]) There is some debate about whether Nero legislated on building heights; he may, of course, simply have repeated Augustus' rule.

It is not clear how much of Nero's work was meant to impose a precedent on the future and how much simply resulted from the way his architects planned their task of rebuilding.[14] Tacitus wrote:

> In the parts of the City unfilled by Nero's palace, reconstruction was not, as after the Gallic sack, without plan or indiscriminate; the alignment of the local quarters was regulated, streets widened, the height of buildings restricted, and, in the cleared spaces, porticoes added to protect the frontages of tenement blocks. . . . He provided rewards, in proportion to rank and resources, for those who succeeded in finishing their houses or tenement blocks within a given time. . . . Buildings must be constructed with a fixed proportion of stone from Gabii or Alba, without timber, because that stone was fireproof. . . .

---

10 Pliny *NH* 16.15.36: Scandula contectam fuisse Romam ad Pyrrhi usque bellum annis 470 Cornelius Nepos auctor est. (Incidentally, Dio 46.31 tells us that in 43 BC, for the war against Caesar's assassins, senators were required to contribute on the basis of the number of roof tiles on the houses they owned, or rented, in the City.)
11 Val. Max. 8.1 *damn*.7, though this was not in Rome.
12 Strabo 5.3.7; cf. Horace *Ep*.1.1.100.
13 Suet. *Aug*.89.
14 Boethius (1932).

There were to be no common walls, but each building
must be surrounded by its own walls.[15]

Further, Suetonius tells us that Nero introduced a new style of
architecture, with porticoes built onto the fronts of tenement
blocks and private houses, from the balconies of which fires
might be fought.[16] The new layout of the roads was permanent
– it is visible on the Marble Plan – and this implies the existence
of what we should call a building line. Balconies might protrude
at times, but at street level the line, whether of house wall or
portico, could be protected by the use of such interdicts as *ne
quid in loco publico vel itinere fiat*,[17] or perhaps through administrative action taken by those in charge of the streets.[18] How the
porticoes could be used for fire-fighting is somewhat obscure.

Unfortunately Tacitus is not specific on the height of the
new building. The absence of timber has generally been taken
to mean that there were not to be the wooden beams which had
customarily been used as frames for brick buildings. How the
ban on common walls was to be applied is a difficult problem
if it was meant to apply to buildings of all sorts.[19] It may have
affected only *domus*, and perhaps public buildings; for *insulae* it
presumably only laid down that each block was to be separate
from its neighbours – but how big is a block? – because
archaeology shows that party walls continued to exist, and they
continued to have legal battles fought over them.[20] (The existence of a time limit, within which someone must complete the
building if he were to get indemnification, seems reasonable.)

Trajan is said, by a late epitomator,[21] to have reduced Augustus'
building height to 60 feet, rather than 70; this too probably only
applied to new buildings fronting on public streets. There is an
enactment of Caracalla in which he gave permission to build
a *balneum* with a dwelling on top of it, provided that the usual

15 Tac. *Annals* 15.43.
16 Suet. *Nero* 16.
17 D.43.8 *passim*: to prevent anything from being done in public places or
ways.
18 D.43.10.1, Papinian; this text is fully discussed in ch. 5.
19 It is notable that at Ostia there are (from personal observation) narrow
alleys between some *insulae*, alleys too narrow for ordinary traffic – even
a laden ass, as still to be seen in Old Jerusalem – since they are roughly
a metre wide, but they do not occur between all *insulae*.
20 E.g. D.8.2.13, Proculus 2 *ep*; h.t.19, Paul 6 *ad Sab*.
21 *Ep. de Caes*.13.13.

height limit was not exceeded.[22] This is a somewhat suspicious text, but since it occurs in the title which contains Zeno's building code, why would the compilers have included this enactment unless it did indeed contain a ruling of this sort? The 'usual height' could perfectly well be Trajan's 60 feet. Depending on whether an *insula* was intended for the upper or lower end of the market, 60 feet would allow for four to six storeys (in Glasgow the middle-class tenements are usually of four storeys and the poorer housing of six). Seneca could write of 'the houses themselves, which they have built upwards to such a degree that, although the homes have been designed for use and shelter, they are now a danger not a protection; so great is the height of the buildings and such the narrowness of the streets that they offer no protection against fire, nor is there a means of escape in any direction if they collapse';[23] Juvenal could complain of the height of cornices and roofs,[24] and Tertullian could joke that the gods of the Valentiniani lived in the attics of a well-known building, the *insula Felicles*.[25]

One device that may have been used to get round the law was to build higher further back than the street line. Wooden structures may have topped many an *insula*, and it is possibly to this that Vitruvius was alluding when he described *craticii* (wattlework) as a wicked material in which to build, like torches ready for kindling, and added that kiln-dried brick was worth the extra expense.[26] He does not, however, seem to imply that there was a law against the use of such materials. Pliny applauded Trajan's restraint over new buildings: 'walls and roofs have stopped shuddering and collapse no longer threatens'.[27] This may only refer to the cessation of Domitian's huge public building programme, but it could perhaps refer to an emperor who was interested in building regulations. On balance, Trajan's 60-foot height limit seems probable, and there may have been other regulations.

The *ambitus* of the Twelve Tables, described by Varro and

---

22 CJ 8.10.1 – Caracalla (no date): observata tamen forma qua ceteri super balnea aedificare permittuntur, id est ut concameratis superinstruas et ipsa concameres nec modum usitatum altitudinis excedas.
23 Seneca *controv*.2.1.11.
24 Juvenal 3.269ff.
25 Tertullian *adversus Val*.7.1–3.
26 Vitruvius 2.8.20.
27 Pliny *Pan*.51.

Festus,[28] was not compatible with the development of the *insula* as the type of dwelling for the majority of the population, a development which seems to have taken place in the first centuries BC and AD, and is visible still at Ostia. Instead, there developed a concept of the space that there should be between buildings to ensure adequate, or at least some, light. Buildings were still too close together for preventing the spread of fire,[29] but the *ambitus* of the early law was replaced by something more in keeping with changed circumstances. Vitruvius quite reasonably remarked that the architect's problem of ensuring that all rooms had adequate light was easier in the country where there were no party walls or narrow streets.[30] Nevertheless, it was precisely because of these difficulties that a way had to be found of overcoming them to some extent if the City were to be habitable for the majority of its population – habitable, but not necessarily comfortable.[31] Caracalla permitted an owner, or someone with his permission, to build on a site which owed no servitude, provided that the lawful space was left between the new building and the neighbouring block.[32] The solution was largely achieved not by express legislation but by the use of the praetor's *imperium*, particularly in the granting of interdicts (but also in the *cautio damni infecti* and the *operis novi nuntiatio*[33]), and by juristic development, especially in the fields of *bona fides* and *iniuria*.

'CIVIL' USE OF URBAN PROPERTY[34]

Most legal concern with building in our period was probably expressed through the interdicts, which protected both private

28 Varro *LL* 5.22; Festus *ambitus* 5L & 15L.
29 Seneca *controv*.2.1.11; Plut. *Crassus* 2; Herodian 7.12.5–7; Ammianus 27.9.8–10.
30 Vitruvius 6.3.11; 6.6.6.
31 D.7.6.1.4, Ulpian 18 *ad Sab*: et puto eas solas praestare compellendum sine quibus omnino uti non potest; sed si cum aliquo incommodo utatur, non esse praestandas.
32 D.8.2.14, Papirius Iustus 1 *de const*: intermisso legitimo spatio a vicina insula. While the term 'legitimo spatio' is almost certainly interpolated by the compilers to accord with Zeno's building code, this does not mean that the sense of the rescript is wrong. The original may well have said something like 'quod ex arbitratu viri boni', etc.
33 These are ways of assuring compensation for an injured neighbour.
34 See Rodger (1972), Rainer (1987b) and Palma (1988) who have written at length on this topic.

and public buildings. The very existence of the interdicts proves that the Romans did think that the public interest made it necessary to control new building activity, and also to ensure the upkeep of existing buildings. The interdicts were issued by the praetor, so it is quite likely that he also had jurisdiction over breaches of the regulations on height or clearance, just as he granted the formula for an action claiming or denying a servitude which permitted building work outside the reasonable limits. Notice of new building work was another means of control. 'We serve a notice [of new work] because we have some right of prevention, . . . or if work of some sort is being carried out contrary to the laws or to imperial edicts issued in reference to limitations on buildings'.[35] But how far did the praetor's jurisdiction overlap with the province of the officials with special responsibility for streets? or of the *curatores operum publicorum?* The Urban Prefect eventually succeeded to a general jurisdiction but, from the tone of Ulpian's writing, this would seem to have been later in the third century.

The element of public interest is naturally not always present in such disputes between private citizens, but it could be, whether from the nature of the construction objected to, such as projecting balconies, or because of the general need for the exercise of reasonableness. For example, the interdict *de cloacis* could be granted to prohibit interference with the cleansing and maintenance of private drains, because such work pertained to public health and safety.[36] A restitutory interdict was available so that a public sewer could be restored to working order after having been obstructed;[37] Labeo even held that this interdict could cover the laying of a new sewer, because of public utility, though properly this fell within the sphere of those in charge of the public streets.[38] Other matters affecting the public amenity also fell within the scope of the interdicts, matters like the smoke

35 D.39.1.1.17, Ulpian 52 *ad ed*: Nuntiamus autem quia ius aliquid prohibendi habemus, . . . aut si quid contra leges edictave principum quae ad modum aedificiorum facta sunt.

36 D.43.23.1.2, Ulpian 71 *ad ed*: Curavit autem praetor per haec interdicta ut cloacae et purgentur et reficiantur, quorum utrumque et ad salubritatem civitatium et ad tutelam pertinet: nam et caelum pestilens et ruinas minantur immunditiae cloacarum si non reficiantur.

37 D.43.23.1.15–16, ibid..

38 D.43.23.2 – Venuleius 1 *interdict*.

coming from a cheese smokery, or a dung-heap;[39] we can only guess that there were controls on tanneries.[40]

The theme of a citizen's duty to his neighbours in the sphere of housing, as enforced predominantly through the private law, has received attentive treatment recently.[41] In the context of the right to light Rodger has said:

> In the classical law in the absence of a servitude *altius non tollendi* to restrain him, an owner was free to build up his house as high as he wished providing that it did not cut off the light to his neighbour's house to an intolerable extent. He had to leave his neighbour at least enough light for ordinary everyday existence. An owner who wished to build without having to leave this usual amount of light for his neighbour would have to obtain a servitude *altius tollendi* over his neighbour's land. This would give him the necessary freedom, though certain limits might be set in any given instance. If a neighbour wished to ensure a greater amount of light than the bare minimum he would have to obtain a servitude *altius non tollendi*, after which the servient owner could not raise his house beyond the limits laid down in the servitude. In the case of both servitudes the exact conditions might vary from case to case. Where an owner, free from any servitude *altius non tollendi*, built in a way which cut off his neighbour's light to an intolerable degree, he could be prevented from building or could be forced to remove what he had built. There were certain rules about which of the parties would be the plaintiff in such cases. Actions on the servitude were available, as also were the *cautio damni infecti* and *operis novi nuntiatio*.[42]

This statement must be amplified to take account of other considerations.

A number of legal texts deal with the need to use one's

39 D.8.5.8.5, Ulpian 17 *ad ed*; h.t.17.2, Alfenus 2 *dig.*
40 Martial 6.93 alleges that Thais smells worse than 'a hide dragged from a dog beyond the Tiber'; Juvenal 14.203 tells his poor man not to despise a trade which has to be banished to the far side of the Tiber.
41 The integrity of the texts has recently been discussed very thoroughly by Rainer (1987b) who sees less public intervention in our period than does Rodger.
42 Rodger (1972): 38.

property in a civilised manner. Someone had a pair of houses, and left as a legacy a usufruct in one of them; the heir, who seems to be living in the other, may build in such a way as to obscure the light of the house in usufruct, only not so as to render it completely dark but to leave enough light for people to live there.[43] It was clear that someone who received inadequate light suffered an actionable loss;[44] arbitration was possible if agreement could not be reached.[45] The loss of a convenience – light, prospect and so on – once enjoyed might also be actionable, at least when it came about through something done on public land;[46] here the remedy was an interdict. Literary and epigraphic texts make the same point, that life must be livable, even if not comfortable.

For the Romans, as much as for at least our nineteenth-century selves, there was an interpenetration of public and private interest, a mixture of legislation and jurisprudence, which controlled their building activities. The crisis of the later third century hastened the change to a much more interventionist society,[47] but in the later Republic and during most of the Principate private law was left to cope with much that in the Dominate came to be regulated.[48]

There must always have been a problem of enforcement. There appears to have been no requirement to notify the authorities, as opposed to possibly interested third parties, of any proposed new structure. In the absence of any mechanism by which the authorities could grant or withhold the equivalent of planning permission, any initiative must be taken by some interested party (which is in practice often true nowadays). It is quite possible that there was somewhat more direct legislation on building in the classical period than has come down to us.

---

43 D.7.1.30, Paul 3 *ad Sab*: Si is qui binas aedes habeat aliarum usum fructum legaverit, posse heredem Marcellus scribit alteras altius tollendo obscurare luminibus, quoniam habitari potest etiam obscuratis aedibus. Quod usque adeo temperandum est ut non in totum aedes obscurentur, sed modicum lumen, quod habitantibus sufficit, habeant. This text is really an abbreviation of D.8.2.10, Marcellus 4 *dig*, which ends by requiring only so much light as 'sufficit habitantibus in usus diurni moderatione'. This is very similar to D.7.6.1.4, already cited. See Palma (1988): 196–8.
44 D.39.2.25, Paul 78 *ad ed*, citing Trebatius.
45 D.8.2.11, Ulpian 1 *de off. consulis*.
46 D.43.8.2.11–12, Ulpian 68 *ad ed*.
47 Cf. MacMullen (1976).
48 Rainer (1987b) regularly stresses this point.

Ammianus Marcellinus reported that the Urban Prefect ordered the removal of *maeniana* 'the building of which in Rome was forbidden by early laws also'.[49] In the context, Ulpian's vagueness seems reasonable:

And Sextius Pedius neatly defined three reasons for a notification of new work: from nature, from public interest, and from imposition. It is from nature when someone inserts something into our building or builds on our land; from public interest whenever statute or resolution of the Senate or imperial enactment is upheld by the notification of new work; from imposition when someone imposes a servitude on his house and subsequently infringes that servitude.[50]

There was hardly any administrative law in the strict sense during the Principate; in the classical period administrative remedies had a tendency to function within the framework of the private law,[51] just as in the Dominate the scope of private law was restricted by the growth of administrative law.

DEMOLITION

There is a final area of subordinate planning to be looked at, the law concerning demolition. We find a general prohibition on demolishing buildings, or on unroofing them – that handy way to make even listed (as of historic interest) buildings fit only to be torn down – in the municipal charters of the late Republic and early Empire.[52] This prohibition applied, explicitly in the Tarentine charter and probably implicitly in the others, unless a building as good or better were put up in the place of the one demolished; in the Flavian charter of Irni and the other Spanish

49 Ammianus 27.9.10; they seem to have been a kind of balcony.
50 D.39.1.5.9, Ulpian 52 *ad ed*: Et belle Sextus Pedius definiit triplicem esse causam operis novi nuntiationis, aut naturalem aut publicam aut impositiciam: naturalem cum in nostras aedes quid immittitur aut aedificatur in nostro; publicam causam quotiens leges aut senatus consulta constitutionesque principum per operis novi nuntiationem tuemur; impositiciam, cum quis . . . contra servitutem fecit.
51 Consider, for example, *nautae caupones stabularii* – D.4.9; 47.5 – considered in ch. 9.
52 For example, at Tarentum between 89 and 62 BC – FIRA i 18 (p.166ff), vv. 32–5; at Urso in 44/43 BC – FIRA i 21 (p.177ff), c. 75; at Irni around AD 82/84 – *JRS* 76 (1986, p.147ff), Tab.VIIA <ch. 62>.

towns it was specified that this must be done within the year. In all these towns the decurions had power to grant a licence to demolish without rebuilding, but if their consent was not obtained, a fine of the value of the loss brought about by the demolition was due to the municipality by an *actio popularis*. At Urso security for the rebuilding must be given to the municipal magistrates, comparable to the *cautio damni infecti* imposed by the praetor at Rome, and there was a quorum laid down if the council was to permit demolition; the Flavian law made clear that the whole built-up area – *continentia* – was covered by the prohibition. By the end of the second century it had become the task of the *curator rei publicae* to see that, in the provinces, houses torn down by their owners were rebuilt.[53]

It is virtually certain that there was such a rule at Rome; a Republican statute from which the charters took their model has been postulated.[54] One can, however, trace some of this line of thinking right back to the Twelve Tables and the prohibition there on demolition in order to recover building materials wrongfully used by another in constructing a house or vineyard; Ulpian explained the ancient ruling as preventing people from demolition on this pretext.[55] A strong argument for this principle has recently been put forward,[56] maintaining that its purpose, originally and throughout the Republic, was to preserve the housing stock in the interests of social stability.

The first actual evidence we have that relates to Rome are two resolutions of the Senate preserved together.[57] The first, the *SC Hosidianum*[58] of AD 44, forbade selling town or country houses for demolition. The wording of the resolution itself, as well as juristic comment on it, makes clear that what was prohibited was demolition in order to make a profit by way of business.[59] The seller was to be fined double the purchase price, and must still answer to the Senate, while the buyer lost his money and the sale was held void. This was a strengthening of the general rule, made necessary by the newer and much more luxurious styles

---

53 D.39.2.46, Paul 1 *sent*: ut dirutae domus a dominis extruantur; or, ' that derelict houses are re-erected by their owners'.
54 By, for example, Phillips (1973); Garnsey (1976), Appendix, p. 133ff.
55 D.47.3.1pr, Ulpian 37 *ad ed*: ne vel aedificia sub hoc praetextu diruantur.
56 Lewis (1989).
57 ILS 6043 (= CIL X 1401).
58 Examined by Rainer (1987a).
59 D.18.1.52, Paul 54 *ad ed*.

of building; it is clear that it was dealings in pretty substantial properties which had given rise to the Senate's resolution. The declared aim was to suppress speculation, and a limited degree of knocking down to rebuild on one's own property was specifically excepted. The *SC Volusianum*, which was found with the first, dates from AD 56 and dealt with a particular case; probably the pair were preserved as a statement of the general law and a record of the licence to waive its application. (The terms of the resolution itself, together with the regular occurrence of the ban in the municipal laws and its origin in the custom described in the Twelve Tables, do not suggest any concern with problems of rural depopulation.[60]) It is likely, however, that the motive behind the new legislation was at least as much to protect the urban display of the glories of Rome as to preserve the housing stock for the poorer elements in society. The pairing of these two resolutions of the Senate suggests that the procedure for obtaining a licence to demolish a *domus* may have been identical in Rome and the municipalities, at least in that period. It seems quite likely that this was the sort of business the Senate handled;[61] according to the Regionary Catalogues, which have no interest in minimising the numbers, there were fewer than 1,800 *domus* in the City.[62] Later it may have been necessary to approach the Emperor himself, as one did for permission to occupy *res sanctae*: 'neither walls nor gates may be occupied as dwellings without imperial permission, because of the fire hazard'.[63]

At Rome in the Republic the enforcement of the ban on demolition may have been rather casual, and quite likely influenced by political factors. Cicero writes quite cheerfully to Atticus about a couple of houses he owned, at Puteoli admittedly, which were falling down – not only the tenants but even the mice were leaving them – and which he reckoned to be able to demolish and rebuild at an eventual profit.[64] Further, Vitruvius talked about the advantage of reusing building stone because it will have weathered.[65] In both cases, however, there is the expectation of rebuilding, as there also is in two texts, recorded

60 As Johnson, Coleman-Norton and Bourne (1961): 142 thought.
61 Cf. SHA *Max. et Balb.* 1.
62 But note Dunn (1914–15).
63 D.43.6.3, Paul 5 *sent*: neque muri neque portae habitari sine permissu principis propter fortuita incendia possunt.
64 Cicero *ad Att*.14.9.1.
65 Vitruvius 2.8.19 – 'ex veteris tegulis'.

in the context of *locatio conductio,* which assume that an *insula* can be demolished.[66]

There are other texts, deriving from somewhat later, which uphold the application of the stricter Senate resolution. It had come to be possible that fixtures and fittings might be more valuable than the whole,[67] so in AD 122 the resolution was amplified to cover legacies of things viewed as an integral part of a building.[68] Hadrian, we are told, laid down that nowhere should houses be demolished to provide cheap building material elsewhere.[69] Further consideration by the Senate led to a prohibition on using either a legacy or *fideicommissum* to leave a building with intent to demolish.[70] The penalty of the *SC Hosidianum* seems to have been modified a little, as we learn that 'if anyone should sell a house, or a part of it, for the purpose of making a commercial profit, and should be condemned for this, it is established that seller and buyer should each pay as a fine the price for which the house was sold. However, it is lawful to convey marble or columns for use in public works.'[71] This makes clear that there was an *actio popularis* at Rome as there was in the municipalities. The permission to re-use building materials from a demolished house in public works implies that the purpose of the law had been modified, and that the aesthetic element had become more significant.

It may also be relevant that the sources in the Principate permitting demolition refer to an *insula,* while three of those forbidding it speak of a *domus*[72] (or *villa*); the others use the neutral *aedes.* It was the pulling down of handsome edifices that the government had become concerned with; *domus* were not likely to suffer *ruina* unless from earthquake or fire, whereas

---

66 D.19.2.30pr, Alfenus 3 *dig a Paulo ep;* h.t.35pr, Africanus 8 *quaest,* citing Servius.
67 Compare the habit of dismantling books (such as Audubon's *Birds of America*) to sell off the individual prints.
68 D.30.41.1, Ulpian 21 *ad Sab*: Sed ea quae aedibus iuncta sunt legari non possunt, quia haec legari non posse senatus censuit.
69 SHA *Hadrian* 18.
70 D.30.114.9, Marcian 8 *inst*: aedes destruendae neque legari neque per fideicommissum relinqui possunt, et ita senatus censuit.
71 D.39.2.48, Marcian, *lib. sing. de delatoribus*: si quis ad demoliendum negotiandi causa vendidisse domum partemve domus fuerit convictus, ut emptor et venditor singuli pretium quo domus distracta est praestent constitutum est. ad opus autem publicum si transferat marmora vel columnas, licito iure facit.
72 Cf. D.43.8.7, Julian 48 *dig.*

water could undermine the many storeys of an *insula*, or cost-cutting in its building could readily lead to collapse. This concern with appearances, which reflected the glory of the individual emperor – and earlier of the Roman people – would also explain why an exception was made for materials re-used for public buildings, in order to beautify them.[73] We know that where someone had built on public land and had not been told to stop, he could not be made to remove what he had built 'ne ruinis urbs deformetur' though he would have to pay a ground rent – *vectigal*.[74]

---

73 In D.9.2.50, Ulpian 6 *opin*. we find: Qui domum alienam, invito domino, demolit . . . without any mention of administrative censure or criminal penalty, but then, this wrecker had built baths.

74 D.43.8.2.17, Ulpian 68 *ad ed*; the same point is made in h.t.7, Ulpian 48 *ad dig*, which adds, however, that anyone who builds in defiance of a praetorian edict must remove the building, so as not to set the praetor's authority at naught.

4

PUBLIC BUILDINGS AND PUBLIC WORKS

Polybius remarked that public building was the chief expense regularly incurred by the state.[1] The range of public buildings in Rome was immense.[2] Plautus described the City's characters in terms of the public places they frequented.[3] Strabo listed the Campus Martius with its grassy areas and porticoes, the three theatres, the amphitheatre (not yet a stone-built structure), Augustus' Mausoleum, the Forums, basilicas and temples, the Capitol and its works of art and those of the Palatium and Livia's Portico.[4] Pliny the Elder mentioned, apart from his praise of the sewers and aqueducts, as among the more important monuments of Rome: the Circus Maximus, basilica Aemilia, Forum of Augustus, Temple of Peace, Agrippa's roofed Diribitorium, Gaius' palace and Nero's *domus Aurea*, and the theatres of Scaurus, and Curio.[5] In 357 the Emperor Constantius paid a visit to Rome and particularly admired the Forum Romanum, the Capitol, the *thermae*, the Colosseum, the Pantheon, Vespasian's Forum with the Temple of Peace, Pompey's Theatre, the Odeum, the Stadium and Trajan's Forum.[6]

There were religious buildings, buildings for popular use, official buildings, commercial buildings, and buildings for leisure; one could add bridges. Public works are somewhat narrowly defined in this chapter, because I have chosen, partly on the

1 Polybius 6.13.3.
2 For a full, if elderly, discussion see de Ruggiero (1925); more recent are Strong (1968); Brunt (1980); Carter (1989); Barton (1989 a and b). See also Boatwright (1987), Thornton (1989) and other citations in ch. 2.
3 Plautus, *Curculio* 470–86, mentioning the Comitium, Venus Cloacina, the basilica, *forum piscarium*, temple of Castor, and the Tuscan quarter.
4 Strabo 5.3.8.
5 Pliny *NH* 36.24.102–3 & 111 & 113–20.
6 Ammianus 16.10.13–15.

basis of the commissions created by Augustus and Tiberius, partly because of their function, to deal with aqueducts and the water supply elsewhere, as also with streets, drains and public baths. The treatment is also restricted because, as with planning, the emperors took so much in this area into their own charge that the formalities of law played rather a small part.

NEW BUILDING IN THE REPUBLIC

In the Republic public building generally, especially secular public building, was the responsibility of the censors;[7] only for the erection of temples did they need to obtain the authorisation of the Senate.[8] Consuls and praetors occasionally engaged in such work, usually with booty gained from successful wars, and always *ex senatusconsulto*, but they commonly restricted themselves to such things as altars, arches and porticoes,[9] except for temples vowed in time of crisis; de Ruggiero counted[10] thirty-six temples with such an origin, before Agrippa's Pantheon. Aediles did not normally initiate any major projects. Although it was the aediles who built, or saw to the building of, the *porticus Aemilia* serving the Emporium, it was the censors who, less than twenty years later, paved the area and repaired the portico.[11] Apart from building financed by booty, and occasionally by fines (such as the *porticus Aemilia*), the Senate provided the relevant magistrates with the money (raised from tribute or taxes) for their public works, whether building, restoration or maintenance.

The work itself was done by contractors. The auction of the contract seems always to have taken place in the Forum; the *praeco* was in charge of the mechanics of the auction, but it was up to the magistrate offering the tender to accept or reject a bid, and the accompanying offer of security.[12] The contract was then registered, and in due course the completed

---

7 Cicero *de leg*.3.3.7 ascribes to them the care of temples, streets and aqueducts, while the aediles have a general care of the city and are responsible for the grain supply and for the games.
8 E.g. Magna Mater – Livy 36.36.4; Diana and Juno Regina – Livy 40.51–2.
9 E.g. Livy 37.3.7; Pliny *NH* 34.7.13. See also ILS 13 (= CIL VI 474), 41 (= VI 1316), 42 (= VI 1301), 59 (= VI 1315).
10 de Ruggiero (1925), ch. 3.
11 Livy 35.10.12; 41.27.8–9.
12 de Ruggiero (1925), ch. ix. Cf. FIRA i 13 (p.140ff) *tabula Heracleensis*, vv. 39–40; *JRS* 76 (1986, p.147ff) *lex Irnitana*, Tab. VIIB <ch. 63>.

work approved by the magistrate.[13] It was on behalf of Caesar, but presumably with the Senate's authorisation, that Cicero and Oppius were doing the preliminary work for widening the Forum and building a colonnade to surround the marble booths proposed for the *comitia tributa's* voting.[14] At the same time Paullus seems to have been restoring the basilica erected by his family at his own expense. (Basilicas, which Vitruvius held should have two storeys, were convenient for *negotiatores*, but *negotiatores* were to be found in all sorts of places, for instance the court of the Temple of Saturn.[15]) The constitutional niceties disappeared in the building work of Sulla, Pompey and, above all, Julius Caesar.[16]

We have ample evidence for the censors' concerning themselves with aqueducts, drains, the repair of temples, basilicas, circuses, bridges and the paving of the streets.[17] On occasion, special commissioners were appointed.[18] In the late Republic, when the censorship was effectively in desuetude, it was mainly the aediles who had to deal with public building as part of their *cura urbis*. It was necessary to arrange the acquisition of a site, its clearance, the putting out to tender of the building work, the raising of the necessary money, whether from *aerarium*, booty, fines, or oblations, the marking out of the limits of the public area, the appointment of men to work on and watch over the new building, and finally its dedication. The aediles had to exercise jurisdiction over all these matters, and also to prevent private persons intruding their buildings on public space.[19]

Major restoration work seems to have counted as building, rather than maintenance; it entitled the restorer to put his name on the building. The consuls (and also the praetors) as holders of *imperium* were sometimes viewed as more suitable than the Senate for the work of restoration, for example in 69 BC on the restoration of Capitoline Jove after the fire which had occurred

13 Cicero *in Verr.* II 1.49.130–58.153.
14 Cicero *ad Att.*4.16.8.
15 Vitruvius 5.1.2 & 4–5; ILS 892 (= CIL I 636): *M. Acilio M. f. Canino q[aestori] urb[ano] negotiatores ex area Saturni.*
16 See ch. 2: Planning.
17 Cicero *de leg.*3.3.7; Livy 39.42 & 44; 40.51; 41.27; 45.15; Frontinus *aq.*5, 6 & 8; ILS 54 (= CIL XI 1827); and see ch. 5: Streets.
18 212 BC, Livy 25.7 records *quinqueviri muris turribus reficiendis et triumviri . . . reficiendis aedibus Fortunae.*
19 Cf. Livy 39.44, on Cato's censorship of 184 BC, when private citizens who had built on public land were given 30 days for demolition.

after Sulla's death;[20] on occasion, however, a curule aedile might not merely restore but also add his own name.[21] When the *curia Hostilia* (where the Senate frequently met[22]) was burned down during riots in 52 BC, the Senate itself, not surprisingly, let out the contract for its rebuilding.[23] (In 44 BC, however, that building was demolished when Caesar determined to rebuild the Senate house.[24])

Maintenance was not in practice clearly split off from new building in the Republic. Its organisation again was the aediles' normal function; maintenance of the temples was in all probability the original purpose of the plebeian aediles. Many public buildings were technically *templa* in that they were places dedicated by the augurs,[25] for example the *curia Hostilia*, or the *atrium Libertatis* from which the censors operated.[26] We also, however, hear of the praetors in this role. Cicero described how Verres had cheated the young heir of someone who had contracted for the maintenance of the temple of Castor. The consuls had put out the contract; neither they nor the praetors assigned to the business had inspected and certified the work,[27] which had in fact been done, so Verres was able to put it out to tender anew and to award the contract to a friend.[28] So uncertain a division of responsibility makes it not surprising that there was confusion in 45 BC over which magistrates were to administer the City in the political crisis following Caesar's absence.[29]

---

20 ILS 35, 35a (= CIL VI 1313–14); Livy *ep*.98; Frontinus *aq*.7 on repair of Appia and Anio Vetus by Marcius. Sometimes in the Empire such work, which is all either restoration or the construction of relatively small monuments, is ascribed to SPQR: ILS 3781 (= CIL VI 89) – restoration of Temple of Concord; ILS 255 (= VI 938) – Temple of Vespasian; ILS 294 (= VI 960) – Trajan's Column; ILS 5386 (= VI 1270) – re-laying a street with public money; Tac. *Annals* 15.18; Dio 51.19 (arch to Augustus after Actium); SHA *Ant. Pius* 6.

21 ILS 43a (= CIL VI 1303–4).

22 Livy 1.30.2; Cicero *pro Mil*.90.

23 Dio 40.49–50.

24 Dio 44.5.

25 Gellius 14.7.7.

26 Certain temples lay outside the City proper, such as that of Venus, to keep off lust, of Vulcan, to prevent fires, and of Mars, to discourage armed quarrels among the citizens – Vitruvius 1.7.1.

27 Cf. D.48.11.7.2, Macer 1 *iud. pub.* on the *lex Julia repetundarum*, forbidding any release to be given for the construction of public works or the maintenance of public buildings before the completed job was approved.

28 Cicero *in Verr*. II 1.49.130–58.153; cf. *ad Att*.4.1.7; 4.2.3–5.

29 Dio 43.48.

NEW BUILDING IN THE PRINCIPATE

Naturally, Augustus, as premier citizen, engaged in the provision of public buildings; they included completing the *curia Julia* as a meeting place for the Senate, the building of a new portico at the Circus Flaminius, the restoration of the Capitol and of Pompey's theatre, and the Forum Augustum.[30] In 34 BC Aemilius Lepidus Paullus rebuilt the basilica Aemilia,[31] but he was a member of the Triumvirate. Agrippa as aedile in 33 BC had repaired all public buildings;[32] but his aedileship was extraordinary both in being held after he had been consul and in its range of public works. Agrippa also dedicated the Saepta (voting enclosures for the tribal assembly of the people) after redecorating them,[33] and he beautified the City generally, at his own expense, with public buildings[34] – but since 21 BC he had been Augustus' son-in-law. However, it was the Senate which resolved on the *ara Pacis*, according to Augustus,[35] who is a possibly disingenuous commentator. Nevertheless, as part of his restoration of the Republic, Augustus encouraged leading citizens to build or to restore out of enemy spoils or their own private resources. He allowed Taurus to build a stone amphitheatre (later burned down), Balbus a theatre, and Philippus to restore the temple of Hercules of the Muses 'to the adornment of Rome for the applause of posterity'.[36] Nevertheless, it was Augustus himself who built on an enormous scale,[37] though we do not know who took detailed control over these works.

As the Empire became established, most work was done in the name of the *princeps*, though we hear, not very reliably, of the Senate discussing public works as late as 238;[38] we know it was erecting triumphal arches in AD 80.[39] Even under Augustus,

---

30 *RG* 19–21.1.
31 Dio 49.42.
32 Dio 49.43.
33 Dio 53.23, of 26 BC.
34 Dio 53.27, of 25 BC, mentioning the basilica of Neptune, a gymnasium (i.e. baths) and the first Pantheon.
35 *RG* 12.2; cf. ILS 81 (= CIL VI 873).
36 Tac. *Annals* 3.72; cf. Suet. *Aug*.29. Also, e.g. ILS 3423 (= CIL VI 30899), 5414 (= VI 30985). Tacitus, however, elsewhere – *Annals* 13.31 – remarks that the erection of public buildings is not worthy of the historian's pen.
37 *RG* 19–21; Suet. *Aug*.29.
38 SHA *Max. & Balb*.1.
39 ILS 264 (= CIL VI 944); Tac. *Annals* 15.18. See also e.g. ILS 348 (= VI 1005), 425 (= VI 1033).

the *campus Agrippae* and the Diribitorium had become public property in 7 BC.[40] Temples and other buildings put up by private persons were taken into the public domain.[41] In AD 22, however – 'for public munificence was still fashionable' – the basilica Pauli was repaired at private expense by Lepidus, after a petition to the Senate,[42] but it was Tiberius who rebuilt the theatre of Pompey after a fire because no member of the family had the resources for such a task.[43] Claudius continued to encourage private persons to construct buildings for the public good, or to repair them, by allowing such people (and no others, except by permission of the Senate) to put up images of themselves;[44] we find this concession mentioned by Ulpian.[45]

From Macer we learn that in the early third century a private citizen – outside Rome – was free to put up some new work at his own expense even without imperial licence, unless it was from rivalry with another city or a source of sedition (which thus excluded a circus, theatre or amphitheatre), but erecting new buildings at public expense did need the emperor's permission; the only name allowed to be inscribed on a public work was that of the emperor or of the citizen who had put it up at his own expense.[46] Antoninus Pius preferred men to leave their money for the upkeep of existing public works rather than the erection of yet more structures that would require expensive maintenance.[47]

Hadrian was a little unusual, we are told, in not putting his name on the buildings he restored,[48] which were many; but this had also been the practice of Tiberius, while Claudius too had

40 Dio 55.8.
41 Moreover, the fisc (imperial treasury) was always the residuary heir: G. 2.150; Ulpian *Reg*.28.7; D.30.96.1, Julian 39 *dig*.
42 Tac. *Annals* 3.72.
43 Velleius 2.130; Tac. *Annals* 3.72; Suet. *Tib*.47.
44 Dio 60.25; hitherto, anyone who wished could have his likeness appear in public, whether in paint, bronze or marble.
45 D.50.10.2pr, Ulpian 3 *opin*.
46 D.50.10.3.2, Macer 2 *de off. praesidis*: Inscribi autem nomen operi publico alterius quam principis aut eius, cuius pecunia id opus factum sit, non licet.
47 D.50.10.7pr, Callistratus 2 *de cogn*; cf. 50.10.5pr, Ulpian *de off.curatoris rei pub*.
48 SHA *Hadrian* 19.9–11; cf. SHA *Sept. Sev*.23, who, it is here said, also usually kept the original inscriptions, though Dio (77.16) said he put his own name to such buildings.

put back the names of the original builders.[49] Domitian, on the other hand, when he restored buildings, allowed only his own name, not that of the original builder, to be inscribed.[50] We can reckon, at least from the reign of Claudius on, that the initiation of public building, actual construction, was becoming steadily more the province of the emperor, except for very minor monuments; major buildings were political propaganda.[51] Some were traditional, if on a new scale, such as the temples of the deified Claudius, Vespasian's Temple of Peace, that of Janus Quadrifons, Hadrian's Temple of Venus and Rome, the basilicas, markets, *horrea* (warehouses), and porticoes. Others were novel, almost revolutionary – the extra forums, the huge *thermae*, the *naumachiae*, the Amphitheatrum Flavium (later known as the Colosseum), the Stadium, the Odeum, and of course the great palaces such as the *domus Aurea*.

It has been pointed out that temples, like arches and porticoes, are simple buildings in general, easy and cheap to construct with a low work load cost.[52] Thornton holds that, apart from Tiberius, the Julio-Claudians 'initiated public works programs with a timing which insured a high and continuous rate of construction and of employment. Whether this is evidence of sophistication or accident we do not know'.[53] The timing does, however, suggest management.[54] Procurators, commissions of equestrians, or imperial freedmen, seem to have been in charge of the construction of individual buildings for the emperors.[55] The Urban Prefect was, of course, the person with overall responsibility from the later Principate and on into the Dominate.[56] Cleander, for example, spent much on houses, baths, and other works of benefit to the public as well as individuals on behalf of Commodus.[57]

---

49 Dio 57.10; 60.6.8.
50 Suet. *Dom*.5.
51 Cf. ch. 2: Planning.
52 Thornton (1986).
53 ibid.: 37.
54 This is also the belief of Brunt (1980).
55 Tac. *Hist*.4.53; Suet. *Titus* 8.
56 E.g. Ammianus 27.3.7 – Lampadius as Urban Prefect put his name on restorations – & 10 – where the seizure of materials by the Urban Prefect without paying caused a riot; Cassiodorus *Variae* 7.15.
57 Dio 73.12.

THE *CURA OPERUM PUBLICORUM*

It was to fulfil the task of maintenance that Augustus created, probably towards the end of his life, the *curatores operum publicorum*.[58] The office was held by a pair of senatorials, usually of praetorian but occasionally of consular rank; sometimes they seem to have been true colleagues, sometimes one had charge of *opera publica* and the other of *aedes sacrae*.[59] The title of the commission does not seem to have been official; we find 'curator/ aedium sacrarum/ et operum/ locorumque publicorum/ populi romani', or any permutation of these,[60] or 'curator aedium sacrarum monumentorumque publicorum tuendorum'.[61] On occasion there seems to have been a senatorial substitute – or perhaps a co-opted member – *vice operum publicorum*.[62] It was Augustus who divorced building and major restoration from maintenance. This limitation on the competence of the curators explains why they are not found exercising a right of *terminatio* – the formal marking off of public land from land susceptible of private ownership – nor jurisdiction.

There is one equestrian recorded, in the very early third century, as *curator aedium sacrarum*,[63] but this may be due to the political confusion of the times. It was the office of sub-curator that was normally held by an equestrian.[64] Individual responsibilities, perhaps at the same level as that of the sub-curator, were held by the *curator operis theatri*[65] or the *procurator operis theatri Pompeiani*;[66] under Constantine there first appeared a (senatorial) *curator statuarum*, reporting to the Urban Prefect.[67] The procurator *operum publicorum* presumably ranked below the sub-curator;[68] this seems to have

58 Suet. *Aug*.37.
59 CIL VI 1854; ILS 452 (= CIL VI 31338a), perhaps the last record of them.
60 ILS 8971; cf. ILS 1098 (= CIL VI 1377), 1080 (= VI 1517), and just *curator aedium*, ILS 366 (= VI 360); or contrast VI 864 with VI 31128, recording the same colleagues.
61 ILS 932 (= CIL IX 3305).
62 ILS 1185 (= CIL XIV 3593) of the third century; he later became curator (*aed. sacr. et oper. pub.*)
63 ILS 8935 (= CIL VI 33856), a *vir clarissimus* under Maxentius.
64 *Eph. ep*. IX 897: *subcurator aedium sacrarum et operum locorumque publicorum*; ILS 1425 (= CIL VII 1054): *subcurator operum publicorum*; cf. Tac. *Hist*.4.53.
65 ILS 1347 (= CIL VIII 822).
66 ILS 1430 (= CIL VIII 1439).
67 ILS 1222 (= CIL VI 1708); cf. *Notitia Dignitatum, Occ*. IV 12–15.
68 ILS 1387 (= CIL X 6657).

become a regular office in the later second century, in the bottom – *sexagenarii* – rank of procuratorships. A distinction seems sometimes to be drawn between *opera maxima* and *opera minora*;[69] the latter perhaps included the responsibility for the putting up of new statues (which in the Later Empire had, as we have seen, their own curator). This had been a matter of some importance in the Republic, when there could be debate about whether someone should be given a public funeral or a public statue.[70] Did the curators themselves, rather than their subordinates, authorise public statues? Did the college of pontiffs continue to have a role? Or was it just the emperor as *pontifex maximus?*

The procurator presumably came to be the official who co-ordinated the shipment and delivery of building materials to Rome, usually by river transport, through the office of the *procurator marmorum*, who had his own staff.[71] We find imperial *rationales* giving permission to the procurator of the column of Marcus Aurelius and Faustina for building on what seems technically to be public land.[72]

There was the usual office staff for the *cura operum publicorum*, whose office seems to have been called the *statio operum publicorum*, and then the *statio urbana*. We have on record *dispensatores, tabularii,* and an *exactor*[73] and *servi publici*;[74] it is reasonable to assume *scribae* and *praecones*, as were employed by the aediles, and by the other commissioners, such as those for distributing grain or for the water supply. Other men were employed as custodians of individual monuments; in a parallel

69 ILS 1250 (= CIL X 6441): *praefecto operum maximorum.* XV 7241 may refer to a *curator operum minorum*, but since he appears to be the tribune of a Praetorian cohort, this would seem to be some military post.

70 Cicero *Phil.* 9.7.16 records the Senate decreeing a statue and a 5-foot length on the benches at the games for the descendants of Servius Sulpicius Rufus – the urban quaestors were to put the job out to tender and see to its completion; cf. ILS 55. Cf. also Cicero *de domo* 51.130–2; 53.136.

71 E.g. ILS 1707 (= CIL VI 410), 1598 (= VI 8483), 1599 (= VI 8184), 1600 (= VI 8486). See also ch. 6 on the Tiber.

72 ILS 5920 (= CIL VI 1585); cf. 5439 (= VI 460).

73 ILS 1604 (= CIL VI 8478), 1605 (= X 529); ILS 1602 (= VI 8479); a *tabularius mensorum aedificiorum* in ILS 1689 (= VI 8933) implies a regular staff of *mensores* or surveyors. Cf. CIL VI 9078, *adiutor tabulariorum rationis urbicae*; VI 8481, *exactor operum.* These are all imperial slaves or freedmen, so they might be working to the emperor rather than the curators.

74 ILS 1968 (= CIL VI 2337); ILS 1969 (= VI 2339).

to the public service, there are members of the imperial *familia* staffing places which remained imperial property.[75] And it would seem to have been the fisc which normally paid.[76] Pertinax is said to have put aside a fixed sum for public works, and Severus Alexander to have taxed pimps and used the profits for the same purpose; the Emperor Tacitus is said to have assigned the revenues from his estates in Mauretania for the maintenance of the Capitol.[77]

PUBLIC BUILDINGS AND THEIR PURPOSE: LIBRARIES, ETC.

While some buildings might have a very general purpose – a temple, for example, could be used for worship, for meetings of the Senate, and for commercial convenience – there were others that were specialised. Originally the Forum had been used for shows of all sorts,[78] but later places of mass public entertainment were constructed. The theatres, amphitheatre and circus have links with law and order, holiday traffic, and so on, but the running of these huge but single-purpose structures was under imperial control, and their upkeep was only marginally a matter of public works.

While hardly 'public' in the sense of nineteenth-century improvements for the working man, there were cultural institutions in Rome which were available to at least a narrow public. It is to be remarked, however, that 'culture' was not normally pursued in buildings dedicated to this single purpose. (Hadrian's Athenaeum does, however, seem to have been built simply for educational activities.[79]) Julius Caesar set out to provide public libraries, Greek and Latin, commissioning Varro to collect on a comprehensive scale,[80] but presumably this project was, like so many others, cut short by Caesar's death.

---

75 ILS 1603 (= CIL XI 3860) *A commentariis operum publicorum et rationum patrimonii*; ILS 1601 (= VI 8480) *exactor operum dominicorum*; ILS 1577 (= VI 8686) *procurator Mausolaei* [of Augustus]; CIL VI 8676, *vilicus thermarum Neronianarum*; ILS 1628 (= VI 8677) *exactor thermarum Traianarum*.
76 ILS 5920 (= CIL VI 1585).
77 SHA *Pert.*9; *Sev. Alex.*24; *Tacitus* 10.
78 Vitruvius 1.1.
79 Dio 74.17; Boatwright (1987): 207–8.
80 Suet. *Julius* 44. Lucullus had thrown open his private library to visiting scholars, especially Greeks, according to Plutarch, *Lucullus* 42.

Pliny tells us that Asinius Pollio founded the first public library in Rome some time after 39 BC, financing it from the spoils of war;[81] this was the one in the *atrium Libertatis* (the site of the censorial office), and it contained both Greek and Latin books. It may also have functioned more generally as a museum, a place for the collection of wonderful things.[82] Dio reports that in 33 BC Augustus used the spoils of the Dalmatian wars to build porticoes and libraries (also in two sections, Greek and Latin), named Octavia after his sister;[83] Plutarch's version[84] is that Augustus' nephew, who died during his aedileship, was commemorated by Augustus' dedication to him of a theatre, and by his mother Octavia's dedication of the library which bears his name. We know that a (freeborn) freedman of Maecenas was, at Augustus' appointment, set to cataloguing it.[85] Two libraries, one Latin, one Greek, were completed on the Palatine in 28 BC, sited in the colonnades of the Temple of Apollo.[86] A very learned freedman of Augustus, C. Iulius Hyginus, was the first librarian,[87] and the contents seem to have included legal works: '[The phrase] "Apollo skilled in the law" [is used] either because the lawyers used to sit and transact their business [which also implies some availability of suitable books] beside the Temple of Apollo, or because Augustus dedicated a library of the civil law and liberal studies there.'[88]

We are told that Domitian, at considerable expense, provided funds for the restoration of fire-damaged libraries.[89] There was a library in the *domus Tiberiana* which the author of the *Historia Augusta* for the life of Probus claimed to have used, as well as the *bibliotheca Ulpia*[90] (in his time located at the Baths of Diocletian) which Trajan established in AD 112 and which was then situated in his Forum.[91] SHA also claimed that the Emperor Tacitus made use of the *bibliotheca Ulpia*.[92] Aulus Gellius and his

---

81 Pliny *NH* 35.2.10; 7.30.115; Ovid *Trist*.3.1.71–2.
82 Pliny *NH* 36.4.23–5 & 33–4.
83 Dio 49.43.
84 Plut. *Marcellus* 30.6.
85 Suet. *gramm*.21; cf. Ovid *Trist*.3.1.69–70.
86 Suet. *Aug*.29; Dio 53.1. Cf. Horace *Ep*.1.3.17; Ovid *Trist*.3.1.63.
87 Suet. *gramm*.20.
88 Scholiast to Juvenal *Juv*. 1.128; see Mayor (1886): 146.
89 Suet. *Dom*.20.
90 SHA *Probus* 2.1; the same was said in SHA *Aurelian* 1 and 8; Gellius 13.20.1.
91 Dio 68.16 records that Trajan built libraries.
92 SHA *Tacitus* 8.1.

friends worked sometimes in the library of the *domus Tiberiana*, but he clearly used a range of libraries: 'as we were by chance sitting in the [Ulpian] library of Trajan's Temple', he was looking up the Edicts of the Praetors; on another occasion he found something in the library of Vespasian's *templum Pacis*.[93] Fronto tells us[94] that Marcus had taken certain books *de Apollinis bibliothecabus* of which the *Tiberianus bibliothecarius* wanted copies. Ammianus in his lament on the decline of modern manners complained that all the libraries were shut while the Romans indulged in music and theatre.[95] The Appendix to the *Curiosum* lists twenty-eight libraries for the mid-fourth century and the *Notitia* twenty-nine.

Paintings and other works of art were also exhibited to the public;[96] porticoes were important for this function. 'In pinacothecam perveni' said Petronius;[97] Pliny tells us that Vespasian put works of art in public places, such as the *templum Pacis*. In other words, in buildings used as libraries one might well expect to find works of art. Pliny devoted quite a lot of space to the artistic glories of Rome; he also said, but it is hard to believe, that Agrippa had suggested nationalising all pictures and statues.[98] It remained a sphere of interest to the state; Cassiodorus said that the *comes Romanus* was in charge of works of art, to prevent vandalism and check theft.[99]

Great men might provide libraries or displays of artistic wealth; as time went on, the only such great men came to be the emperors. Particular officials to look after them might be appointed; as we have seen, librarians appear to have come from the imperial *familia*. But the buildings which housed the books or works of art seem to have fallen simply to the care of the *curatores aedium et operum* and their staff; a task for the works department, even if there were technical specialists as well for certain posts.

93 Gellius 11.17.1; cf. 5.21.9; 16.8.2.
94 Fronto *ad Marcum* 4.5 (Naber p.68, Loeb p.178–9).
95 Ammianus 14.6.18.
96 Van Buren (1956).
97 Petronius *Sat.*83.
98 Pliny *NH* 34.19.84; 35.7.19–10.28; 36.4.27. *NH* 35.9.26 is the reference to Agrippa's proposal; for an explanation, see Tortorici (1991): 120.
99 Cassiodorus *Variae* 7.13.

5

STREETS AND THOROUGHFARES

Dionysius of Halicarnassus wrote: 'In my opinion, indeed, the three most magnificent works of Rome, in which the greatness of her empire is best seen, are the aqueducts, the paved roads, and the construction of the sewers'.[1] Strabo too remarked that the major concern of the Romans was with streets, aqueducts and drains.[2] On the topic of streets and their maintenance, as well as the traffic using them, we are fortunate in having the detailed rules of the *tabula Heracleensis*.[3] The care of the sewers and drains in the Republic and for the first century or so of the Empire, until it was attached under Trajan to the *cura alvei Tiberis et riparum*, went along with the supervision of the streets, but this chapter concerns them only so far as was necessary for keeping the surface of the City clean. (They are dealt with in more detail under Public Health – see chapter 8.)

REPAIR AND MAINTENANCE IN THE JULIAN LAW

S.7[4] of the Julian law deals with streets within the City and a mile beyond – i.e. in the built-up area.[5] Frontagers are to keep the streets in repair in accordance with the judgement of the relevant aedile in charge of that quarter of the City. This is

1 DH 3.67.5.
2 Strabo 5.3.8.
3 FIRA i 13 (p.140ff). Recent discussions of the inscription are referred to in ch. 1, footnote 24; see particularly Frederiksen (1965). I accept the mid-sections as legislation for Rome, proposed by Julius Caesar, which therefore can be referred to as the Julian law. It will be cited in this chapter simply as *Tab. Hera*. The Latin texts, in the order discussed, are placed as an Appendix to this chapter.
4 *Tab. Hera*. vv. 20–3.
5 See ch. 1.

a matter for the aedile to supervise – naturally enough, if it must be done to his satisfaction. Nor is water to stand in the streets, impeding the passage of the populace. So, clearly, the drains must not be clogged or damaged, even accidentally in the course of repair. One does not know the defence that could be put forward by a frontager whose part of the street had an adequate gutter but from which there was no effective drainage; while he was responsible for any drain serving his own house, this extended only up to the junction with the main drain. Presumably the aedile will have sent along a gang to clear the drain, or else called in the contractor who had taken on street works to send his gang.

In s.8[6] the aediles (who, within five days of taking office, must divide among themselves their geographical sphere of duty[7]) are each required to see to the general repair, as well as maintenance, specifically paving, of the public streets; so one can deduce that some streets were unadopted, and so not in the full sense public. (This may well have continued to be the case when we consider T. Flavius Germanus, who flourished under Commodus, procurator of a Region or Regions of the City, to whose duty was added the paving of two-thirds of the City's streets[8] – unless it was really repair.)

In s.9[9] the law considers streets with public buildings or land adjoining them on one side and private property on the other. This does not affect the responsibility of the private owner, but the aedile is to let out the contract for the maintenance of the public side of the street. It does not seem to be the responsibility of any temple authorities, nor of the censors or the consuls; presumably this is part of the general *cura urbis* exercised by the aediles. It is, of course, too early for there to be commissioners for the upkeep of public buildings.

S.10[10] deals with an all too likely problem: that the frontagers would not carry out their duty – by reason of poverty, age, sickness, absenteeism, idleness, or incompetence. The aedile is authorised to see to this. He is to contract out the maintenance of the street, giving at least ten days' notice of this intention in

---

6 *Tab. Hera.* vv. 25–8.
7 The four *regiones* of the Republic: Collina, Suburana, Esquilina, Palatina.
8 ILS 1420 (= CIL XIV 2922) – *proc. reg. urbi.*
9 *Tab. Hera.* vv. 29–31.
10 *Tab. Hera.* vv. 32–46.

a public poster – drawn up, presumably, by a *scriba* – which also names the street and the defaulting frontager. Would the tender for the contract vary with the credit-worthiness of the frontager? It seems quite likely. Notice must also be given to the frontager, or his procurator. The contract is let through the urban quaestor[11] or the minor magistrate (probably one of the *III/IVviri auro argento aere flando feriundo*) in charge of the *aerarium*; this official is acting publicly in the Forum, and equally the record of the debt due from the frontager is public. The frontager must pay, or at least give security to, the contractor within thirty days after he becomes aware of the notice of assessment; otherwise he must pay the cost of the tender plus a penalty of 50 per cent. The contractor is able to recover this from him by ordinary process of law, with the sum due being treated as a straightforward loan.

S.11[12] deals with cases where such a contract has been let. The contractor is responsible to the aedile for the carrying out of the work to a reasonable standard; the quaestor's role is akin to that of the legal staff in a modern city, in that he must see that the proper formalities have been observed.

Why s.13,[13] which is also on maintenance, should not follow directly but come after the section on cleansing is not clear. Despite the phrase 'ante aedificium', the section seems more likely to refer to alleys than pavements.[14] Alleys are not quite so likely to be used by the general public, and safe passage was the ostensible reason given for the prohibition on standing water. But the paving here required may be demanded explicitly because it is precisely in a lane or alley that one might think a lesser standard would do. It is clear from archaeology that decent paving, with stone blocks set into a foundation, was normal on city streets, even if the problems of open drains, cartwheel ruts, winter mud, rubbish, and so on might diminish the effect. The frontager would know what was expected of him concerning the upkeep of the street in front of his house. (The efficiency of the work of maintenance was, of course, no more guaranteed than was cleanliness.

11 Cf. Cicero *Phil.* 9.7.16, where the quaestors are to let out the contract for putting up a statue.
12 *Tab. Hera.* vv. 47–9.
13 *Tab. Hera.* vv. 53–5.
14 Many, perhaps most, streets were not wide enough to have pavements, and there are few archaeological traces of 'sidewalks'; the existing streets of many Italian or French towns manage without.

Petronius' heroes cut their feet on the misplaced paving stones as well as the broken crocks;[15] Ammianus, who admittedly wants to draw a gloomy picture, while acknowledging that the streets of Rome were broad, refers to the uneven paving – *subversas silices*.[16])

So much is specifically on maintenance in the Julian law; we can add various details. In the Republic Livy records the censors paving the streets,[17] but he also refers more than once to this as an aedilician function.[18] Varro[19] tells us that the Clivus Publicius was so called because it had been constructed with the money from fines, so that vehicles could have access to the Aventine, by two brothers of that name who were aediles around 238 BC; he adds that two other *clivi* were named after the 'viocuri' who built them. An inscription simply records: 'The Senate and Roman people saw to the re-levelling of the Clivus Martius at public expense'.[20] There seems to have been a *lex Visellia*,[21] of 72 BC, giving a *cura viarum* to the tribunes, but this may have applied, like the Augustan one, to roads outside the City. Agrippa as aedile (a special consular aedile) repaired all the City streets in 33 BC.[22] In 20 BC Augustus himself as commissioner for highways in the neighbourhood of Rome had the Golden Milestone erected as a terminus for all roads, but two ex-praetors, each with two lictors, actually supervised the work.[23]

REPAIR AND MAINTENANCE
UNDER THE PRINCIPATE

Dio further informs us that in 6 BC there were appointed officials chosen from among the people, 'whom we call street commissioners (*stenoparchoi*)'. These men were entitled to wear official dress and to be attended by two lictors, but only on certain days

15 Petronius, *Sat*.79.
16 Ammianus 14.6.16.
17 Livy 38.28.3 (189 BC) and 41.27.5 (174 BC).
18 Livy 10.23 (296 BC) and 10.47 (293 BC). See also Cicero *de leg*.3.3.7 on their respective roles.
19 Varro *LL* 5.158.
20 ILS 5386 (= CIL VI 1270).
21 CIL I 593: *cur viar e lege visellia de conl sen . . .* [three names] *. . . opus consta.*
22 Dio 49.43.
23 Dio 54.8.

and in those quarters of the City in which they held authority. They were put in charge of the corps of slaves which had formerly been under the orders of the aediles with the task of saving buildings which had caught fire.[24] These cannot be the *IVviri viis in urbe purgandis* (with or without the *IIviri viis extra urbem purgandis*), for those were normally young men of senatorial family and, even if (as Dio himself tells us[25]) a resolution of the Senate in 13 BC opened the vigintivirate to those of equestrian status, it was still a first step on the senatorial career. The *stenoparchoi* must be some lesser persons, probably, as the reference to 'official dress' rather implies, the *vicomagistri*,[26] here exercising a new function; though it remains possible that they were a short-lived experiment in the year following the creation of Augustus' XIV Regions. Efficiency was clearly intended, since they were to control an organised body of slaves who would actually wield the picks, shovels and brushes.

Dio goes on to explain that in each of the XIV Regions an aedile, praetor or tribune was put in charge, after the distribution of lots. This was not a new idea; in 49, 36 and 28 BC Dio had recorded praetors and tribunes carrying out the aedilician functions, and so Augustus was recognising recent practice. Nevertheless, when referring to AD 38, Dio still describes the aediles as being the magistrates in charge of keeping the streets and alleys clean.[27]

The *cura viarum*[28] of the Principate applied only to the streets and roads outside the (Servian) walls of the City. Within the walls there was no special commission created; streets there remained a matter either for the aediles or for the officials in charge of the XIV Regions. Under Claudius there seems to be some involvement of the quaestors in the paving of the streets;[29] this may hark back to the Julian law or it may refer to roads outside Rome. The record of Nero's reign is a special case because it is dominated by the rebuilding of the

---

24 Dio 55.8.
25 Dio 54.26.5–7.
26 Livy 34.7 described them as 'Hic Romae infimo generi magistris vicorum', but yet entitled to wear the *toga praetexta*; see ch. 1.
27 Dio 59.12.
28 Dio 59.15; 60.17.
29 Suet. *Claudius* 24.

City after the Great Fire;[30] even he, however, seems mostly (outside the monumental centre) to have reconstructed what was there before – witness the continuing names of many roads, unchanged from Republic to Late Empire. Despite Tacitus' report of people grumbling because the new streets were so broad that they gave no shelter from the sun, archaeological evidence suggests that most remained narrow and not particularly straight. Vespasian took an interest: 'He restored at his own expense the city streets decayed through the negligence of former times'.[31] This is perhaps a little surprising, following so soon on the Neronian rebuilding of the City, and even more so when one remembers Vespasian himself had been aedile.[32] A little later, Martial praised Domitian for turning footpaths into roads, and for clearing the streets themselves so that shops and cafés did not spill out into the roadway, making passage difficult.[33]

Marcus Aurelius as a 'good emperor' was concerned with the maintenance of the City streets,[34] as was Pertinax and, of course, Severus Alexander, who restored many bridges.[35] Caracalla built a new and beautiful street – the via Nova, parallel to the via Appia – alongside his Baths;[36] it was only major building works, which were inevitably imperial after the earlier Principate, which could make space for the construction of a genuinely new street within the City.

Who then in the Empire actually organised the work? It was the function of the aediles originally; they were helped from some unknown date (which may be Caesarian) by the *IVviri viis in urbe purgandis* and the *IIviri viis extra urbem purgandis*, but the latter college was abolished under Augustus.[37] The creation of the XIV Regions divided responsibility into geographical (or topographical) areas. Augustus' establishment of the *curatores viarum* to supervise the maintenance of the great trunk roads, a senatorial or equestrian office depend-

30 Tac. *Annals* 15.38–43; see ch. 2.
31 ILS 245.
32 Suet. *Vesp*.5.
33 Martial 7.61.
34 SHA *M. Ant. Aurelius* 11.
35 SHA *Pertinax* 9; *Sev. Alex*.26.
36 SHA *Caracalla* 9; cf. Aurelius Victor 21.4.
37 Tac. *Annals* 3.29 demonstrates that there was only a vigintivirate under Tiberius; Dio 54.26.7 dates the change to 13 BC. Mommsen (1887): II 603–4.

ing on the status of the road, will have affected the ordinary inhabitants of the City by making access easier for the market gardeners around Rome, and for improving communication with Ostia[38] (although the river remained the best route for heavy loads). Aediles (or the other senatorial magistrates in charge of the Regions) continued to head the urban service, and just as the *IIIviri capitales* still assisted them in their police duties, so did the *IVviri* with the care of the streets; all these were gentlemanly occupations, fit for senators. The aediles themselves were perhaps largely concerned with jurisdiction – indeed, did they specialise in litigation arising from market business?

Other subordinates were needed for the more practical details of supervision. Dessau has four citations of equestrian officials concerned with the City's streets. Hence we find that T. Flavius Germanus (who was responsible for the organisation of Commodus' triumph in 180), between being *procurator ludi magni* and *ludi matutini* and procurator for the 5 per cent inheritance tax in Umbria and elsewhere, was *procurator reg. urbi. adiuncto sibi officio viarum sternendarum urbis partibus duabus*.[39] T. Cl. Xenophons, later sub-prefect of the grain supply, who also seems to have lived during Commodus' reign, was *procurator viarum urbis* at the start of his official career.[40] T. Claudius Ulpian was *procurator silicum viarum sacrae urbis*, then sub-prefect of the Night Watch.[41] Another man, originally an imperial slave, having started as *a cubiculo*, then *nutritor* of Lucius Verus, was granted equestrian status by Antoninus Pius, and became *procurator ad silic.* (and *praefectus vehiculorum*).[42] From this we can gather that by around the middle of the second century there was a subordinate procurator for one or more of the senators in charge of the Regions, who might exercise a specific task outside his own Region, that there might be a subordinate, appointed presumably for all XIV Regions, with the specific task of street maintenance, and that a procurator might be appointed to have charge of the equivalent of the modern highway engineer's depot, the *castra*

38 ILS 1401 (= CIL X 1795): *proc Aug viae Ost et Camp.*
39 ILS 1420 (= CIL XIV 2922, cf. 2955).
40 ILS 1421 (= CIL III S. 7127, cf. 8042).
41 ILS 1422 (= CIL XI 6337).
42 ILS 1740 (= CIL VI 1598).

silicaria as the Regionary calls them. The evidence for the rest of these men's careers shows that they were the usual generalists, and not specialist engineers or architects. However, since the *cura aquarum* employed architects and surveyors as well as specialist craftsmen, it is by no means unlikely that there were such in either the aediles' office or in that of the curator of the Regions.

In these aedilician offices we hear frequently of scribes, *praecones, viatores* and others[43] (for example, in the Republic, the scribe and the *viator* for whose thefts from the *aerarium* the curule aedile who employed them was held responsible[44]). Some civil servants explicitly held office under the *IVviri viarum curandarum*,[45] and one can reasonably assume that many more did so, since we know of others serving the vigintivirate.[46] There must have been considerable paperwork involved in the putting out to tender of specific matters of street maintenance and cleaning. And some of these clerical officers may well be included in those referred to in sections 18, 20 and 21 of the Julian law, to which we shall come under Open Spaces.

Although Ulpian firmly points out that the praetor's interdict *Ne quid in loco publico vel itinere fiat* applies only to rural, not urban, roads: 'For the care of urban streets belongs to the magistrates',[47] yet its terms give us some further information about what such care involved. The maintenance of a road involved keeping it at its proper breadth and depth, removing all obstacles from its surface and cleaning it; while contractors engaged in such a task were no more allowed to pave a dirt road with stone than to turn a paved into a dirt road, urban magistrates presumably had the implicit power, if granted the money by Senate or council, to pave their streets.[48]

---

43 E.g. ILS 1879 (= CIL VI 103); 1880 (= VI 1068); 1883 (= VI 1843); 1908 (= VI 1869); 1923 (= VI 1933); 1936 (= VI 1946).

44 Livy 30.39.

45 ILS 1898 (= CIL VI 1808); 1929 (= VI 1936); 1930 (= VI 466).

46 ILS 1900 (= CIL VI 1840); 1901; 1909 (= X 5917).

47 D.43.8.2.24, Ulpian 68 *ad ed.*

48 D.43.11.1pr-2, Ulpian 68 *ad ed*: 'The praetor says: "I forbid the use of force to prevent anyone from opening up or repairing a public road or way, as long as that road or way is not made worse". 1. To open up a road is to restore it to its old breadth and depth. It is a part of its repair to clean it. Cleaning it is, properly speaking, to reduce it to its proper level by clearing away all that is upon it. Repair includes opening it up and cleaning it and everything that is done to restore it to its original state.

We may note the place of contractors in the Julian law; their needs were recognised in the grant of public open spaces for their use.

Among the relevant legal texts, the most prominent is Papinian, on the Care of Cities, concerned with the maintenance and repair of the streets.

The city overseers (*astunomikoi* – translated into Latin as *curatores urbium*) are to take care of the streets of the city so that they are kept level, so that the houses are not damaged by overflows (*flumina – rheumata*), and so that there are bridges where they are needed. 1. And they are to take care that private walls and enclosure walls of houses facing the street are not in bad repair, so that the owners should clean and repair them as necessary. If they do not clean or repair them, [the overseers] are to fine them until they make them safe. 2. They are to take care that nobody digs holes in the streets, encumbers them, or builds anything on them. In the case of contravention, a slave may be beaten by anyone who detects him, a free man must be denounced to the overseers and the overseers are to fine him according to law and make good the damage. 3. Each person is to keep the public street outside his own house in repair and clean out the open gutters and ensure that no vehicle is prevented from access. Occupiers of rented accommodation must carry out these repairs themselves, if the owner fails to do so, and deduct their expenses from the rent.[49]

2. If anyone makes the road worse under pretext of repairing it, force can be used against him with impunity. Because of this, the employer of the interdict cannot make the road broader or longer, higher or lower, on the pretext of repair, or lay gravel on a road, pave a dirt road with stone, or turn a stone-paved road into a dirt road.' One presumes contractors are meant, rather than magistrates, as similarly with the interdict *de ripa munienda*, where we are told 'It is extremely useful to repair and build up the banks of public rivers. So just as an interdict is provided for the repair of a public road, another had to be provided for building up the bank of a river' (D.43. 15.1.1, Ulpian 68 *ad ed*). Security had to be given to neighbours of the proposed work, which included those on the other side of the river. (These rules were also extended to lakes, canals and pools.)

49 D.43,10.1, Papinian *ek tou astunomikou monobiblou*. Schulz (1953): 247 could not accept that this was Papinian's own work, but it seems rash to believe that the jurists of the Severan period were exclusively concerned with Rome and Italy.

It seems unlikely that Papinian wrote this for Rome. He may have been asked to provide something for the cities of the Greek-speaking east, where the magistrates charged with city housekeeping were called *astunomikoi*. It must be debatable how far it reflected the law at Rome. The rules are often quite different from those of the Julian law; but it is by no means impossible that things should have changed over a period of two and a half centuries. The equivalence of these overseers to the *IVviri viarum curandarum*, as the *IVviri viis in urbe purgandis* had become known, is highly probable; the powers they exercise make it unlikely that they are to be equated with the *vicomagistri* (or – if they are different – with the *stenoparchoi* mentioned by Dio[50]).

In the Julian law the frontagers are admittedly to make sure there is no standing water, but this last seems rather different from the streams or overflows – *flumina* – which Papinian's city overseers are to prevent from harming the buildings. It was the duty of the *curator aquarum* to see that there was sufficient surplus water to hose down the streets and sewers; it was the duty of the *curator alvei Tiberis*, from the time of Trajan, to keep the drains and sewers functioning; to what at Rome could these particular streams refer?

Further, the reference to seeing that there are bridges where there is need can hardly apply to city streets; the existence of bridges over the Tiber was surely always a matter not even for the aediles, but for a higher authority such as Senate or Emperor. (Could Papinian here be thinking also of the *curatores viarum*, whose jurisdiction was over the imperial roads in Italy, not within the City? This would fit with the bridges.) And his statement relates more closely to the subject matter of the interdicts (where Ulpian makes the point that repair by private contribution is perfectly in accord with a road being public, since its 'public' nature lies in the authoritative definition of its length and fixed limits of width).

Papinian's magistrates are to fine those citizens who do not clean and repair the walls of their property until they make them safe; under the Julian law the magistrates were to put out such work to tender, and the contractor recovered what he spent direct from the householder, sometimes with a penal element

---

50 Dio 55.8. Mommsen (1887): II 498.

added. But putting out contracts for public works may well have been rarer, and direct intervention more common, by 200 AD.

In the state of affairs envisaged by Papinian a slave can be flogged by anyone who catches him in the act of digging holes or building something in the street, or even encumbering it. It is possible that there is here an implicit assumption that 'anyone' means anyone official since, even taking into account that such a slave was behaving contrary to *bonos mores*, it might appear a case of *iniuria* if done by a private citizen;[51] after all, in some circumstances even a magistrate might be liable to a slave's owner.[52]

Papinian's magistrates have powers to fine, powers which would seem reasonable for the *IVviri* who rank on a level with the *IIIviri capitales*. More, the magistrates are to demolish whatever has been wrongfully erected; here we can contrast Ulpian: 'If someone builds in a public place and nobody prevents him, he cannot then be compelled to demolish for fear of ruins disfiguring the City, and because the interdict is for prohibition not restitution. But if his building obstructs public use, it must certainly be demolished by the official in charge of public works – *qui operibus publicis procurat*. If it does not, [the official] must impose a ground rent on it.'[53] If Papinian was writing for cities other than Rome, as also for the *Urbs*, it would allow the term 'magistrates' to include not only those of Rome and the *curatores viarum*, but also municipal aediles; the powers recorded seem reasonable for them as well as for members of the vigintivirate, for in the municipalities too the general prohibition on demolition applied.[54]

CLEANING THE STREETS

A section of the Julian law, s.12,[55] dealt with the cleaning of the streets. This is clearly distinguished from maintenance; a

---

51 D.47.10.15.34 & 38, Ulpian 77 [*sic*] *ad ed*: for such beating to be 'adversus bonos mores' leaves room for debate.
52 D.47.10.15.39, ibid. citing Labeo; h.t.17.2, Ulpian 57 *ad ed*, citing Mela and Labeo.
53 D.43.8.2.17, Ulpian 68 *ad ed*. Elsewhere in his own writings, Ulpian had held that the praetor must have power to obtain the demolition of buildings put up despite his interdict, otherwise his power would be empty and derisory (h.t.7, 48 *dig*). Cf. the section on Demolition in ch. 3.
54 See ch.3.
55 *Tab:Hera*. vv. 50–2.

different verb is used – *'purgare'* not *'tueri'*; the law refers to special minor magistrates to assist the aediles in this task. This is in fact the first reference to the *IVviri* (and the *IIviri*), and it is possible that their office was created by this law. The silence about them in earlier sources does not prove their previous non-existence;[56] on the other hand, Julius Caesar was certainly responsible for a number of modifications to the constitution.[57] I think that, as well as the contractors used for particular jobs, one has to posit some sort of street sweepers at their disposal;[58] these may have descended from the ex-aedilician crew given to the *vicomagistri*, and it seems probable that they came to be available to the heads of the XIV Regions.

What further information have we on cleaning the streets? It was traditionally always a matter for the aediles or their subordinates. From Plautus we gather that the aediles would wish to keep the streets clear of (live) pigs;[59] Plautus also describes someone cleaning and scrubbing as 'exercising an aedileship'.[60] There are other references to dirt and obstructions. As already mentioned, Petronius' heroes cut their feet on broken crocks as well as uneven paving stones.[61] Martial, talking of Domitian in flattering terms for enforcing the planning laws and keeping the streets clear, says that the praetor – even! – is no longer forced to walk in the mud.[62] Juvenal too talks of the mud thick on his shins, as well as of tiles sliding from roofs and garbage chucked out of windows.[63]

The existence of the quasi-delictual action *de effusis vel deiectis* should not be forgotten in this context, although its terms were aimed at compensation for damage or injury rather than keeping the streets clean; moreover, Labeo is said to have argued that it did not apply at night, though Paul commented that there were places people did go by night.[64] It was not

---

56 D.1.2.2.30, Pomponius *enchiridion*, is valueless in this context.
57 E.g. the creation of the *aediles cereales*, recorded by Pomponius, D.1.2.2.32; also Suet. *Julius* 41.
58 E.g. 'Barney': ILS 1964 (= CIL VI 2342) *Barnaeus de familia publica reg. VIII.*
59 Plautus *Captivi* 791f.
60 Plautus *Stich.*352.
61 Petronius *Sat.*79.
62 Martial 7.61, cited above; Seneca *de ira* 3.35.5 talks of uneven and muddy alleys – *scabras lutosasque semitas.*
63 Juvenal 3.247 & 268–77.
64 D.9.3.6.1, Paul 19 *ad ed.*

helped of course by the streets being unlit, except when, on certain festivals, some streets seem to have had temporary illumination; one only has to consider the public's readiness to dump in the lanes and back alleys of a modern city, where the dumper cannot readily be seen.

The aediles had the powers to enforce the co-operation of the frontagers, and they had the staff, as we learn from the text on the removal of beds[65] which were presumably obstructing the street; it is inconceivable that the removal was carried out by the aediles in person, and it seems more likely that *apparitores* or public slaves should be used than their own personal slaves. It is arguable from the texts that the frontagers' duty was passive – not to make a mess – while the authorities actively cleared up what was inevitable. The aediles continued in charge of this aspect of maintenance, as Dio tells us[66] in the famous story of how the Emperor Caligula ordered his soldiers to stuff mud down Vespasian's toga when the latter was aedile and the streets were clearly dirty.

Our Papinian text includes street cleaning with repairs; so too did the praetor when granting interdicts: 'It is a part of its repair to clean it. Cleaning it is, properly speaking, to reduce it to its proper level by clearing away all that is upon it.'[67] In Papinian's text the owners of houses of which the walls, including any garden walls, faced on the street were to clean them as well as keep them in repair – does this mean also cleaning off posters and graffiti? The fragment continues:

> Each person is to keep the public street outside his own house in repair and clean out the open gutters and ensure that no vehicle is prevented from access. . . . They [the *astunomikoi*] must see to it that nothing is left outside workshops, except for a fuller leaving out clothing to dry or a carpenter putting out wheels; and these are not by doing so to prevent a vehicle from passing. They are not to allow anyone to fight in the streets, or to fling dung, or to throw out any dead animals or skins.[68]

65 D.18.6.13(12)-14(13), Paul 3 *Alfeni epit*; note that the aedile may be liable under the *lex Aquilia* if he has acted 'non iure'.
66 Dio 59.12, of AD 38; also told in Suet. *Vesp*.5.
67 D.43.11.1.1, Ulpian 68 *ad ed*.
68 D.43.10.1.3–5, Papinian *de cura urbium*; the provenance of the text has been discussed above.

Fighting in the street seems here to be being viewed as something that would frighten the horses and obstruct passers-by, rather than as an offence against public order. In Rome itself there may not have been open drains by the later Principate (although Pliny mentions them in Bithynian cities at the beginning of the second century), except perhaps in the outskirts. Dung flinging was forbidden, we know, in the burial grounds on the Esquiline; how much more must this have been the case in the streets of the City. 'Dead animals' in this context are not butchers' carcasses but the bodies of overworked asses, run-over dogs, and mysteriously dead cats – animals which had met a fairly natural death rather than being slaughtered. The prohibition on skins was probably because of the highly unpleasant smell associated with tanning,[69] even if fullers got away with their trade. The stress on free access and free passage – two different verbs in the Greek – of vehicles again is mildly suggestive of application to other cities as well as Rome. Surely at Rome the carpenter would have had to bring his wheels in towards evening when the heavy goods traffic could enter the City and, further, were Roman thieves so unenterprising that wheels could safely be left overnight in the streets?

Supervision of the drainage system was originally an element of the care of the streets, whether carried out by censors, aediles, or officials of some other sort, but under Trajan this duty was transferred to the commission for the bed and banks of the Tiber. The cleaning and repair of a particular existing drain was a matter for the private citizen, with his right to carry out this duty protected by interdict, but the construction of a new drain was for 'cui viarum publicarum cura sit' to concede.[70] Perhaps the *IVviri qui curam viarum agerent/viis in urbe purgandis* would (if they were in existence) have issued such a licence in the Republic, but more likely it would have been a matter for the aediles, or even the censors. Private ownership covered each branch until it joined the main sewer. Drains were primarily for carrying off rain water; it would seem to have been their character as constructions lying beneath or issuing onto the streets which was the concern of the aediles, or the private owners.[71] The provision of adequate water for their flushing,

69 Restriction to Trastevere is implied in Martial 6.93; Juvenal 14.203.
70 D.43.23.2, Venuleius 1 *interdict*, citing Labeo.
71 Pliny *NH* 36.2.6.

as well as of running water to those places which did receive it, was from the time of Augustus a matter for the *cura aquarum*.

TRAFFIC

The Julian law then moves to deal with traffic.[72] We do not know at what time of year the law was passed, but the opening sentence of this section, bringing it into force on 1 January next, clearly was designed to give people time to rearrange their habits. For the greater part of the day wagons, i.e. heavy goods traffic, were forbidden to move on the streets of Rome; deliveries and removals must take place in the late afternoons and after nightfall. The legislator is therefore careless of disturbing the sleep of the City's inhabitants,[73] but rather concerned with not hindering people walking around on their daily business – or leisure. (Provision for the citizens' leisure could itself create problems; we are told that for Julius Caesar's *naumachia* 'such crowds flooded in to the City that people had to put up in tents pitched in the streets or along the roads', and that many, including two senators, were crushed to death.[74])

Not surprisingly, some exceptions were made. Building materials for temples – restricted presumably by the words 'of the most holy gods' to temples of the official Roman gods – or for public works, such as aqueducts, could be transported. It was also permissible to move the rubbish from demolitions carried out by contractors under a public tender. We know of two wagons being pulled by mules up the *clivus Capitolinus*,[75] but not of their business, nor of the time of day. But specified drivers needed to get licences for the particular purpose,[76] presumably until a particular job was finished rather than on a weekly or monthly basis; it must have caused some difficulties when a driver was sick or absent if a replacement could not do his job. This raises some unanswerable questions: who supervised this? who would get the sweetener when some unofficial Gaius Seius stepped in? who had power to stop the wagon and demand to see its and the driver's licence? who would charge whom and with what offence? Where were the licences issued? – presumably

72 *Tab. Hera.* vv. 56–61.
73 As Juvenal emphasises in *Satire* 3.
74 Suet. *Julius* 39.4.
75 D.9.2.52.2, Alfenus 2 *dig*; he was a jurist of the Late Republic.
76 *Tab. Hera.* v. 61.

from the aediles' office; were these open every working day or only during certain times of year?

There were certain other exceptions to the ban on heavy goods vehicles.[77] Wagons – still specifically the heavy wagons known as *plostra* or *plaustra* – needed for the official religious observances of the Roman people, and also for triumphs, and for public games and their preliminary rituals, were not covered by the ban on daytime use, when employed for these purposes or at these times. Presumably, therefore, if a rehearsal was needed – as our experience suggests was possible – a licence would need to be obtained.

Hygiene was also considered. Wagons which had entered the City by night could lawfully leave if empty, or if carrying out ordures, with no apparent check on the time of their passage.[78] We hear in the literary texts of carts used for taking away various kinds of refuse, which must include night soil.[79] Refuse disposal was probably an early morning trade, one hardly suitable for the heat of the day or the press of crowds. It seems unlikely, however, that there was much of a rush hour at Rome, though there must have been some time when pedestrian traffic increased – at the usual hour when the shops opened, or a little before. But there is a slight problem here. The City was so huge that it must have been hard to decide sometimes whether someone was driving around or driving out. Was this check on wagons something that only took place at the *portoria*? That would simplify the problem of enforcement, even if it did not control abuse of the law within the urban area itself.

It is not clear that there were any traffic restrictions before the Julian Act. If one believes Dio's story,[80] referring to 36 BC, of the senator who used to go to dinner parties riding on an elephant, one can see the need for their introduction. From a variety of texts it is clear that litters were normal for women and old men from the beginning of the Principate;[81] Augustus used a closed litter when he was in the City informally while holding the consulship, in order not to cause a stir.[82]

77 *Tab. Hera.* vv. 62–5.
78 *Tab. Hera.* vv. 66–7.
79 Val. Max. 1.7 *ext.*10; Tac. *Annals* 11.32.
80 Dio 49.7.
81 Petronius *Sat.*28; Juvenal 6.349.
82 Suet. *Aug.*53; similar stories are told of Trajan and Hadrian (Pliny *Pan.*20; Dio 69.7).

Covered chairs, of the kind Pliny the Elder used in Rome so that he could go on working while travelling, seem only to have become fashionable under Claudius.[83] Horse-drawn carriages for reasons of expense, and also the inconveniences of stabling, were reserved for the upper classes – compare the proportion who kept a town-carriage in the much more sprawling town of eighteenth-century London; stables where horses could be hired were attached to the inns near the City gates.[84] The Oppian sumptuary law of the Hannibalic War had forbidden women to ride in such carriages, except on religious occasions; one feels this must have been more of a symbolic than a practical restriction, but perhaps carriages were of more use then than later when the City had grown.

The Julian law seems to have dealt only with heavy goods traffic; it mentioned wagons – *plostra*, so the lighter carts, which asses or mules more commonly drew,[85] were presumably outside its original terms, though these may well have been extended. Caligula, sending despatches to announce the defection to the Romans of a British king's son, ordered the *speculatores* to go straight on to the Forum and Senate House in their carriage,[86] which could imply that this was forbidden, but it may merely have been arrogant. It seems to have been Claudius who widened the prohibition to cover Italy; in an edict he laid down that travellers should not pass through towns in Italy except on foot, or in a chair or litter,[87] which Dio implies was extended to the towns from the City. Certainly Petronius' *tabellarius* gets out of his vehicle at an inn, and so probably on the edge of the City.[88] Juvenal tells us of the poet who, when he moves house, can fit all his belongings in one *rheda*[89] – would this be after the tenth hour? or was the vehicle too humble to count? Juvenal also complains of the ill dying from insomnia; of wheels creaking all night while the carters yell; the rich go about in carriages but most people are stuck in the traffic. Some carts carry whole trees, and others are laden with marble

83 Dio 60.2.3; Suet. *Nero* 26.
84 Kléberg (1957): 49 on the siting of stables at Pompeii; Lafaye (1909).
85 E.g. Dio 77.4.
86 Suet. *Caligula* 44.
87 Suet. *Claudius* 25; cf. Dio 60(61).29.
88 Petronius *Sat*.79.
89 Juvenal 3.10.

which could crush by-standers to a pulp.[90] Trajan showed his unassumingness by accepting lifts in the carriages of friends as well as offering them rides with him in his own,[91] which suggests that there were exemptions for rank, since a 'good' emperor would not have flouted the law. Hadrian seems to have repeated the prohibition on goods vehicles, or at least it was thought proper that he should have, even though one can hardly accept his ban literally: 'He prohibited vehicles with heavy loads from entering the City, and did not permit horses to be ridden in towns.'[92] On the other hand, we hear that if traffic were excluded from a public road or the road were narrowed, the magistrates should intervene.[93]

The point that such restrictions were the mark of a 'good' emperor is confirmed by Marcus Aurelius also being alleged to have prohibited riding and driving in carriages in towns, and Severus Alexander specifically allowing to senators the privilege of using *raedae* and *carrucae*.[94] Some confirmation of the continuing restrictions on commercial traffic may be gathered from the implication of the mention that at the start of the Marcomannic War 'there was in fact so great a pestilence that corpses were carried out of the City on wagons and carts'.[95] A late historian tells that Commodus' body, after his murder, was put in a cart that was at the entrance to the palace and taken to the outskirts of the City during the night.[96] Among the illustrations Ammianus uses of the decadence of the times and as an example of luxury are unusually high carriages, horses being galloped through the open spaces and paved streets of the City, women in closed litters, and the huge escorts for carriages, but then he was looking for proof that times were getting worse.[97] Certainly the Codes tell us that the use of *carrucae* in the City – here Constantinople is meant – was permitted to *honorati*, and by implication denied to others.[98]

90 Juvenal 3.232–45 and 254–61.
91 Eutropius 8.4.
92 SHA *Hadrian* 22.
93 D.43.8.2.25, Ulpian 68 *ad ed.*
94 SHA *M. Ant. Aurelius* 23; *Sev. Alex.*43; cf. *Aurelian* 4.
95 SHA *M. Ant. Aurelius* 13, *vehicula* and *sarraca*.
96 Herodian 2.1.2.
97 Ammianus 14.6.
98 CTh 14.12.1 – AD 386 (= CJ 11.20.1).

OPEN SPACES

Another section in the *lex Julia* then deals with public places and porticoes.[99] Its link with streets seems clear from the fact that the charge of such places is the care of the magistrates responsible for the streets and their cleaning. These are public spaces and arcades bordering on roads, places which people are accustomed to frequent which are not more specifically described – as are fora or temples. Again, it is free passage which is important, and the reason why there is to be no building in such places. S. 18 talks of the censors or other magistrates who let out some of these spaces for the yielding of public revenue; such use is not prohibited by the statute.[100] The following section sets out another, more specific, exception to the ban on building on or otherwise blocking public spaces – temporary erections for the shows and spectacles.[101] The days of the games would be known, and the permission to erect such obstacles to public passage (though they are not described as such in this clause) would in the nature of things be temporary.

The final two sections of the Julian law which are relevant to the running of the City deal with the public spaces used by magistrates' staffs (scribes and copyists) and, specifically, the censors' slaves.[102] One can imagine that the availability to the public of such persons would be a convenience easily outweighing the hindrance created by their stalls or booths, which I presume is the class of obstacle required for their activities,[103] such as the issuing of licences and the keeping of records, even if these became in effect permanent. Anyway, the justification would be the demands of the *res publica*. The remainder of the so-called Julian law is irrelevant for the present purpose.

There is some general information from the municipal charters,[104] but it is insufficiently detailed. The Digest tells us more

99 *Tab. Hera.* vv. 68–72.
100 *Tab. Hera.* vv. 73–6.
101 *Tab. Hera.* vv. 77–9.
102 *Tab. Hera.* vv. 80–2.
103 The *schola Xanthi*, the office of the aedilician staff, for example, would seem from its site between the arch of Tiberius and the Rostra to have been on public land.
104 FIRA i 18 (p.166ff) *lex municipii Tarentini*, vv. 39–42; FIRA i 21 (p.177ff) *lex Ursonensis*, cc. 77 & 78; JRS 76 (1986, p.147ff) *lex Irnitana*, Tab. IXA <ch. 82>.

about the legal control of public spaces. 'It is open to anyone to claim for public use what belongs to the use of all, such as public roads and public ways. Therefore, interdicts are available to safeguard these at anyone's demand.'[105] And the same is amplified by the interdict on not obstructing public places or public passage. The praetor forbids building in public places; any such action needs permission by statute, resolution of the Senate or imperial enactment, not just a magistrate's authority. For public places serve both public and private uses. 'The term "public place" should be understood, as defined by Labeo, to apply to public open spaces, tenement buildings, fields, roads and highways.'[106] The interdict was normally available if the authorised new work damaged someone's legally claimable interests, because an authorisation usually specified that such injury should not happen. Restitution as well as prohibition applied to *res sacrae*. Drainage, otherwise good, could make a public road worse, as indeed could its absence if water were allowed to collect. A bad smell did not justify recourse to the interdict.[107] Such interdicts were not temporary because they were a matter of public welfare.

Slightly curiously, until one thinks of sections 18 and 19 of the Julian law, there was an interdict aimed at protecting public works contractors.

> The praetor says: 'I forbid violence to be used to prevent a lessee or his partner from enjoying under the law of lease a public place which he has leased from someone entitled to let it.' It is obvious that this interdict is provided for public welfare. For in forbidding force against the lessee it safeguards the public revenue. . . . The praetor says 'to prevent from enjoying under the law of lease'. He rightly says 'under the law of lease'. For anyone wishing to enjoy beyond the law or contrary to it should not be heard.[108]

---

105 D.43.7.1, Pomponius 30 *ad Sab*: Cuilibet in publicum petere permittendum est id quod ad usum omnium pertineat, veluti vias publicas, itinera publica; et ideo quolibet postulante de his interdicitur. H.t.2, Julian 48 *dig.* adds that nobody may erect a funerary monument in a public road – Nemini licet in via publica monumentum exstruere.

106 D.43.8.2.3, Ulpian 68 *ad ed*, citing Labeo. In s.6 we are told that an interdict could be brought about an awning over a balcony which interfered with a neighbour's light.

107 D.43.8.2.29, ibid. citing Nerva.

108 D.43.9.1, Ulpian 68 *ad ed*.

Finally, we are told: 'It is usual to permit public erection of images and statues that will be an ornament to the community'.[109] This seems to imply a general assumption that such things will be a good, rather than any requirement for permission in individual cases. But who would order the taking down of an image which was not an ornament, and how would this be defined? Could there be scope here for aesthetic judgement? I should guess that it would be whoever was in charge of the streets and open spaces in the relevant quarter; although, of course, he would be the most likely person to wish to erect a statue or image.

APPENDIX: *TABULA HERACLEENSIS*, vv. 20–82

Repair and maintenance

Tab. Hera. vv. 20–3: Quae viae in urbe Roma propiusve urbem Romam passus M, ubi continente habitabitur, sunt erunt, cuius ante aedificium earum quae via erit, is eam viam arbitratu eius aedilis, cui ea pars urbis hac lege obvenerit, tueatur; isque aedilis curato uti, quorum ante aedificium erit, quamquam viam hac lege quemque tueri oportebit, ei omnes eam viam arbitratu eius tueantur, neve eo loco aqua consistat, quominus commode populus ea via utatur.

Tab. Hera. vv. 25–8: . . . qua in parte urbis quisque eorum vias publicas in urbem Romam, propiusve urbem Romam passus M, reficiundas sternendas curet, eiusque rei procurationem habeat. quae pars cuique aedili ita hac lege obvenerit, eius aedilis in eis locis, quae in ea parte erunt, viarum reficiendarum tuemdarum procuratio esto, uti hac lege oportebit.

Tab. Hera. vv. 29–31: Quae via inter aedem sacram et aedificium locumve publicum et inter aedificium privatum est erit, eius viae partem dimidiam is aedilis, cui ea pars urbis obvenerit, in qua parte ea aedis sacra erit sive aedificium publicum sive locus publicus, tuemdam locato.

Tab. Hera. vv. 32–46: Quemcumque ante suum aedificium viam publicam h. l. tueri oportebit, qui eorum eam viam arbitratu eius aedilis, cuius oportuerit, non tuebitur, eam viam aedilis, cuius arbitratu eam tueri oportuerit, tuendam locato;

---

109 D.43.9.2, Paul 5 *sent*: Concedi solet ut imagines et statuae quae ornamenta rei publicae sunt futurae in publicum ponantur.

isque aedilis diebus ne minus X, antequam locet apud forum ante tribunale suum propositum habeto, quam viam tuendam et quo die locaturus sit, et quorum ante aedificium ea via sit; eisque, quorum ante aedificium ea via erit, procuratoribusve eorum domum denuntietur facito, se eam viam locaturum, et quo die locaturus sit; eamque locationem palam in foro per quaestionem urbanum eumve qui aerario praeerit facito. Quanta pecunia eam viam locaverit tantae pecuniae eum eosque quorum ante aedificium ea via erit pro portioni, quantum cuiusque ante aedificium viae in longitudine et in latitudine erit, quaestor urbanus cuive aerario praerit in tabulas publicas pecuniae factae referendum curato. Ei qui eam viam tuemdam redemerit, tantae pecuniae eum eosque adtribuito sine dolo malo. Si is qui adtributus erit eam pecuniam diebus XXX proximis quibus ipse aut procurator eius sciet adtributionem factam esse, ei cui adtributus erit non solverit neque satis fecerit, is quantae pecuniae adtributus erit tantam pecuniam et eius dimidium ei cui adtributus erit dare debeto, inque eam rem is quo quemque de ea re aditum erit iudicem iudiciumve ita dato, uti de pecunia credita iudicem iudiciumve dari oportebit.

Tab. Hera. vv. 47–9: Quam viam h. l. tuemdam locari oportebit, aedilis quem eam viam tuendam locare oportebit, is eam viam per quaestorem urbanum quive aerario praerit tuemdam locato, uti eam viam arbitratu eius qui eam viam locandam curaverit tueatur. Quantum pecuniam ita quaeque via locata erit, tantam pecuniam quaestor urbanus quive aerario praerit redemptori, cui e lege locationis dare oportebit, heredive eius dandam adtribuendam curato.

Tab. Hera. vv. 53–5: Cuius ante aedificium semita in loco erit, is eam semitam eo aedificio perpetuo lapidibus perpetuis integris continentem constratam recte habeto arbitratu eius aedilis cuius in ea parte h. l. viarum procuratio erit.

Cleaning

Tab. Hera. vv. 50–2: Quo minus aediles et ivviri viis in urbem purgandis, iiviri viis extra propiusve urbem Romam passus M purgandis, quicumque erunt, vias publicas purgandas curent eiusque rei potestatem habeant, ita uti legibus plebeiscitis senatusve consultis oporte oportebit, eius h. l. nihilum rogatur.

Traffic

Tab. Hera. vv. 56–61: Quae viae in urbe Roma sunt erunt intra ea loca, ubi continenti habitabitur, ne quis in eis viis post kalendas Januarii primas plostrum interdiu post solem ortum neve ante horam x diei ducito agito, nisi quod aedium sacrarum deorum immortalium causa aedificandarum operisve publice faciumdi causa advehi portari oportebit, aut quod ex urbe exve iis locis earum rerum, quae publice demoliendae locatae erunt, publice exportari oportebit, et quarum rerum causa plostra hac lege certis hominibus certis de causis agere ducere licebit.

Tab.Hera. vv. 62–5: Quibus diebus virgines Vestales, regem sacrorum, flamines plostris in urbe sacrorum publicorum populi Romani causa vehi oportebit, quaeque plostra triumphi causa, quo die quisque triumphabit, duci oportebit, quaeque plostra ludorum, qui Romae aut urbi Romae propius passus M publice fient, inve pompam ludis circensibus duci agi opus erit: quo minus earum rerum causa eisque diebus plostra interdiu in urbe ducantur agantur, eius hac lege nihilum rogatur.

Tab. Hera. vv. 66–7: Quae plostra noctu in urbem inducta erunt, quo minus ea plostra inania aut stercoris exportandei caussa post solem ortum horis X diei bubus iumenteisve iuncta in urbe Roma et ab urbe Roma passus M esse liceat, eius hac lege nihilum rogatur.

Open spaces

Tab. Hera. vv. 68–72: Quae loca publica porticusve publicae in urbe Roma propiusve urbi Romae passus M sunt erunt, quorum locorum cuiusque porticus aedilium eorumve magistratuum qui viis locisque publicis urbis Romae propiusve urbi Romae passus M purgandis praeerunt, legibus procuratio est erit ne quis in iis locis inve iis porticibus quid inaedificatum inmolitumve habeto neve ea loca porticumve quam possideto neve eorum quod saeptum clausumve habeto quo minus eis locis porticibusque populus utatur pateantve, nisi quibus utique legibus pleb-eivescitis senatusve consultis concessum permissumve est.

Tab. Hera. vv. 73–6: Quibus locis ex lege locationis quam censor aliusve quis magistratus publicis vectigalibus ultrove tributis fruendis tuendisve dixet dixerit, eis qui ea fruenda tuendave conducta habebunt ut uti frui liceat aut uti ea ab eis custodiantur cautum est; ei quo minus iis locis utantur fruantur ita uti quoique eorum ex lege locationis iis sine dolo malo uti frui licebit ex hac lege nihilum rogatur.

Tab. Hera. vv. 77–9: Quos ludos quisque Romae propiusve urbi Romae passus M faciet, quo minus ei eorum ludorum causa scaenam pulpitum ceteraque quae ad eos ludos opus erunt, in loco publico ponere statuere eisque diebus quibus eos faciet, loco publico uti liceat, eius hac lege nihilum rogatur.

Tab. Hera. vv. 80–2: Qui scribae librarii magistratibus apparebunt ei quo minus locis publicis ubi is quoi quisque eorum apparebunt juserit apparendi causa utantur, eius hac lege nihilum rogatur. Quae loca servis publicis ab censoribus habitandi utendi causa adtributa sunt, ei quo minus eis locis utantur eius hac lege nihilum rogatur.

6

THE TIBER

From the earliest times the Tiber[1] was of interest to whoever governed Rome, for at least two somewhat contrary reasons: it was both an obstacle which, certainly for trading purposes, needed to be crossed, and yet, at the same time, it was a permanently navigable river, with other – profitable – uses. It was also a source of danger when it flooded. The first point to be considered is the river simply as an obstacle. There may have been ferries across the river at Rome;[2] at the end of the Republic and in the early Empire there were certainly pleasure boats plying on it.[3] But the normal way to overcome such an obstacle was by building a bridge. And Rome grew partly because it lies on what was until relatively recently the lowest bridgeable point on the river.

BRIDGES

Bridges are functionally an extension of the streets or roads, and this, indeed, appears to be how they were regarded from the point of view of administration. The bridges were not, however, central to the City's life. Rome was not a city which grew along the axis of the river; it developed on the left bank, eastwards from the Tiber's course, as can clearly be seen from the layout of the City revealed by the lines of the Servian and Aurelian Walls. Nevertheless, there was access to both banks, and so to a variety of land routes. The oldest bridge, the *pons Sublicius*, is traditionally ascribed to the age of the kings, in particular to

1 The principal monograph is Le Gall (1953).
2 Lanciani (1897): 26.
3 Ovid *fast*.6.773–84; Juvenal 9.130–2; Suet. *Nero* 27.3.

Ancus Marcius.[4] It was built of wood alone, without metal, and was always rebuilt in this style when necessary.[5] (It was off this bridge that the curious ceremony of the *Argei* was performed, when twenty-seven rush figures were thrown each year into the Tiber by the priests.[6])

In the Republic, the construction of bridges, as of other public works, was a decision taken by the Senate, and carried out through the agency of the censors. The *pons Aemilius* owes its name to M. Aemilius Lepidus, one of the censors of 179 BC, who, as well as providing docks, saw to the putting in of piles for a bridge; the arches, however, were not added until the censorship in 142 BC of P. Scipio Africanus and L. Mummius.[7] It was repaired by Augustus.[8] The *pons Milvius*, where the via Flaminia crosses the river just before entering the City from the north, is almost certainly considerably older. While Ammianus in the fourth century AD ascribed it to the censor of 109 BC,[9] this must concern a restoration, since Livy refers to it as existing in 207 BC;[10] no third-century BC censor was called Milvius, so presumably it dates from an unknown censor of the fourth century BC.

The *pons Fabricius*, joining the *insula Tiberina* to the City, was built by L. Fabricius, *curator viarum*, in 62 BC; it was scrutinised and approved on the orders of the Senate by the consuls of 21 BC.[11] The *pons Cestius*, from the island to the right bank, was constructed towards the middle of the first century BC, when the Cestii were prominent and one of them may well have been *curator viarum*;[12] it was restored by Antoninus Pius in AD 152[13] (and again very thoroughly around 367 by Valentinian, Valens and Gratian[14]). Agrippa built a bridge in 25 BC, south-west from the Campus Martius;[15] this too

4 Livy 1.33.6.
5 Pliny *NH* 36.23.100.
6 Varro *LL* 7.44.
7 Livy 40.51.4.
8 CIL VI 878.
9 Ammianus 27.3.4; Aurelius Victor *de viris ill.*72.8.
10 Livy 27.51.2, when a throng from the City, awaiting news of the battle against Hasdrubal, stretched so far.
11 ILS 5892 (= CIL VI 1305). It may have replaced an earlier wooden bridge – P & A: 400.
12 Le Gall (1953): 209.
13 *Inscr. It.*XIII i 152.12–13.
14 ILS 771–2 (= CIL VI 1175–6): for the use of the Senate and people of Rome.
15 ILS 5926 (= CIL VI 31545).

was restored by Antoninus Pius.[16]

In the Principate bridges were built only by emperors. This was done by Nero for access to his Vatican circus,[17] and by Hadrian to link his mausoleum with the City.[18] Other bridges were built, or possibly only rebuilt, in the Later Empire: the *pons Valentiniani*, dedicated by Symmachus, which may originally have been the work of Marcus Aurelius,[19] and the *pons Theodosii*, which was probably the former *pons Probi*.[20] Since the maintenance of the bridges continued to be linked with that of the streets, this aspect of the Tiber does not call for separate treatment.[21]

SEWERS

Also linked with the care of the streets in the Republic and early Principate was the care of the sewers.[22] Under Trajan this duty was made over to the *curator riparum et alvei Tiberis*.[23] When Labeo, who lived under Augustus, wrote of the sewers, he naturally wrote in the context of the care of the streets. Labeo remarked that the interdict *de cloacis* applied to repairing old sewers but that there should be a similar interdict to protect the building of new ones, although the granting of permission for laying new sewers was a matter for him 'cui viarum publicarum cura sit'; in the later second century Venuleius cited this opinion without any qualification or reference to other authority.[24]

The responsibility for the sewers must have involved, at the very least, liaison between the Tiber commissioner and the aediles and the *IVviri viis purgandis*, whose street cleansing duties continued to make use of the sewers, even though they were no longer responsible for them. There must also have been

16 *Inscr. It.*XIII i 147.12. He also is said to have restored the *pons Sublicius* – SHA *Ant.Pius* 8.
17 Le Gall (1953): 211.
18 CIL VI 973; Dio 69.23; SHA *Hadrian* 19.
19 ILS 769; Ammianus 27.3.3; P & A: 398–9.
20 Symmachus *Rel.*25–6; Le Gall (1953): 310f.
21 ILS 5893 (= CIL VI 31543) was found in the foundations of the *pons Cestius*, but since it says that the earliest board 'ex s. c. reficiendam curaverunt', it refers to 'ripam'.
22 See further ch. 5 on Streets and ch. 8 on Public Health.
23 ILS 5930 & 5932 (= CIL VI 31549 & 31553) concerning Julius Ferox, who held office between 101 and 103, or longer. The establishment of this commission is dealt with in the next section.
24 D.43.23.2, Venuleius 1 *interdict*.

a need for continuing co-operation with the *curator aquarum*, whose duty it was to see that there was sufficient surplus water to flush the drains.[25] Did the *curator riparum et alvei Tiberis et cloacarum urbis* use the same gangs for their cleansing and maintenance as were employed in keeping the banks in repair? There seems to be no evidence for how this function was carried out, but the commissions established in the early Principate did generally have their own gangs of workmen, as well as contracting major jobs out.

FLOOD PROTECTION AND THE CREATION OF THE *CURA TIBERIS*

The maintenance of the banks of the Tiber was of importance for two reasons: flood prevention; and access for the ships and boats that brought in Rome's supplies of food and other essentials, and also of luxuries. The necessity of flood prevention, or at least flood damage limitation, was the motive for the creation of the commission for the Tiber, the *cura riparum et alvei Tiberis*. The river had always been a threat as well as a benefit to the citizens of Rome. We hear of the danger of floods and attempts to alleviate their consequences on a number of occasions. For example, Livy tells of storms in 193 BC which flooded the lower parts of the City and led to the collapse of some buildings; the following year there were worse floods in which the river washed away two bridges and many houses.[26]

A century or so later we hear of further serious floods. In 60 BC the *pons Sublicius* was destroyed and many boats on the Tiber sunk; in 54 BC there were floods with much loss of life, human and animal, and many houses collapsed.[27] In 27 BC the Tiber flooded again, and again in 23 when the *pons Sublicius* was carried away once more, and for three days the City was navigable by boat.[28] In 22 BC the floods were one of the factors leading to the crisis in the food supply for which

---

25 Frontinus *aq*.111. In the third century the link with the *cura aquarum* may have been made stronger; more than once a man held office as *curator Tiberis* shortly before being water commissioner – ILS 1182 (= CIL XIV 3900); 1186 (= XIV 3902).

26 Livy 35.9.2; 35.21.5.

27 Dio 37.58; 39.61.

28 Dio 53.20; 53.33.

Augustus appointed *praefecti frumenti dandi*.[29] Naturally it was the low-lying areas around the Campus Martius which were worst affected; the Emporium and Rome's dockland, while not perhaps the most vulnerable, were probably most critical in the effect they had on the life of the City. Hence it is not surprising that attempts were made to control the waters.

It has been suggested that during the Republic the state was more directly involved in the management of the Tiber than our surviving sources indicate, particularly because the river was for long the main water supply.[30] What we do hear is that Augustus, 'to restrict flooding, dredged and cleared the bed of the Tiber, which had become filled with rubble and narrowed by projecting buildings'.[31] Flooding, however, continued.[32] Suetonius' view[33] that it was Augustus who set up the commission to regulate the banks of the Tiber seems, however, to be mistaken, though it is just possible that he established a more limited *cura riparum*, which was soon absorbed into the larger commission.[34]

Both Tacitus and Dio think that the creation of a commission was the work of Tiberius. Tacitus tells us that as a result of a flood 'Ateius Capito and Lucius Arruntius were instructed to find means to restrict the river', but that their plans for diverting various tributaries of the Tiber were rejected.[35] Dio recounts that in AD 15 there was a flood and that people had been going around in boats; therefore five senators, chosen by lot, were to constitute a permanent board to look after the river, so that it should neither overflow in winter nor fail in summer.[36] The argument in favour of a date around AD 15 is somewhat strengthened by the fact that it was originally a five-man commission; the only other board with this number of members was the purely Tiberian *curatores locorum publicorum iudicandorum*, whereas there were only three men on Augustus' *cura aquarum* and two on the *cura aedium sacrarum et operum*

29 Dio 54.1.
30 Viganò (1972).
31 Suet. *Aug*.30.1.
32 Dio 54.25; Dio 55.22, when the City was navigable for seven days; Dio 56.27.4, when the Circus was under water.
33 Suet. *Aug*.37.
34 Palma (1980): 236, and literature cited there.
35 Tac. *Annals* 1.76 & 79.
36 Dio 57.14.7–8.

locorumque publicorum. There continued to be five senators on the commission, under the presidency of a consular, for the first four boards;[37] thereafter, from the time of Vespasian, the principle of collegiality seems to have been abandoned and the office held by one man,[38] of consular status, who apparently continued to have no fixed term of service. The *cura Tiberis* can be traced down to the fourth century, when it became subordinated to the Urban Prefecture.[39]

As with the other commissions established in the early Principate, the senators appointed to the *cura* of the Tiber banks and bed were given administrative support. The curator certainly had an office, with the normal staff, down at Ostia,[40] as well as at Rome.[41] The Ostian office may have been headed by his deputy; as early as AD 41–4 we hear of an equestrian *praefectus* to the commission[42] and by 180 there was at Ostia an equestrian *adiutor curatoris alvei Tiberis et cloacarum*.[43] To assume that the curator was based in Rome with someone fairly senior at Ostia seems not unreasonable. Of clerical staff, a *commentariensis*[44] is known at Ostia; his presence sufficiently implies a full office staff, with *scribae, praecones*, and other minor functionaries for the needs of a commissioner of consular rank. The *aerarium*, the treasury controlled by the Senate, presumably funded this *cura* originally, since its work was authorised by the Senate; even after the phrase *ex SCo* disappears it is by no means unlikely that this state of affairs continued, since the joint approach between emperor and Senate in matters essential to the City is widely evidenced – although so is the increasing dominance of the imperial role.[45]

37 ILS 5893 (= CIL VI 31543); 5925 (= VI 31544) between 16 and 24; XIV 4704, between 23 and 41; ILS 5926 (= VI 31545) between 41 and 44.
38 ILS 5927 (= CIL VI 31546) in 73; 5928 (= VI 31547) later in 73; 5929 (= VI 31548) during 74; 8969 (= IX 4194) around 75; 5930–2 (= VI 31549–51 & 31553) concerning Julius Ferox, when *'cloacarum'* was added; ILS 2927 (= V 5262) and others concerning Pliny the Younger, who held the office after his consulate and before he went to Bithynia, and cf. *Ep.*5,14; ILS 1092 (= VI 1523) after AD 159; 5894 (= VI 1242) under Diocletian.
39 *Notitia Dignitatum, Occ.*IV 6.
40 CIL XIV 5384.
41 CIL VI 1224.
42 ILS 5004 (= CIL X 797). NB that Claudius created the office of *procurator aquarum*.
43 ILS 1429 (= CIL XIV 172); XIV 5345.
44 ILS 1560 (= CIL II 6085).
45 Chilver (1949); Rickman (1980): 213–17; Talbert (1984): 372–9.

Certainly some of the embankments designed to control the floodwaters, and also to act as wharves, seem to date from the early years of the first century AD; literary sources on the anti-flood work done by the curators are lacking, as are juristic and epigraphic sources, and hence we must largely rely on the scant archaeological evidence.[46] There is, however, plenty of literary evidence that floods continued. We hear, for instance, of them in AD 36,[47] in 69 when the *pons Sublicius* collapsed again and backed up the waters,[48] and under Trajan – a much worse flood than that under Nerva – when Pliny the Younger was *curator alvei Tiberis et riparum et cloacarum urbis*.[49] In one letter Pliny tells us that there was still considerable damage from the Anio and the Tiber, despite Trajan's efforts – 'he made a cut by which the floods which so regularly distressed the City might be diverted into a permanent channel'.[50] However, further major floods are recorded, for instance, one under Marcus Aurelius, causing famine and the death of many animals, another in 217, when people even in the Forum were swept away by the force of the waters, and again in 374,[51] though on that occasion there was no starvation because of the many small boats able to transport food.

The legal texts too reflect the fact of flooding. Ulpian cites the Republican jurist Trebatius: 'When the Tiber flooded and carried a great deal of property belonging to many people into other peoples' houses, an interdict was granted by the praetor to prevent force being used against the owners to stop them taking away their possessions, provided they gave security for possible damage'.[52] It is difficult to assess the scale of the measures taken for flood control since much of the archaeological evidence has faded in the course of time. It is even more difficult to judge whether they were of any great effect, and whether indeed success was technically within the power of the authorities.

46 Largely destroyed by the embankment of the Tiber at the end of the nineteenth century.
47 Dio 58.26.5.
48 Tac. *Hist*.1.86; Suet. *Otho* 8.3.
49 ILS 2927 (= CIL V 5262); *Ep. de Caes*.13.12.
50 ILS 5797a (= CIL XIV 88); cf. Pliny *Ep*.8.17.
51 SHA *M. Ant. Aurelius* 8; Dio 79.25; *Ep. de Caes*.32.3; Ammianus 29.6.17–18.
52 D.39.2.9.1, Ulpian 53 *ad ed*.

THE ZONE OF PUBLIC ACCESS

There was a legal right of access to the banks of the river.

> Indeed, all rivers and harbours are public, and so the right
> of fishing in the harbour and rivers is open to everyone. . . .
> The use of river banks is also public by the law of all
> peoples, as is the use of the actual river. . . . But the
> ownership of the banks vests in those whose lands adjoin
> the river.[53]

Matters were, of course, a little more complicated than that, as
the legal texts illustrate. Furthermore, the Marble Plan shows
that many properties backed onto the water, and thus public
access to the river banks within the City was frequently denied.
Those areas which were kept public were marked out.

Even before the creation of a commission for the Tiber, *cippi*
had marked the area delimited for public use. The earliest of
these markers which survive are those put up by the censors
on the authorisation of the Senate in 55/54 BC,[54] which are
found on both banks. Cippi were again erected in 8 BC by
the two consuls *ex senatusconsulto;*[55] those of 7/6 BC[56] were
erected by Augustus himself, again *ex senatusconsulto*. From
AD 15 this task had become that of the *curatores riparum et
alvei Tiberis*,[57] who restored the *cippi* of Augustus.[58] Under
Claudius the *cippi* become authorised by the emperor rather
than the Senate.[59] Under the *divi fratres*, the curator no longer
appears in the nominative on the *cippi*, but in the ablative –
curante – as the emperor's delegate; this, however, was reversed
under Severus – though no reason is apparent. *Cippi* continued
to be erected, perhaps as much the result of alluvion adding
to the banks as of floods washing them away; old ones were

---

53 *Inst.* 2.1.2 & 4; cf. ILS 9376 (= CIL XIV suppl. 4702), where a pre-
Sullan urban praetor had, on the authority of the Senate, made public
property of riparian land at Ostia. Cf. also ILS 5989 (= VI 29782) of
the Augustan period: ab angulo qui ripam contingit usque at viam
Flaminiam . . . privata.
54 ILS 5922 (= CIL VI 31540.l); 5923 (= VI 31541. g,h,o,s,u); 5924 (= VI
31542.s).
55 ILS 5923 (= CIL VI 31541).
56 ILS 5924a-d (= CIL VI 31542).
57 ILS 5893 (= CIL VI 31543).
58 ILS 5924d.
59 ILS 5926 (= CIL VI 31545): five curators – in the nominative – 'ex
auctoritate . . . principis sui ripam cippis positis terminaverunt'.

replaced only as there was need.[60] The inscriptions on them are our best, and frequently only, source for the names of those who exercised this commission, which seems not to have received much attention from contemporaries.

Ulpian distinguished between streams and rivers and between public and private rivers in his discussion of the praetor's interdicts to prevent anything being done to hamper navigation on a public river;[61] one does not have to assume that mention of a river necessarily means the Tiber (since he even mentions the Nile). Scaevola pointed out that someone owning land on either bank of a public river did not have a right to bridge it.[62] Ulpian's passage on the praetor's interdict *de ripa munienda*, protecting those who wished to repair and build up the banks of public rivers,[63] seems even less likely to have had application within Rome, as indeed Ulpian pointed out in the comparable case of interdicts concerning public roads or streets.[64] The implication that private persons are responsible for the protection of the banks, together with the requirement of security to be given to neighbours and to those who possess land on the opposite bank, would suggest that the interdict was designed for the Tiber upstream of the City and for rivers elsewhere. Downstream must have been, to some extent at least, the affair of the curator, since both banks had towpaths along which oxen pulled ships up to Rome against the current;[65] he may have had a limited jurisdiction over the local riparian owners rather than direct powers.

NAVIGATION

The curators were responsible for the bed of the Tiber, which must also include the river flowing in it. This task presumably involved some sort of regular dredging; we know that Augustus did this, and we are told that Aurelian dredged the river and renewed its embankments for the sake of the grain supply.[66] It also implied the clearance of wrecks and other obstacles to

---

60 E.g. ILS 5894 (= CIL VI 1242), in the reign of Diocletian, where the bank had collapsed.
61 D.43.12.1, Ulpian 68 *ad ed*; cf. 43.14.1, Ulpian 68 *ad ed*.
62 D.43.12.4, Scaevola 5 *resp*.
63 D.43.15.1, Ulp.68 *ad ed*.
64 D.43.8.2.24: in the City it was a matter for the magistrates.
65 Procopius *BG* 5.26.10–12.
66 Suet. *Aug.*30; SHA *Aurelian* 47.2–3.

navigation within the stream; Aulus Gellius tells us of an early praetorian edict by which public contracts were let 'flumina retanda', which he interprets as clearing out fallen trees. This may have included less pleasant things on occasion. Tacitus reports that in the bloody aftermath of Sejanus' downfall (in AD 33), many were executed and 'the putrid bodies were thrown into the Tiber to be driven at the mercy of the winds and waves. Some were carried away by the current, others grounded, but none was allowed burial'.[67] Keeping the river free for navigation would seem to have been a duty taken over by the curators after the administrative breakdown of the first century BC.[68] We know there were divers – *urinatores* – who presumably worked on removing obstacles as well as recovering things which had fallen overboard; it is possible that their expertise was used for work on the foundations of the bridges, even if these were in theory dealt with as streets.

The banks have earlier been considered as constructions for flood control. But the lower-lying areas, such as the Emporium and also the *forum boarium* and the *forum Holitorium* – commercial developments of the second century BC[69] – were also the most suitable for quays or wharves where boats could tie up and discharge their cargoes. Rickman's work on the corn supply and on warehouses has led him to reckon that about a million tons a year came in through the docks of Rome.[70] There must have been huge numbers of small ships,[71] some specialist, others not, and even huger numbers of men, since the layout of the wharves and *horrea* strongly suggests the use of porters humping loads, not carts.

The competence of the curator extended to Ostia and the sea,[72] as well as upstream at least to the Milvian Bridge. It therefore seems reasonable to assume that the curator was responsible for the maintenance, directly or indirectly, of the towpaths on the banks of the Tiber. Procopius recorded that in his day the towpath down the left bank (which led to Ostia) had disappeared, but that the right one (leading to Portus) was still fit for use.[73]

---

67 Tac. *Annals* 6.19.
68 Viganò (1969).
69 E.g. Livy 35.10; 40.51; 41.27.
70 Rickman (1971): 10.
71 E.g. Tac. *Annals* 15.18.3.
72 CIL XIV 192; 254; 4704; 5320. See also Meiggs (1973): 303.
73 Procopius *BG* 5.26.8–9 & 13.

It is not clear from our sources how far it was part of the office of the curator to act as harbour master for the City; we do not hear of anyone else in a position to fulfil such duties, and yet 'the congestion on the river at times must have been intense and there must have been attempts at organisation'.[74] It seems safe to assume a constant co-operation with the *praefectus annonae*, the *curatores operum publicorum*, and also with other officials, such as those in charge of bringing in wild animals for the shows, since we hear of animals being unloaded at Rome's docks.[75]

What powers, if any, the curator may have had over the various boatmen on the river are unfortunately obscure;[76] Rickman, however, seems convinced that they existed, though Meiggs was doubtful. We hear, for instance, in AD 206 of a lictor, who was patron of the guild (as authorised by resolution of the Senate) of fishermen and divers of the whole Tiber basin, who had had some dealings with the boatmen and their rights of navigation.[77] Did any jurisdiction of the curator cover pleasure boats as well as cargo ships? There were ferries near the river mouth,[78] crossing the two arms of the Tiber, and communicating with the Isola Sacra; at Rome, however, considering the relative unimportance of Trastevere, the bridges were probably adequate for the traffic.

OTHER USES OF THE RIVER

'For four hundred and forty-one years from the foundation of the City, the Romans were satisfied with the use of such waters as they drew from the Tiber, from wells, or from springs.'[79] As the aqueducts were brought in, the number of inhabitants who continued to fetch water (whether for drinking, cooking or washing) from the river must have diminished sharply; fountains would have been easier to use, as well as cleaner. Pomponius tells us that it was not permitted to draw off water from a navigable river, but he seems to have structures such as

74 Rickman (1980): 20.
75 Pliny *NH* 36.4.40.
76 CIL XIV 254 & 5320 show the curator granting permission to certain boatmen in guild affairs; ILS 1442 (= XIV 4459) procurator ferriarum et annonae Ostis . . . lyntr . . .
77 ILS 7266 (= CIL VI 1872): praesertim cum navigatio scapharum diligentia eius adquisita et confirmata sit.
78 CIL XIV 254.
79 Frontinus *aq*.4. See also ch. 7.

aqueducts in mind rather than buckets.[80]

Similarly, while the river doubtless continued to be used as a bathing place, particularly one imagines by local boys, the provision of the great imperial *thermae*, as well as of private *balnea*, will have greatly diminished its importance in this regard.[81]

Fish, some of them highly prized, were at one time to be caught in the Tiber (indeed, the commercial fishermen had their own special holiday in June[82]); their gastronomic reputation clearly declined,[83] perhaps as a result of pollution, and it seems unlikely that during the Empire the river made a significant contribution towards the City's food supply.

There appears to have been no regulation of these uses of the Tiber, apart from the maintenance of the right of free access to the banks. However, it must have been the curator of the Tiber who controlled the taking of sand from the river bed for building purposes, though this seems to have been a consular duty in the Republic.[84]

CO-OPERATION

While we know very little directly about the functioning of the *cura Tiberis*, its very existence is interesting because it implies the close liaison that there must have been between the various branches of the City's administration. The great volume of imports, which included wood for fuel, wild animals and building materials, as well as foodstuffs, must have involved regular co-operation with the controllers of the baths, those responsible for the animals at the shows, the *procurator marmorum* and the *curatores operum publicorum*, as well as the *praefectus annonae*. For the efficient care of the sewers and the bridges there must have been easy communication between the curator of the Tiber and his colleagues in charge of the water supply and of the streets. In fact, if there is one thing that emerges from a glance at the functions of the curator of the Tiber, it is the need that there must have been for sensible arrangements between the various branches of the City's administration.

80 D.43.12.2, Pomponius 34 *ad Sab.*
81 See ch. 8.
82 Festus 274L: games were given for them in Trastevere by the Urban Praetor.
83 Macrobius *Sat.*3.16.11–18. Also CIL VI 29700, 29702, which record the doings of the guild of fishermen and divers.
84 CIL XV 7150.

7

WATER AND FIRE

Water[1] has always been recognised as the most essential pre-requisite for human settlement, whether in New Mexico or in the ancient Mediterranean. That government should be concerned with a city's water supply is taken completely for granted, alike in classical Athens and eighteenth-century London; urban living is not possible without adequate water (though the definition of 'adequate' can vary widely). Effective fire prevention is also very dependent on the availability of ample water and, while the supplies of water to Rome have been estimated variously, they seem to have been more lavish than those of modern western cities.[2] At Rome the water commission that came into being under Augustus was concerned with 'not merely the convenience but also the health and even the safety of the City'.[3] An increased supply led to the improved health of the City, and 'not even the superfluous water is wasted but the appearance of the City is cleanlier, the air purer and the causes of the unwholesome atmosphere . . . are removed'.[4]

THE REPUBLICAN PROVISION OF WATER

In the Republic the bringing in of an external water supply, once there came to be such a need – for the Tiber, springs and

1 See Robinson (1980); Bruun (1991); Trevor-Hodge (1992).
2 Blackman (1978) estimates 600,000 cubic metres daily from the four largest aqueducts, and Hodge (1989) seems to accept a million or so cubic metres, drawn from all sources.
3 Frontinus *de aquis urbis Romae*, hereafter cited simply as Frontinus, 1. In D.43.21.4, Venuleius, 1 *interdict*, points out that if roads are not repaired men can go round another way, but that if river banks are not maintained, men die of thirst.
4 Frontinus 88.

wells long satisfied the population of Rome[5] – was the duty of the censors. This was entirely the case with *aqua Appia* (started in 312 BC) and *aqua Tepula* (125 BC). The censors' work might be supplemented if necessary by *duumviri aquae perducendae*, as with *Anio Vetus* (begun in 273), or replaced by the praetor on the commission of the Senate, as with *aqua Marcia*, built from 144 BC over some five years.[6] *Aqua Appia* was (probably) financed by tribute, *Anio Vetus* by the proceeds from the victory over Pyrrhus, *Marcia* by a specific grant of the Senate, and *Tepula* presumably from general revenue. The procedure for bringing in aqueducts was probably roughly like that described in the *lex Ursonensis*.[7] The censors had the regular oversight of contracting for public works in the City; the reason for the Senate's commissioning the Urban Praetor for such a task is obscure, and presumably political. These four were the only Republican aqueducts.

The censors were also concerned both with the repair and maintenance of the fabric and with the distribution of an adequate supply; for example, we hear of Cato in 184 BC claiming back water supplies for public use, as well as repairing the channels and reservoirs.[8] However, in the three and a half year periods (sometimes longer) in which there were normally no censors operating, the responsibility for granting the right to take water was given to the aediles by default. Among those whom Frontinus describes as the *veteres*, meaning the men of the Republic, private grants of water were only made from the surplus from the public basins (*lacus*),[9] and even that was sold (with the fee paid into the *aerarium*) only to baths and fullers, apart from grants to some leading citizens. (The procedure was presumably similar to that laid down in the *lex Ursonensis*,[10]

---

5 Frontinus 4; e.g the spring of Juturna, near the temple of Castor and Pollux, of which the water was famed for its healing qualities – Varro *LL* 5.71.

6 Frontinus 5, and Livy 9.29; Frontinus 8; Frontinus 6; Frontinus 7.

7 FIRA i 21 (p.177ff) c.99. The magistrate proposed his work and its route to the town council, of whom two-thirds must be present; a simple majority vote was sufficient to authorise its being brought in, though not through any buildings.

8 Livy 39.44; Plutarch *Cato maior* 19.

9 Nash (1981): 9ff and 18ff.

10 FIRA i 21 (p.177ff), c.100. Application must be made to the local *duumvir*, who would refer the request to the town council, of which a quorum must be present. If the majority of those present approved, the private citizen was empowered to take public water 'sine privati iniuria', and presumably subject to the supervision of the local magistrates.

since it is likely that this was based on Roman practice.)
Furthermore, it was for the aediles, in the absence of censors,
to give permission for such things as watering the Circus Maximus when games were being held there, and this right is said
to have survived Augustus' creation of the *cura aquarum*.[11]

Maintenance of the structure of the aqueducts and of the
supply was put out to contract by the censors. The contractors,
the *aquarii*, had to employ a fixed number of slaves both outside
and inside the City – there were nearly 200 kilometres above and
below ground to maintain – and to enter in the public records the
names of those they employed according to district. The censors
naturally were primarily responsible for inspecting the work of
the contractors, but the duty could devolve on the aediles as part
of their *cura urbis*, or sometimes on the quaestors.[12] We know
from himself, and also from Frontinus, of M. Caelius Rufus'
battles with the *aquarii* when he was aedile.[13] Moreover, the
curule aediles had a duty to appoint two men from each *vicus*,
either resident or property-holding within it, to oversee the
public fountains. (In contrast to provincial cities, there is no
other evidence at Rome for private citizens exercising responsibility concerning the water supply.[14]) The purpose of this local
control, according to Frontinus, was to prevent pollution of the
water supply, or to ensure that it was punished; the aediles
must have been the magistrates to impose the heavy fines for
the unlawful taking of public water or for its pollution – we are
even told that unlawfully irrigated land might be made public
property.[15]

Some degree of control in matters concerning distribution
may have been exercised by the Urban Praetor. He was responsible for granting interdicts which concerned public as well as
private law, such as 'Nothing shall hinder water being drawn
from a public river (unless the emperor or the Senate shall so
forbid) as long as that water be not dedicated to public use';[16]

11 Frontinus 94–5 & 97.
12 Frontinus 96.
13 Cicero *ad fam.*8.6.4; Frontinus 76.
14 Unless perhaps in the obscure *lex Sulpicia rivalicia* – FIRA i 5 (p.81):
   [*mon*]*tani paganive si*[*fis aquam dividunto*]; this, however, may have applied
   only to the suburbs, for Frontinus tells us that in his day a third of the
   total water-supply was used outside the city – Frontinus 78.
15 Frontinus 97.
16 D.43.12.2, Pomponius 34 *ad Sab*; cf. D.43.13 *passim*.

again, the praetor granted an interdict on *aqua cottidiana* which applied whether the water was inside or outside the city, and which later could apply to water drawn from a reservoir by imperial licence.[17] There would be nobody else in a position to exercise control over any disputed use of the springs and wells – and indeed waters leaking from aqueducts[18] – which will have continued to provide some water for private persons. It seems possible that the praetor also had discretion over grants for private use;[19] in Augustus' edict concerning the aqueduct at Venafrum (a town not far from Monte Cassino) it is the Peregrine Praetor who is to have jurisdiction in matters beyond the competence of the local magistrates,[20] as was the case at Rome under the *lex Quinctia* once the *curator aquarum* ceased to exercise his jurisdiction for the year.[21]

THE ARTERIAL WATER SUPPLY UNDER AUGUSTUS AND AFTER

Under Augustus more aqueducts were added to the Republican four, *Julia* and *Virgo* by Agrippa, and then *Alsietina* and several supplementary channels, mostly called *Augusta*.[22] Agrippa may have been praetor or he may have been aedile – an unprecedented consular aedile – when he brought in *Julia*; it was as Augustus' son-in-law rather than through any office that he brought in *Virgo*, chiefly, it seems, for supplying his new Baths, but also complementing the existing provision by, for the first time, bringing in an aqueduct for the Campus Martius area. Thereafter new aqueducts were all built in the emperor's name: *Claudia* and *Anio Novus*, begun by Caligula, were finished under Claudius; *Traiana* under Trajan, to supplement *Alsietina* in Trastevere;[23] *Alexandriana* by Severus Alexander, to supply the *thermae Neronianae* which he restored.[24] Claudius also rebuilt *Virgo* where it had been torn down for Caligula's construction

17 D.43.20.1.14 & 40–2, Ulpian 70 *ad ed.*
18 Frontinus 65.
19 ILS 5742 (= CIL X 8236): Q. Folvius Q. f. M. hance aquam indeixsit aput P. Atilium L. f. praetorem urbanum; cf. Frontinus 94.
20 FIRA i 67 (p.400ff).
21 Frontinus 101.
22 Frontinus 9 and Dio 48.32, differing as to date; Frontinus 10; Frontinus 11; Frontinus 12 & 5 & 21.
23 Nash (1981): 52f.
24 P & A: 20.

work in the Campus Martius; Nero extended *Claudia* (to the Aventine and Trastevere[25]), as did Domitian; Nerva rebuilt *Marcia* and extended it; Trajan modified the source of *Anio Novus*; Caracalla brought in a new branch of *Marcia*.[26] The growing population and, in particular, the expanding role of the public baths explain the necessity for the greatly increased water supply in the early Principate. New mains were accompanied by new fountains, apparently plentiful; when the mob complained of the high price of wine, Augustus said – approximately – 'let them drink water'.[27]

Strabo remarked:[28] 'Water is brought into the City through the aqueducts in such quantities that veritable rivers flow through the City and its sewers; almost every house has cisterns and siphon pipes and copious fountains.' He may have been exaggerating, but Frontinus complained of the diversion of public water through bribery of the *aquarii* which led to his having found 'fields, shops, garrets too, and even houses of ill fame' all fitted up with running water supplies.[29] 'With such an array of indispensable vast enterprises carrying so many waters, compare the superfluous pyramids, or the useless though famous works of the Greeks.'[30] Pliny the Elder had said that 'if we take into careful account the abundant supplies of water in public buildings, baths, pools, conduits, houses, gardens, suburban estates, if we reckon from how far the water comes, the raised arches, the tunnelled mountains, the levelled valleys, we shall admit there has never been anything more marvellous in the whole world'.[31]

THE ADMINISTRATION OF THE WATER SUPPLY

Agrippa also supervised the aqueducts, both his own and the existing ones. He saw to their repair and maintained them with his own gang of slaves, which he bequeathed to Augustus – who made them public property. He provided fountains, and made

25 Frontinus 20.
26 Frontinus 76 & 87 for Nero's, Nerva's and Trajan's work; P & A: 26 for Claudius' work; P & A: 29 for Caracalla's.
27 Suet. *Aug*.42.
28 Strabo 5.3.8.
29 Frontinus 76.
30 Frontinus 16.
31 Pliny *NH* 36.24.123; cf. Propertius 2.32.14–16.

the decisions on the allotment of water to public buildings, to basins, and to private persons.[32] He or Vitruvius, or more likely the pair of them, introduced the standard measurement of the *quinaria*.[33]

The office of the *curatores aquarum*, or water commissioners, was established by Augustus to continue Agrippa's work and to provide clear control over the water supply. There was to be a commission of three, operating under a president. The curators were to administer the water supply in accordance with the resolutions of the Senate of 11 BC and the *lex Quinctia* of 9 BC, and also an edict of Augustus concerning the aqueduct of Venafrum in Campania. Outside the City they were each to have the use of two lictors, three public slaves and an architect; otherwise their staff was to consist of the architects (and the public slaves) and also senior clerks, copyists, orderlies and criers in the same numbers as the *praefecti frumenti dandi*. A list of these attendants was to be submitted to the *aerarium* within ten days of their taking office; rations and pay would subsequently be authorised by the praetors of the treasury (a new use for praetors; they were replaced by quaestors by Claudius). The commissioners could also draw stationery and other office materials. Three months of the year were set aside for the exercise of their jurisdiction, as with the *curatores viarum* and the *praefecti frumenti dandi*, thereafter, in accordance with the *lex Quinctia*, the Peregrine Praetor had jurisdiction.[34]

It came to be the *procurator aquarum*, an office created under Claudius,[35] who was in executive charge of the water supply, and concerned with it permanently, whereas the commissioners might be pursuing their senatorial careers elsewhere much of

32 Frontinus 98.
33 This was a particular size of cross-section which, normally in multiples, defined the size of an ajutage, the pipe nozzle or valve through which water was drawn from an aqueduct – Frontinus 25 & 26–63.
34 Frontinus 99–101. Certainly we find commissioners holding other posts at the same time, among them the jurist Ateius Capito, who was also concerned with the Tiber, A. Didius Gallus, who seems to have been simultaneously legate of Moesia, and L. Calpurnius Piso who was also a member of the commission supervising the *vectigalia*. This may help explain why Frontinus sometimes complained about his predecessors' neglect of their duties.
35 Frontinus 105.

the time. His name appears on many surviving lead water pipes, presumably as authorising their laying.[36] He also put into effect the grants of water to private citizens.[37] Until the time of Trajan the post was filled by an imperial freedman, but it then became equestrian, as was the general tendency; the procurator seems to have been nominated by the curators.

The headquarters of the water service, the *statio aquarum*, was fixed at the *porticus Minucia* after the apparent bringing together of the two services of water and grain supply under Commodus or Septimius Severus;[38] from the fourth century it seems to have been at the *lacus Juturnae*, between the temples of Vesta and Castor,[39] and during the course of the century grain and water supplies were separated again. (Further, the responsibility for water was itself divided, under the overall control of the Urban Prefect; the *comes formarum* came to have charge of the infrastructure and the *consularis aquarum* of the distribution.)[40] Headquarters staff included the architects and engineers attached to the commission, and various clerks,[41] as well as the usual *apparitores*, *praecones*, etc. The records of the water commission were clearly essential for controlling maintenance work and checking on the flow of water, as well as for keeping track of grants. Frontinus used to prepare a written schedule, assigning the work for the following day.[42] The architects were there to give advice about correct priorities concerning repairs, extensions and construction work.[43] Major work seems to have been put out to contract, since it would need to employ many more men than the regular staff, and the latter could not safely be taken from their routine duties.[44]

36 Frontinus 112 (implicitly); e.g. ILS 8678; 8679 (= CIL XV 7279); 8684 (= XV 7309).
37 Frontinus 105.
38 ILS 1128 (= CIL V 7783); 1186 (= XIV 3902); 1191 (= VI 1532). See also P & A: 424ff; Pavis d'Escurac (1976): 35.
39 ILS 8943; 9050.
40 CJ 11.43(42).1 – AD 330; ILS 5791 (= CIL VI 3866); *Notitia Dignitatum Occ.*IV 5 & 11; Cassiodorus *Variae* 7.6.
41 *Rationalis* – ILS 8686 & 8688 (= CIL XIV 2008a & 1981); *a commentariis* – ILS 1609 (= VI 8487); *tabularii* – ILS 1607 (= VI 8488); *scribae* and *librarii* – Frontinus 100.
42 Frontinus 117.
43 Frontinus 119–24.
44 E.g. ILS 3512 (= CIL XIV 3530) of AD 88.

As well as their architects, the commissioners had technical staff drawn from the slave gangs assigned to the care of the aqueducts, of which Frontinus says there were two: one of around 240 men, descended from Agrippa's – this is the state gang, the property of the *populus romanus* – and the other of 460 men which had been created by Claudius and remained imperial property.[45] They seem to have comprised both crafts-men[46] and labourers with their *vilici* or foremen;[47] at the head of each gang was a *praepositus*. The wages for the state gang were paid from the *aerarium*, which itself received the water rents and possibly also a tax from establishments adjoining the aqueducts; Domitian took these into the fisc, but Nerva restored the earlier practice. Caesar's gang were paid from the fisc, which also paid for lead and other expenses,[48] such as the materials needed for the maintenance of the structures, including any necessary compulsory purchases.[49]

The commission's prime function was the maintenance of the supply,[50] within and outside Rome, described by Frontinus as the guardianship of the aqueducts.[51] To this end it was the duty of the commissioners to make frequent rounds of the channels and reservoirs,[52] and to oversee the correct diversion or bringing together of the various aqueducts, so that worse water was not mixed with better, and each was reserved, as far as possible, for its most suitable use.[53] Unauthorised or secret branch pipes must be destroyed, and 'puncturing' stopped, preventing fraud by either the *aquarii* or the public.[54]

45 Frontinus 116.
46 *Circitores* (inspectors), *silicarii* (pavers), *tectores* (plasterers) – Frontinus 117; *libratores* (levellers) – Frontinus 105; *plumbarii* (plumbers) – ILS 1637 & 8705 (= CIL VI 8461 & XV 7647).
47 Frontinus 117; ILS 1610–14 (= CIL VI 8491, 8495, 8494, 8497), 1975 (= VI 2345).
48 Frontinus 118.
49 Frontinus 125.
50 E.g. letting *Alsietina*, normally used only for irrigation, supply Trastevere when, through bridge repairs or some other cause, the usual supply to the right bank was cut off – Frontinus 11.
51 Frontinus 17, and he refers to the maps and plans he had had drawn up for his office.
52 Frontinus 103.
53 Frontinus 91–2; Frontinus had found *Marcia* serving baths, fullers, and '*relatu quoque foedis ministeriis*'; it was reorganised so that its purity provided drinking water, while *Anio Vetus* could be used for watering parks and gardens and for the baser services of the City.
54 Frontinus 9 and 114–15.

The prevention of fraud, whether simple diversion of the supply or something more complicated, was a matter of permanent concern for the commissioners.[55] The proper clearance zones must be left around the course of the aqueducts, to save them from damage from such things as tree roots, to keep away squatters and to allow ready access.[56] Probably, as at Venafrum, the land and fences of adjoining proprietors were to be respected, except in so far as was necessary for inspection and repairs.

The commission was also, in the emperor's name, concerned with the control of distribution. In the first place there was the division between public and private use. Rather more than a third of the aqueducts' total supply was used outside the City. Of the water brought within to the 247 reservoirs, the emperor took nearly a sixth, private persons more than a third, and the rest was divided among the basins, ornamental fountains, and public buildings, including barracks (and presumably also the imperial baths, the *thermae*, unless these were classed under Caesar's water).[57] 'The water commissioners . . . shall take pains that the public fountains may deliver water as continuously as possible for the use of the people day and night.'[58] According to the resolution of the Senate of 11 BC, the number of public fountains was to remain unchanged, but this seems not to have remained in force;[59] unfortunately, we have no knowledge of the planning of their sites or of the designing of their form. The public fountains – *salientes* – were free, and the majority of the population must have drawn their water from them, or from the basins, for drinking, cooking, washing, and keeping in reserve against fire. In grander houses there were special slaves whose duty was to keep a domestic cistern full.[60]

Private persons could get licences to draw water from the public supplies for particular premises only after an approach

55 Frontinus 69, 72 and 75–7.
56 Frontinus 126–9.
57 Frontinus 78; in 79–86 he breaks down the distribution among the individual aqueducts.
58 Frontinus 103–4, citing the SC.
59 Frontinus 88 on the increase in all kinds of water-works, including reservoirs, fountains and basins, under Nerva.
60 D.33.7.12.42, Ulpian 20 *ad Sab.*

to the emperor, so it must have been very much a privilege (even if we sometimes find it granted – outside Rome – to poets[61]). Armed with a letter from him, they could approach the curator, who would presumably record the recipient and the quantity and source, and then order the *procurator* to put the grant into effect. The foremen of the gangs were to be informed, and a leveller employed to check that the correct valve was installed together with 50 feet of pipe of the correct gauge.[62] Water must not be withdrawn from the channels, but only from reservoirs; it was one of the duties of the commissioners to decide where in the City such reservoirs for private use should be established.[63] Such a right to take public water was personal, and could not be transmitted to an heir, or passed on to a buyer of the property so favoured. When the right expired, this fact must be announced to the commission's office and entered in their records; a grant was then available to the next applicant in the queue, though there was a 30-day period of grace before the water was cut off from the outgoing licensee.[64] The public baths alone had the privilege that water once granted them was theirs in perpetuity.[65]

Aquae caducae, the overflow from the reservoirs, was granted only very sparingly; it was valued 'for it not only is relevant to the wholesomeness of our City, but also is of use in flushing the sewers'.[66] The general advantages of a supply of fresh water were well understood; Frontinus talked of 'the improved health of the City as a result of the increase in the number of reservoirs, water works, fountains and basins'.[67] (It is interesting that we also find Frontinus complaining about shops, cheap lodgings and even brothels receiving water from the mains;[68] presumably their offence was as much non-payment as lack of suitability, but one cannot be sure.) The other feature of the ample supplies of water was the contribution to public safety in fire-fighting. (As an incidental point, the Romans were well aware of the dangers

61 Statius *Silv*.3.1.61ff.
62 Frontinus 103–5; see also 36 and 112–13 on the right positioning of valves and pipes.
63 Frontinus 106.
64 Frontinus 107–9.
65 Frontinus 108–9.
66 Frontinus 110–11.
67 Frontinus 88.
68 Frontinus 76.

of lead poisoning, but their technology meant that this was a risk which had to be accepted.[69])

FIRE CONTROL IN THE REPUBLIC[70]

In the old days the business of preventing fires was supervised by a commission of three who, because they kept watch at night, were called *tresviri nocturni*; sometimes aediles and plebeian tribunes took a part in the service. There was a body of public slaves stationed about the gates and walls who could be called out if necessary, and there were privately owned gangs of slaves who put out fires either for pay or gratis.[71]

The *tresviri nocturni*, who are identical with the *triumviri capitales*, are not frequently recorded in this fire-fighting role. Livy mentioned them as being so busy with their normal duties in 186 BC as to need special helpers in the hunting out of the Bacchanalian conspirators.[72] Valerius Maximus wrote that in 169 BC all three were condemned because they came too late to extinguish a fire in the Via Sacra, and that another was condemned in 56 BC for being negligent in his watch.[73] The aediles' share in this duty would fit with their regular *cura urbis*. Indeed, an aedile of 26 BC, Egnatius Rufus, set up his own fire brigade from his slaves and others whom he hired; the people voted him his expenses, and elected him as praetor out of the normal order. His boasting of these feats enraged Augustus and the better sort.[74] There was also some planning against fire;[75] as far back as the Twelve Tables of the fifth century BC cremations were forbidden within the City for this reason, and we find this echoed in the municipal charters.[76]

Augustus, however, confirmed that the control of fires was

69 E.g. Vitruvius 8.6.10f; Pliny *NH* 34.50.167.
70 Robinson (1977).
71 D.1.15.1, Paul *de off. praef. vig*; cf. Plut. *Crassus* 2; Scholiast to Juvenal 14.305, and see Mayor (1881): 344f.
72 Livy 39.14.10.
73 Val.Max. 8.1 *damn*.5 & 6.
74 Velleius 2.91, against Dio 53.24 on the date.
75 See ch. 3, concerning height limits, ambit and party walls.
76 XII T.10. 1 & 9; Cicero *de leg*.2.23.58; 2.24.61; *lex Ursonensis* – FIRA i 21, (p.177ff), cc. 73–4.

part of the aediles' *cura urbis*; four years later, in 22 BC, he again laid this duty on the curule aediles, and added a force of 600 slaves to assist them in its performance.[77] Then, as with so much else, there was innovation. The task of fire-fighting seems to have been given temporarily to the *vicomagistri* in 7 BC,[78] unless – which is less likely – a new magistracy was then established which rapidly disappeared. Overall supervision would have rested with the aediles and plebeian tribunes who, together with the praetors, were responsible for the fourteen new Regions. This experiment was clearly not successful, but the next one – the institution of the *vigiles* – survived until the fourth century.[79] Nevertheless, in order to maintain popular morale, the emperors had to be seen to be intervening personally from time to time.[80]

THE *VIGILES*[81]

In AD 6 seven cohorts of a night watch were organised, at first as a temporary measure; they were recruited from the freedman class but commanded by a man of equestrian rank appointed by the emperor. This remained their permanent form, seven cohorts, paid from the *aerarium* (through a 4 per cent tax on the sale of slaves), each with a tribune in command, under the *praefectus vigilum*.[82] Each cohort seems to have consisted at their establishment of a notional 500 men; this number was later doubled, as were the cohorts of the other City-based troops.[83] Each cohort had only seven centuries,

77 Dio 54.2.
78 Dio 55.8, if his account can be trusted.
79 When they seem to have given way to *collegiati*, or guilds; cf. Pliny *Ep*.10.33–4; FIRA i 87 (p.444f); Symmachus *Rel*.14.
80 E.g. Suet. *Tib*.48 & 50; Dio 58.26.5; 59.9.4; Suet. *Claudius* 18; *Vesp*.8; *Dom*.5; Dio 73.24.3; most notably Nero's relief measures after the Great Fire of 64 – Tac. *Annals* 15.39; Suet. *Nero* 38.
81 Reynolds (1926); Rainbird (1976); Rainbird has professional knowledge of modern fire-fighting. Cf. Fire Services Act, 1947, c.41, s.1
82 Strabo 5.3.7; Suet. *Aug*.25; Appian *BC* 5.132 (who is clearly wrong in placing their creation in 36 BC); Dio 55.26 & 31; D.1.15.3pr, Paul *de off. praef. vig*.
83 The size of the cohorts, and other questions which relate also to the Praetorian and Urban cohorts, are treated in ch. 12. Rainbird (1976) ch. v, and (1986): 150, is certain that the early cohorts were composed of centuries consisting of 60–80 men, and that they were doubled under Septimius Severus; Cagnat (1919): 867 held that they were miliary cohorts from the start.

a peculiarity of the *vigiles*.[84] They continued to be recruited mainly but not exclusively from freedmen,[85] and indeed six years' completed service – later reduced to three – would give citizenship to a Junian Latin.[86] This provenance was hardly surprising considering that they succeeded a gang of slaves. Their status was para-military rather than military, although they did in a number of respects benefit from regular military privileges.[87]

Each cohort had two Regions to protect, and initially the men seem to have been billeted throughout the City, as also were the Praetorian and Urban cohorts.[88] They came in from their billets to barracks of cohort size, one for each pair of Regions that the cohort protected, with *excubitoria* (for which we do not have indisputable evidence until Caracalla's reign) perhaps in both, perhaps only in the other of the pair. The *vigiles* functioned as a fire brigade by intensive patrolling throughout the night.[89] Householders were required to keep a supply of water in their apartments;[90] the awkwardness of having to strike a light meant that many households would have lamps or a brazier permanently alight.[91] ('Industrial' risks would normally be at ground-floor level.) We also hear about fire-fighting apparatus in private houses; it counted as *instrumenta* – fixtures and fittings – things designed to keep out the weather or fight fires, not just ornaments. 'Most authorities, including Pegasus, say that vinegar too, when it is intended to put out fires, is included [under *instrumenta*], likewise rag mats, siphons, also poles and

---

84 E.g. ILS 2156 (= CIL VI 1056).
85 E.g. ILS 2163 (= CIL VI 220). This inscription also records the individuals' eligibility to receive the public corn, as had the other City-based troops since the time of Nero – Tac. *Annals* 15.72.
86 G. 1.32b, under the *lex Visellia*; Ulpian *Reg*.3.5. Rainbird (1976) ch. viii, seems convinced that they did have this short term of service – on operational grounds.
87 For instance, Tac. *Annals* 4.5 does not list them in his review of the Roman army's numbers. And they did not count fully as veterans – D.27.1.8.4, Modestinus 3 *excus.* – although they did have the right to make a military will – D 37.13.1.1, Ulpian 45 *ad ed*; see also *FV* 140 & 144.
88 Suet. *Aug*.49; *Tib*.37.
89 D.1.15.3.3, Paul *de off. praef. vig.* Cf. CIL VI 32327, vv. 21–2; Petronius *Sat*.78. Rainbird (1986): 151.
90 D.1.15.3.4, Paul *de off. praef. vig.* It is quite possible that this requirement was imposed by Nero after the Great Fire.
91 Juvenal 3.197–202 on the risk of fire; Rainbird (1976) ch. vii.

ladders, mats, sponges, buckets and brooms.'[92] Security against possible damage might also be ordered where there was a fire hazard.[93] Water was generally available throughout the City, from the public fountains and basins – 591 of the latter in Frontinus' time[94] – from the baths, and to some extent from private establishments; Nero, after the Great Fire, tried to preserve the natural springs for public use.[95]

Rainbird has pointed out that there is a concentration of recorded fires in *Regiones* VIII, IX and X.[96] The stationing of the cohorts seems to have been in line with the perceived risk, concentrating them close to the danger areas. The Great Fire of 64, which seems to have created a fire-storm – like the bombing of Dresden – he reckons at a one in eleven million occurrence. There were, of course, other major fires, which devastated areas of the City; we hear particularly of those of 80, of 192, of 217, when, after a fire caused by a lightning strike, the Colosseum was shut for many years for rebuilding, and of 238, as a consequence of severe rioting.[97] He estimates that there were up to 100 fires daily, with 20 being large, that is, more than petty, and 2 serious;[98] early intervention by a patrol would usually be successful. He thinks it unlikely from modern experience that there would have been more than four of these larger fires at a time and the strength in which the *vigiles* patrolled and the distribution of their forces was designed to cope with that. A half-century or century would suffice for most outbreaks, and a cohort would be right for a larger fire. The population increase, and its accompanying hazards, in the early Principate was probably counterbalanced by the increased use of concrete and brick. The *vigiles* were a night watch, and it is clear that the streets were relatively empty after dark; in fighting daytime fires they might be hampered by the press of people.[99] It was quiet scouting and using their noses which was the correct approach,

92 D.33.7.12.16 & 18, Ulpian 20 *ad Sab*; alum was also known as a fire retardant – Gellius 15.1, and larch as a fire-resistant wood – Vitruvius 2.9.16.
93 D.9.2.27.10, Ulpian 18 *ad ed.*
94 Frontinus 78.
95 Tac. *Annals* 15.43. Cf. the Fire Services Act, 1947, s. 13, on the duty of the relevant authority to arrange provision of adequate water supplies.
96 Rainbird (1976) ch. vii, p.346f.
97 Dio 66.24 on AD 80; Dio 73.24 and Herodian 1.14.3–5 on 192; Dio 79.25 on 217; Herodian 7.12 on 238.
98 Modern Glasgow has sixty or so calls daily.
99 Herodian 7.12.5.

as even the jokes imply; both Seneca and Tertullian explain that it is the smell of smoke that brings the firemen – the *sparteoli* – in on a dinner-party.[100]

The *vigiles* had plentiful access to water, but they had to rely on man and bucket power, partly because there was so low a pressure in the gravity-fed mains, and partly since there were no flexible hoses – technologically not yet feasible for use in a crisis – so the water needed to be close at hand. They were equipped with buckets (*hamae*), with pumping engines (*sifoni*)[101] – two to each cohort, with ceiling hooks (*uncini*) and grappling hooks (*falces*), mattocks (*dolabres*) for clearing away and axes (*secures*) for breaking in,[102] mats (*centones*) that could be used to smother flames, and possibly mats onto which people could jump. (Their equipment was presumably also suited to dealing with the aftermath of earth tremors, which frequently cause fires as well as collapse.) Each cohort also had three *ballistae*, which seem to have been used for making fire-breaks;[103] there may also have been supplies of vinegar,[104] as in private houses. But 'manpower had to make up for equipment', and it was the scale of the patrols which was, and is, unique, and also effective, since catching a fire early gives the best chance of extinction. There also seem to have been, at least by the Severan period, four *medici* to each cohort; these were probably qualified doctors, not just medical orderlies, to judge from their place in the inscriptions.[105] This number suggests that they would tend casualties among the public, not just their own men;[106] to keep the *vigiles* themselves

---

100 Seneca *Ep*.64.1; Tertullian *apol*.39.
101 Vitruvius 10.7.1–4: machina quae in altitudinem aquam educit; ILS 2172 (= CIL VI 2994) records a *'siponarius'*.
102 Petronius *Sat*.78 recounts a patrol of *vigiles* breaking down a door in order to reach a suspected fire. Cf. Fire Services Act, 1947, s.30, which gives powers to firemen to break into any premises 'where a fire has or is reasonably believed to have broken out, or any premises or place which it is necessary to enter for the purpose of extinguishing a fire' without needing the consent of owner or occupier.
103 D.47.9.3.7, Ulpian 56 *ad ed*; 43.24.7.4, Ulpian 71 *ad ed*; 9.2.49.1, Ulpian 9 *disp*, referring to the same opinion of Celsus. Even nowadays demolition to create a fire-break is the only effective method of quelling a really serious fire.
104 This may be what the obscure *'emb'* (for *'embamma'*) refers to in the lists, e.g. in ILS 2157 (= CIL VI 1058) in the centuries of both Romulus and Sohaemus.
105 See also Cheesman (1914): 43–4.
106 Suggested by Reynolds (1926): 73.

fit there appear to have been physiotherapists (*unctores*) within the individual cohorts.

The *praefectus vigilum* was primarily the commander of Rome's fire-fighting force, though he also had a jurisdiction, connected with these duties, as a subordinate of the Urban Prefect.[107] His duty to patrol all night, properly shod and equipped with buckets and mattocks,[108] is presumably a metaphor for the Night Watch, since earlier it had not been considered proper for even such junior magistrates as the *triumviri capitales* to be on duty all night.[109] This, however, is not certain; in the early days of the *vigiles*, when fire-fighting was probably truly his main duty and a wider jurisdiction had not been imposed on him, it might have been expected of a professional equestrian that he actually patrol. The cohort tribunes, who were almost exclusively promoted senior centurions (*primipilares*), must have worked nights.

The prefect had a headquarters and an office staff. In the second century, under Trajan, he acquired a sub-prefect; the first known dates from 113.[110] On at least one occasion this appointment may have been to provide a legal expert;[111] it is quite likely that the sub-prefect was not concerned with fire-fighting at all. The sub-prefecture ranked as a procuratorship of the second class – *centenarii* – and could follow an administrative career or the senior centurion post of a legion. The sub-prefect had his own staff within the office. In the third century there was another sub-prefect down at Ostia,[112] and also recorded was a *curator cohortium vigilum*, whose function is obscure but who is listed before the cohort tribune.[113] In the office staff there were *cornicularii* and *a commentariis praefecti*, and the *beneficiarii* appointed by the officer to whom they were attached, prefect, sub-prefect, or cohort tribune, and there were also *immunes* (junior NCOs); we read too of *tabularii*, and also of *librarii*, *codicillarii* and *actarii*.[114] There seems indeed to have been the normal military organisation.

107 See ch. 12.
108 D.1.15.3.3, Paul *de off. praef. vig.*
109 D.1.2.2.30–1, Pomponius *enchiridion*.
110 ILS 2160 (= CIL VI 221); see also 1456 (= VI 1628).
111 ILS 1422 (= CIL XI 6337); VI 1621, C. Laeccanus Novatilianus *iuris peritus*.
112 ILS 2159 (= CIL XIV 4398).
113 CIL VI 1092.
114 ILS 2157 (= CIL VI 1058); summarised by Reynolds (1926): Appendix C, 129–30.

8

PUBLIC HEALTH

Of the matters which fell under the general heading of the promotion of public health, as far as was possible in a large and crowded city, the first and most important of all was the water supply (which has been dealt with separately), and the provision of baths open to the public, sometimes free and at all events (at least in the Principate) cheap, to enable people of all classes to keep clean. With these went a system of drains and sewers, along with public latrines, and cleansing services. There was also the encouragement of exercise, at the *palaestra* attached to the baths or in the Campus Martius, and the recognition of the importance of parks and gardens as open spaces. Burials too were controlled in the interests of hygiene; eventually medical services came into the civic domain and hospitals became available. Besides these developments, the legal framework within which people lived gave interdicts to protect the public's rights and allowed actions to assert such things as access to light or to prevent the emission of noxious fumes.

ATTITUDES TO HEALTH

First it must be made clear that the Romans did have a concept of public hygiene; indeed, they were concerned rather more with public than private health. Private medicine was mostly learned from the Greeks, but there was a preference for native folk remedies. Celsus[1] gave the basic – and enduring – rules for healthy living. His and other medical writings show awareness of the importance of cleanliness, diet, exercise and fresh air. (Martial in describing the good life includes exercise,

1 Celsus 1.1–2.

the best aqueduct and the baths in his list.[2]) Diet, however, for all Romans was essentially cereal-based and deficient in vitamins, especially for urban dwellers who did not go out much in the sun, so rickets was common among children, according to Soranus.[3] It seems that the aediles' control of the market, although primarily concerned with adequate provision of supplies,[4] also involved, presumably on grounds of hygiene, the rejection of unfit wares; more specifically we hear of stinking fish and aged lamb.[5] Apuleius has a municipal aedile getting one of his staff to jump on fish that was allegedly not fresh.[6]

Vitruvius was concerned with healthy living from an architect's point of view.[7] An architect must know the medical consequences of climate, situation, water supply and other factors when deciding where a city should be built; he must be wary of the 'poisoned breath of marsh animals' and conscious of the prevailing winds with their differing effects upon health. Seneca vividly describes the pollution of the City: 'No sooner had I left behind the oppressive atmosphere of the City and that reek of smoking cookers which pour out, along with a cloud of ashes, all the poisonous fumes they've accumulated in their interiors whenever they're started up, than I noticed the change in my condition at once.'[8]

Livy described the stench and overcrowding which attended the plague of 463 BC, when 'contact itself propagated the disease';[9] he may have been modelling himself on Thuycydides' famous description of the plague of 430 BC at Athens, but if so, it still suggests a common stock of knowledge. Just as there is very little record of real famine, as opposed to hunger,[10] at Rome, so we hear relatively little of virulent plague as contrasted with ordinary epidemics, though disease was endemic. The major plagues in our period seem to have taken place under Nero, under Domitian, under Marcus Aurelius – the notorious one

2 Martial 5.20.
3 Cited by Rickman (1980): 7.
4 DH 6.90; see chs 9 and 10.
5 Plautus, *Rudens* 373–4; *Capt.*823.
6 Apuleius *Met.*1.24–5.
7 Vitruvius 1.1.10; 1.4.1–8; 1.6.1–3.
8 Seneca *Ep.*104.
9 Livy 3.6.3.
10 Garnsey (1988) Preface, p.x.

– and in 189 under Commodus.[11] Flight was really the only remedy against serious epidemics, and that was not available to the majority. We learn from Ammianus Marcellinus that maladies were more severe at Rome than elsewhere because the City attracted men to it, and that medical art often could not ease them; attempts were made to isolate the sick, and slaves sent to enquire about a sufferer's progress must wash thoroughly before their return.[12] In the Later Empire we even find concern expressed about hygiene in prisons. An accused person when incarcerated 'must not suffer the darkness of an inner prison, but he must be kept in good health by the enjoyment of light, and when night doubles the necessity for his guard, he shall be taken back into the vestibules of the prisons and into healthful places'.[13] On Sundays provincial governors were to inspect prisons, to ensure that food was supplied to those who did not have it from a private source; moreover, 'Prisoners must be conducted to the bath under trustworthy guard'.[14]

BATHS[15]

Water has been dealt with separately, but it is clear that one of the main uses of the water brought into the City was for the public baths; indeed, they were the principal cause of the need to increase the water supply which, Frontinus reckoned,[16] had already doubled in the later second century BC. The ready availability of baths is one of the clearest indications of the positive Roman attitude towards health. Baths were certainly a pleasure, but by the Empire they were viewed as more than a luxury; otherwise how are we to explain why they should have been made so accessible to all, even to women – and slaves. The negative link between cleanliness and disease was understood, even if the risk of disease being spread at the baths was not. Cleanliness, however, was relatively easy to achieve in public places, whereas in the private dwellings of the urban poor it

11 Suet. *Nero* 39; Dio 67.11; SHA *M. Ant. Aurelius* 13 & 21 and Herodian 1.12; Dio 72.14; see Gilliam (1961).
12 Ammianus 14.6.23.
13 CTh 9.3.1 – AD 320.
14 CTh 9.3.7 – AD 409.
15 See Robinson (1984).
16 Frontinus *aq.*65–8.

must have been nearly impossible.[17] But the normal Roman garments for both sexes, being simple, were generally conducive to health and reasonably easy to keep clean.

Baths open to the public seem to have been in existence by the end of the third century BC; Plautus suggests that Roman audiences would not find them unfamiliar.[18] They began as simple wash-places,[19] but by the end of the Republic they had changed from a merely useful amenity to a social necessity. These early baths were almost certainly run for profit; Agrippa's munificence in 33 BC, when he provided bathing free for his year as aedile in all the baths, not just the great baths he built at his own expense, seems to have been a novelty.[20] Subsidised, if not free, bathing soon, however, came to be the accepted norm for Rome, thanks to imperial benificence.

In the provinces, individual magistrates or leading persons provided free bathing from time to time but, in general, costs had to be covered. Baths privately owned and charging a fee continued to flourish in the Empire, as we learn from both literary[21] and legal[22] sources, but it seems that the great imperial *thermae*[23] set the standards, as exemplified by those of Agrippa, Nero (rebuilt by Severus Alexander) and Trajan.[24] Nero, indeed, may have been the first to link athletic facilities with baths.[25] Although they were provided for the inhabitants of Rome and for its visitors by the emperors, it seems fair to view this as a municipal provision, because it is comparable to similar if smaller scale munificence in lesser towns.[26] The building of the great *thermae* was presumably from the emperors' own resources; about their upkeep we know that Agrippa,

17 Yavetz (1958); Scobie (1986); there is some reason to believe that things may have improved slightly in the Empire, precisely because of the increase in baths, etc.

18 E.g. Plautus *Rudens* 527ff.

19 Seneca *Ep*.86.12.

20 Dio 49.43.

21 E.g. Fronto *Ep.Gr*.5.

22 E.g. D.7.1.13.8, Ulpian 18 *ad Sab*; 25.1.14.2, Ulpian 5 *reg*; 32.91.4, Papinian 7 *resp*.

23 This term is applied to the 'leisure complexes' built by the emperors; simpler establishments, *balnea*, continued to be provided.

24 Nash (1981): 429–33; 460–4; 472–7; P & A: 518–20; 531–2; 534–6. Caracalla was another grandiose builder of baths in the Principate.

25 Tac. *Annals* 14.47.3, if the dedication of the gymnasium is to be taken with the grant of oil.

26 ILS 5664 (= CIL X 4884); 5671 (= IX 5074); 5672 (= XIV 2979).

for instance, in his will left to Augustus certain estates to maintain his baths, and that Augustus at once made these estates over to the people, that is, to the *aerarium*.[27] Severus Alexander is alleged to have assigned a whole range of taxes for the maintenance of his own and other *thermae*.[28] In the Later Empire the *collegiati*, compulsory and hereditary corporations, were responsible for the baths to the Urban Prefect, and it is possible that particular taxes were used for this purpose.[29]

In the Republic, as we learn from Seneca,[30] baths were an area of aedilician responsibility. It is made clear that private as well as contracted-out services were subject to official control, even to the extent of the regulation of the heat. We do not hear explicitly of any replacement for the aediles in this field in the early Principate, any more than in connection with markets and eating houses, but at some stage, though perhaps not until the reign of Constantine, overall responsibility passed to the Urban Prefect.[31] It is possible too that the *praefectus vigilum* had a role here; he exercised a jurisdiction over various thieves, and specifically over the *capsarii* who minded the clothes of the bathers.[32] On the other hand, it was the praetor who protected the individual citizen's right of access to the public baths, granting an action for *iniuria* – defamation – if anyone was refused admission to the baths, the theatre or the playing fields.[33]

The regulations for the baths at Vipasca, an imperial mining village in Portugal, are well known to us from an inscription,[34] and they are probably exemplary in outline. There the sexes were segregated in time not space, but Vitruvius wrote that men's and women's baths should adjoin so that they could share the same furnaces.[35] Certainly respectable women did frequent public baths, for example, Augustus' mother.[36] Mixed

27 Dio 54.29.
28 SHA *Sev. Alex*.24.5.
29 As at Constantinople: CJ 8.11.19 – AD 424.
30 Seneca *Ep*.86.10; *de beata vita* 7.3.
31 Chastagnol (1960): 361; see e.g. ILS 5703 (= CIL VI 1750); 5715 (= VI 1703); 5716 (= VI 1670).
32 D.1.15.3.1 & 5, Paul *de off. praef. vig*; cf. Apuleius *Met*.4.8.
33 D.43.8.2.9, Ulpian 68 *ad ed*: qui in campo publico ludere vel in publico balineo lavare aut in theatro spectare arceatur.
34 FIRA i 105 (p.502ff), *lex metallis Vipascensis*, vv. 19–31.
35 Vitruvius 5.10.1. Archaeological evidence, e.g. at Caracalla's Baths, often seems to show separate changing rooms but shared facilities otherwise; at Herculaneum there are separate women's baths.
36 Suet. *Aug*.94.4.

bathing, which seems to have become normal in the early Empire, perhaps always appeared a little fast to some people; Hadrian forbade it,[37] and Marcus Aurelius confirmed the ban.[38] But clearly this prohibition was not to discourage bathing by both sexes, any more than was the higher charge for women, which seems explicable on grounds of hygiene – long hair and menstruation. The traditional admission charge for an adult man was a *quadrans*,[39] a quarter of an *as*, while boys were admitted free, as perhaps were girls below puberty. Further needs, such as oil, probably had to be paid for. As long as there were ample supplies of water, and also of fuel for the furnaces, which was an important item in the traffic at the Tiber docks, public baths were a very suitable way of promoting public health. The one problem they produced was fumes from the furnaces. Ulpian records the view of the jurist Aristo that an *interdictum utile* should be given for the repair and maintenance of the flues carrying off these fumes.[40] Such pipes might be a nuisance to neighbours,[41] and it might even be necessary to acquire a servitude right to control steam from baths.[42]

FRESH AIR

A part of the positive approach to health, as evidenced widely by Martial, Petronius and Seneca, was the Roman recognition that exercise – which often took place at the baths – was generally a good thing, as also was the taking of fresh air in parks and gardens. Exercise was definitely recognised as beneficial to the health of the individual; the provision of facilities for the citizens to exercise indicates the concern for public health. Similarly, nearly all Romans seem to have enjoyed parks and gardens;[43] the fact that they were widespread throughout the City may be merely a happy coincidence, but it probably included a politic recognition of their benefit to the citizens' health and

37 Dio 69.8; SHA *Hadrian* 18.
38 SHA *M. Ant. Aurelius* 23.
39 Cicero *pro Caelio* 26; Horace *Sat.*1.3.137; Seneca *Ep.*86.9; Martial 1.59; 3.30.
40 D.43.21.3.6, Ulpian 70 *ad ed.*
41 Fronto *ad Marcum* 1.3; D.8.2.13pr, Proculus 2 *ep*; h.t.19pr, Paul 6 *ad Sab.*
42 D.8.5.8.7, Ulpian 17 *ad ed.*
43 Grimal (1969); Toynbee (1971), ch. iv, mentions 'the general passion of the Romans for gardens'.

temper. Julius Caesar left his gardens beside the Tiber to the people for their use and enjoyment;[44] Agrippa too bequeathed gardens to the people.[45] When Augustus built his Mausoleum he made over the surrounding woods and walks for the use of the people.[46] Vespasian, a hard-working emperor, yet spent much of his time in the Gardens of Sallust.[47] On a smaller scale, porticoes provided an amenity, sheltered from the weather, yet in the open; their arcades, or rooms off them, could provide a suitable setting for works of art or even libraries. The concept of 'lungs' for a city is not new.

DRAINS AND SEWERS

The Cloaca Maxima is one of the oldest constructions in Rome; in a sense, its building for the drainage of the Forum area marks the urban foundation of Rome just as much as does the dedication of the Capitol. Drainage made usable both the Campus Martius and the Circus Maximus areas.[48] The drainage of the marshy lands around the City by Agrippa and Augustus, Claudius, and Nerva was also important for public health.

Dionysius of Halicarnassus greatly admired Rome's paved streets and aqueducts, and also 'the construction of the sewers. . . . [It is alleged] that once, when the sewers had been neglected and were no longer passable for the water, the censors let out the contract for the cleaning and repairing of them at a thousand talents!'[49] Strabo was similarly impressed by the roads, aqueducts and drains of Rome; some sewers were large enough for a hay wagon, and all were plentifully washed by water from the aqueducts.[50] This account links with that of Pliny the Elder who recorded that there were admirable sewers which were navigated by Agrippa in his aedileship[51] (an event

44 Dio 44.35; Plutarch *Brutus* 20.
45 Dio 54.29.
46 Suet. *Aug.*100.
47 Dio 65.10.
48 Lanciani (1888): 55–6; (1897): 29–31; Ammerman (1990).
49 DH 3.67.5.
50 Strabo 5.3.8.
51 Pliny *NH* 36.24.104: mirabantur praeterea cloacas, opus omnium dictu maximum, sub fossis montibus atque urbe pensili subterque navigata M. Agrippae in aedilitate post consulatum.

also recounted by Dio Cassius[52]). Pliny also praised other parts of the drainage system. There were seven streams which flushed the City and, when thrust forward by rain water as well, these battered the bottoms and sides of the sewers; sometimes the Tiber when in flood backed up the sewers, and even so their construction was strong enough to withstand this, for the Cloaca Maxima had endured since the Tarquins.[53] (Not that all the sewers were on such a scale; we hear of unsuccessful attempts to push hated bodies into them, when they proved too narrow;[54] this does seem to prove the existence of manholes or hatches giving access to the sewers.[55])

In the Republic, and under the Principate until Trajan, the responsibility for sewers and drains was viewed as part of the care of the streets, and so fell into the charge of the censors or the aediles; it has been discussed in that context in chapter 5. Then, under Tiberius a board of commissioners was set up to control the Tiber;[56] under Trajan their remit was extended to include the sewers.[57] The cleaning and maintenance work probably continued to be put out to tender[58] since we do not hear of any substantial gang belonging to the commission, unlike the *cura aquarum*. There must have been some public slaves attached, however, since there was a normal office staff.[59]

While the main sewers must always have been publicly maintained, whether through censors, aediles, or commissioners of some sort, their tributaries often fell within the control of the private citizen, with the public aspect protected by interdict.

The praetor has taken care by means of these interdicts [both prohibitory and restitutory] for the cleaning and the repair of drains. Both pertain to the health and safety of cities. For drains choked with filth threaten pestilence of

52 Dio 49.43. After repairing all the public buildings and all the streets, Agrippa cleaned out all the sewers and sailed through them underground.
53 Pliny *NH* 36.24.105–6.
54 Herodian 1.13.6; 5.8.9; SHA *Elagabalus* 17; *Gordian* 13; *Ep. de Caes.*39. Cf. Suet. *Nero* 26.
55 Lanciani (1888): 56, with illustration – the Bocca di Verità.
56 Tac. *Annals* 1.76; Dio 57.14.7–8. See ch. 6.
57 ILS 5930 & 5932 (= CIL VI 31549 & 31553).
58 Juvenal 3.31–2 & 37–8; Fronto *ad M. de or.*10.3 (Nab.155); cf. Pliny *Ep.* 10.32, which shows penal slaves cleaning baths and sewers, as well as maintaining streets and highways.
59 See ch. 6.

the atmosphere and ruin, if they are not repaired. This interdict is provided for private drains, as public drains deserve public care. . . . And Pomponius also writes that if anyone wishes to make a drain so that it has an outlet into the public drain, he is not to be hindered. . . . This interdict applies to public drains, so that you should have nothing that is done or inserted in a public drain by which it is or shall be made worse.[60]

Moreover,

although the repair of a drain, but not the building of a new drain, is included in this interdict, nevertheless Labeo said that there should be a similar interdict against the use of force to prevent the building of a drain of the same usefulness; for the praetor had issued an interdict of this kind, forbidding the use of force to prevent the building of a drain in public land; and this had met with the approval of Ofilius and Trebatius. Labeo himself stated that it should be said that the cleaning and repair of a drain already built should be permitted by interdict, but that the building of a new one was for those who had charge of the public streets to concede.[61]

Some rules about drains fell purely within the private sphere; for instance, the usufructuary not the owner had the burden of maintaining the sewers of a property which was the subject of the usufruct.[62] Again, an heir was liable to pay any outstanding tax, including what was levied for sewerage or water supply, on land which had been left as a legacy.[63]

LATRINES

Many houses, and certainly most tenement blocks, do not appear from archaeological evidence to have had main drainage (and if they did, it seems to have been only at ground-floor level). This is hardly surprising, since most houses in Rome

---

60 D.43.23 *de cloacis* 1.2–3 & 9 & 16, Ulpian 71 *ad ed.*
61 D.43.23.2, Venuleius 1 *interdict.*
62 D.7.1.27.3, Ulpian 18 *ad Sab.*
63 D.30.39.5, Ulpian 21 *ad Sab*: . . . vectigal praeteritum vel tributum vel solarium vel cloacarium vel pro aquae forma.

did not have a running water supply,[64] but water was fetched from the street fountains or basins. At Pompeii, as at Ostia,[65] there are more traces than in Rome of connection to the public sewers. Anything resembling water closets,[66] seats sited over running water, must have been rare in private housing. Some houses seem to have had cess-pits,[67] but mostly people must have used commodes[68] or just chamber pots[69] which slaves will have emptied down the drain, or perhaps loaded on the wagons taking out the night soil – we shall consider these in a moment under cleansing services. The references which we do have on the siting of latrines probably refer to the country;[70] Cicero said that architects must keep from the eyes and noses of householders 'those fluid substances which would unavoidably contain an element of offensiveness'.[71]

There were however public latrines, 144 according to the *Breviarium* of the *Curiosum Urbis*[72] of the Later Empire. Dio reports that the Senate ordered the room in the Curia Pompeia where Caesar had been murdered to be turned into a public latrine.[73] They seem to have been a normal concomitant of public baths, with which they could share water supply and drainage, and presumably of private ones for the same reasons; they were also likely to be found at other convenient sites.[74] It seems likely that access was free, but perhaps there was a token payment when they were separate from the baths; it seems reasonable

64 Martial 8.67: Caldam poscis aquam; nondum mihi frigida venit. See ch. 7.
65 Meiggs (1973): 143; Richardson (1988): 59–62.
66 Thédénat (1904a).
67 Lanciani (1897): 32, fig.15; common at Pompeii according to Mygind's article in *Janus* 25 (1921) cited by Scobie (1986): 400ff; Richardson (1988): 61.
68 Horace *Sat.*1.6.109 – *lasanum*; Petronius *Sat.*41 & 47.
69 Petronius *Sat.*27; Martial 6.89; cf. 3.82.15–17; 14.119.
70 Certainly in the case of Columella 9.5.1 – near an apiary – and Varro *RR* 1.13.4 & 1.6.24.
71 Cicero *nat. deorum* 2.56.141.
72 *Breviarium* 6.10; their size is unknown. There are 116 *necessariae* listed in Richter's *Topographie* as sited along the Aurelian Wall, but these were, almost certainly, classed separately. On *foricarii*, Lanciani (1897): 32; 81; Nash (1981) plate 159.
73 Dio 47.19; cf. Martial 12.61; 12.77.
74 For instance, the author has photographs of the splendid set beside the forum at Vaison la Romaine. In Petronius fragment xiv(xiii) the term *aumatium* seems to refer to the kind of privy to be found at the theatre or Circus.

to suppose that the entrance fee to private baths would cover the latrines as well. We do not know the location for Suetonius' story of Lucan as a young man who had fallen out of favour with the emperor and was speaking his mind: 'once in the public lavatories, after a too-evident rumble from his belly, he uttered a half-line of Nero's which caused his fellow-sitters to leave en masse: "Would you suppose that it was thundering under the ground?"'.[75] Public lavatories were clearly often comfortable places, warm and well decorated,[76] where one might sit and read or otherwise amuse oneself sociably, hoping for invitations even.[77] (This picture does not fit with the stories told of 'bad' emperors, under whom it might even be construed as treason to carry into a latrine or brothel a coin or ring bearing the emperor's portrait.[78] One suspects literary exaggeration here.[79])

Public urinals, on the other hand, seem simply to have been large jars, *dolia*, cut short for convenience and hence often called *dolia curta*,[80] which were regularly emptied and the contents sold to the fullers; there is the famous story that Titus complained when Vespasian imposed a tax – *urinae vectigal* – and Vespasian asked him if the money smelled bad.[81] One gathers from both literary[82] and legal[83] texts that public contracts were let to those who collected and sold the urine; the fisc demanded interest from them if their payments were late. Since these *dolia* were

---

75 Suet. *de perd. lib. rel.* (Teubner, p. 299): adeo ut quondam in latrinis publicis clariore cum strepitu ventris emissi hemistichium Neronis magna consessorum fuga pronuntiavit: 'Sub terris tonuisse putes?'.
76 Meiggs (1973): 411.
77 Martial 11.77:
   Why does Vacerra spend his hours
   In all the privies, and day-long sit?
   He wants a supper, not a shit.
   Cf. 5.44; 12.19.
78 Suet. *Tib*.58, though Suetonius does class this as a far-fetched accusation. This may be the origin of the unlikely allegation that it might even be held treasonable to urinate where there were statues or portraits of the emperor – SHA *Caracalla* 5. Cf. Dio 58 *post*, fr. 2.
79 The jurists held that a chance-flung stone which hit an imperial statue did not make the thrower guilty. D.48.4.5.1, Marcian 5 *reg*.
80 Lucretius 4.1026–9; Propertius 4.5.73; Martial 6.93; Macrobius 3.16.15, claiming to cite a Republican authority.
81 Suet. *Vesp*.23; cf. Martial 6.93.1–2.
82 Juvenal 3.38, and Scholiast.
83 D.22.1.17.5, Paul *de usuris*.

in the streets, their overall supervision presumably fell to the magistrates responsible for the streets, aediles or the *IVviri*; other public latrines were probably also the concern of the aediles, since the regulation of the baths was in their charge, and then of their successors in this function. 'Committing a nuisance' is not a new problem; there is the grave with the hopeful plea inscibed on it: 'Ne quis hic urinam faciat', and Juvenal was unkind about the problems of women returning home.[84] (One wonders if at least some *popinae* and *tabernae* had a chamber pot for the use of female customers or staff; proper inns and hotels will have been equipped to the same extent as any other house.)

Urine was bought by the fullers as it was used particularly for cleaning woollen material, such as togas. (It seems likely that many fullers were also laundrymen,[85] particularly as we do not hear of public wash-places for women, though the Tiber may have been used where it was not embanked for docks and other purposes.) The disposal of excrement not washed down the sewers must have been a problem. The quantity must have been very considerable, in view of the population. The agricultural writers point out that it could be aged into useful manure;[86] there were market gardens all round Rome. It was presumably often taken out of the City as night soil; some was dumped in the open pits on the Esquiline (and doubtless other places) into which all sorts of refuse, including the bodies of the poor and animal carcasses, was also thrown.[87]

CLEANSING SERVICES

We know that water was important for the regular cleansing of streets and sewers. We hear too of carts used for taking away various kinds of refuse, including night-soil, as we have mentioned when considering the regulation of traffic.[88] Valerius

---

84 ILS 8203 (= CIL VI 3413); Juvenal 6.309–13; cf. Juvenal 1.131.
85 D.12.7.2, Ulpian 32 *ad ed*; 39.3.3pr, Ulpian 53 *ad ed*.
86 Columella 11.3.12. In summer it would presumably have dried to a crumble reasonably quickly – cowshed information from Israel – but human manure is slower to degrade than that of grass-eaters; the Roman diet was, however, cereal-based.
87 Lanciani (1888): 65–7.
88 FIRA i 13 (p.140ff), *tab. Heracleensis* v. 66: plostra . . . stercoris exportandei caussa.

Maximus tells of the body of a man murdered by an innkeeper and just at that moment being carried off, covered with night-soil, in a wagon to the gate.[89] Messalina escaped to Ostia in 'a vehicle in which the refuse of the gardens is removed'.[90] The abusive potential of night-soil is magnificently recorded in the famous case from Cnidos.[91] The Romans were admittedly better off than we are in terms of litter – plastic and gift-wrapping alike being unknown to them; we do, however, hear of fish being wrapped in paper and the same of olives.[92] However, I can think of no reference to dog dirt – and there were plenty of dogs.[93] What happened to old copies of *Acta Diurna*?

In the Republic and the early Empire it was the aediles who were responsible for keeping the streets clean.[94] We have already mentioned in this context the Julian law and Papinian's fragment on streets and drains.[95] If, as seems likely on *a priori* grounds, the cleansing service was let out by the aediles, these contractors, like the *foricarii*, would have been concerned with making a living, and the customer must have paid. There may possibly have been regular routes for refuse carts; there may perhaps have been local dumps, from which the cleansing services would collect.[96] It seems logical to assume that there were rag and bone men, but these are unevidenced. What is noticeable is that there has not survived any expression of Roman satisfaction – or otherwise – with rubbish collection or refuse disposal; this may be chance, or it may be that it left no monumental remains to admire – no aqueducts, baths, sewers – or because the Romans did not see this as a matter for public concern. But something must have been done, whether

---

89 Val. Max. 1.7 *ext*.10.
90 Tac. *Annals* 11.32; but this may already have been outside the City boundary. Ulpian's context is admittedly the country not the City, but he tells us that among the working tools – *instrumenta* – of a farm are to be classed the wagons which carry away the dung – D.33.7.12.10, Ulpian 20 *ad Sab*.
91 FIRA iii 185 (p.582ff). A chamber pot was flung out of an upstairs window onto a man below, who was being persistently abusive; unfortunately, it killed him.
92 Catullus 95.8; Persius 1.43; Martial 13.1.
93 E.g. D.9.1.2.1, Paul 22 *ad ed*; Toynbee (1973): 107–22.
94 See ch. 5.
95 FIRA i 13 (p.140ff), *tab.Heracleensis* vv. 20–3; 50–2; 56–61; 66–7; D.43.10.1, Papinian *de cura urbium*.
96 Scobie (1986): 414, cites a recent graffito from Herculaneum recording payment for the removal of ordure: exemta ste[r]cora a[ssibus] XI.

by public slaves or by contractors, if the aediles and other magistrates were to fulfil their duty.

BURIALS[97]

Burials may seem a somewhat odd topic to precede rather than succeed medical care, but the link is really with refuse disposal and cleansing services. What about the human hand the dog dropped in front of Vespasian[98]? In fact, from at least the time of the Twelve Tables, hygienic considerations had led the Romans to prohibit burials and cremations within the City.[99] That this was not a taboo, a moral uncleanness, is indicated by the presence of a few inhumations within the *pomerium*; Vestal Virgins and some other privileged persons continued to be, or to have the right to be, buried within the City. Cicero supposes that the prohibition in the Twelve Tables was because of the danger of fire; certainly pyres or burning mounds were forbidden within 60 feet of another's building, except with his consent.[100]

Cicero also records that the college of pontiffs had prohibited graves in public places; indeed, the pontiffs had ordered large-scale exhumations in the area outside the Colline Gate, but this was because it was not felt proper that private citizens should be able to change the legal status of public property. Outside the City and its immediate environment there seems to have been no general control of burial grounds; all that was required was that no-one be buried in another's land without permission, and that land once consecrated by such use be not subject to ordinary commercial dealings.[101] There are immense cemeteries outside Ostia and, very visibly, along the via Appia. These and other suburban areas provided burial space for the rich and their dependents and for the moderately well-to-do. Their rights were protected by the interdict *de mortuis inferendis*.[102]

The Romans seem to have felt no need for economy in their use of land for this purpose. But to acquire such a site cost

97 See Robinson (1975); Kaser (1978).
98 Dio 65.1. Or the corpse in the road at which Nero's horse shied – Suet. *Nero* 48.
99 Cicero *de leg*.2.23.58.
100 ibid., 2.24.61.
101 D.11.7.2, Ulpian 25 *ad ed*; cf. ILS 8391 (= CIL X 3334), the *sententia Senecionis*.
102 D.11.8 *passim*.

money which the ordinary urban poor, let alone the vagrants and homeless, could hardly have afforded. Their corpses seem simply to have been cast into open pits, and presumably these were lightly covered at fairly regular intervals. The Esquiline Field was one of the burial places of the poor. Notices from around 80 BC on boundary stones which were posted there by a praetor on the recommendation of the Senate give warning that on the City side there were to be no cremation fires nor were corpses or refuse to be dumped.[103] Another inscription from the Esquiline Field[104] records a resolution of the Senate which imposed on the plebeian aediles some jurisdiction over those who had the duty of making sure that no fires were lit nor refuse dumped there. Presumably this too applied to the City side. The aediles had the care of the City in their charge, but a praetor's threat could be backed by his *imperium*.

This and other burial areas were covered with four to eight metres of earth and converted into gardens at the beginning of the Principate[105] – Lanciani said it still smelled when excavated at the end of the nineteenth century[106] – and the process will have started again further out from the City and presumably on a scale suited to the locality. The earth removed in the creation of Trajan's Forum was used to cover the burial ground between the old and the new via Salaria; however, the land remained 'religious' it seems.[107] The size of Rome's population seems to have defeated the authorities, in the Late Republic anyway, in disposing of human remains, but at least the exclusion of burials from the City proper will have fulfilled some of the demands of hygiene. It is generally reckoned that cremation (which, of course, also caused pollution) decreased relative to burials about the end of the first century AD;[108] perhaps the invention of *columbaria* helped deal with the problem of the disposal of human remains.

While the praetor dealt with the disputes of private citizens

---

103 ILS 8208 (= CIL VI 31614): L. Sentius C. f. pr[aetor] de Sen. sent. loca terminanda coer. Nei quis intra terminos propius urbem ustrinam fecisse velit nive stercus cadaver iniecisse velit.
104 ILS 6082 (= CIL VI 3823).
105 Horace *Sat*.1.8; Lanciani (1897): 405–6; 411–12.
106 Lanciani (1888): 67.
107 Homo (1971): 42–3.
108 Festus, 29L, *bustum*; e.g. Hopkins (1983): 211, n.14.

over funerary matters, and in particular funeral expenses,[109] the aediles might be the magistrates – delegated by the pontiffs? or appointed by the family? – to whom the power was given to modify private rights by permitting further burials in a family tomb.[110] Their edict *de funeribus* is mentioned by Cicero.[111] They seem to have been responsible for the general supervision of decency in graveyards and at funerals.[112] For regulation elsewhere than at Rome the *lex Ursonensis*[113] would seem exemplary. It forbade the introduction of bodies, burials or cremations within the town's boundaries, and also the building of funeral monuments; new burning mounds were to be at least half a mile from the town.

The pontiffs exercised a control in determining religious questions, such as when there was good reason, for example permanent flooding, for the re-inhumation of a corpse,[114] and perhaps also in deciding whether an authorised burial had made a place *religiosus* or merely put it into the public domain.[115] But the emperor, perhaps as *pontifex maximus*, perhaps from secular interest, claimed some degree of control.[116] Marcian quotes[117] a decree of the *divi fratres* forbidding disturbance of a corpse, but permitting the transfer of a coffin with its contents to some more convenient place if circumstances required; this may perhaps have referred to a provincial case.[118] It is possible that an inscription[119] recording the removal of a body *permissu trib. plebis* refers to the emperor's tribunician power. The pontiffs had also controlled the repair of tombs and monuments.[120] The imperial enactments preserved in Justinian's Code on funerary matters[121] are largely from the pagan Empire and show the emperors acting with pontifical power, confirming particular applications of the general rules.

109 D.11.7 *passim*.
110 ILS 8388 (= CIL VI 12389).
111 Cicero *Phil*.9.7.17, where its operation is remitted, to allow the burial of Servius Sulpicius Rufus within the City.
112 E.g. Ovid *fast*.6.663–4.
113 FIRA i 21 (p.177ff), *lex Ursonensis*, cc. 73–4.
114 e.g. ILS 8380 (= CIL VI 2120), or FIRA iii 85e (p.275).
115 Cicero *de leg*.2.23.58.
116 D.11.7.8pr, Ulpian 25 *ad ed*.
117 D.11.7.39, Marcian 3 *inst*.
118 Cf. Pliny *Ep*.10.68–9.
119 ILS 8389 (= CIL VI 20863).
120 E.g. ILS 8382 (= CIL VI 2963); D.11.8.5.1, Ulpian 1 *opin*.
121 CJ 3.44 *passim*.

MEDICAL SERVICES

This topic hardly has a place in an account of public health at Rome between the last century BC and the end of the Principate, for it was only in the fourth century that medical services and anything approaching hospitals became normal for civilians. The temple to Asclepius was built on the island in the Tiber because of the plague of 295 BC;[122] this provided the first area set aside for the sick, but it was no more than a waiting-room for prayer. Sick slaves who were abandoned there by their masters were freed (as Latins) by an edict of Claudius.[123] The language of all the medical treatises, except that of Celsus, is Greek; if one considers the various words for hospitals and the like – *xenodochium, nosocomium, brephotrophium, orphanotrophium* – only *valetudinarium* is a Latin word. The owners of large estates, the heads of great households, felt able and obliged to care for their dependants, making use of sick-bays and convalescent areas; we see this in the agricultural writings of Cato, Varro and Columella, and even in Martial we find a *narthecium* (medicine chest) mentioned as a suitable gift.[124] And the major Latin author, Celsus, was probably an amateur not a professional. Even in the legions, it was only under the Empire that persons claiming to be trained[125] in medicine came to have a reasonably high status, as can be deduced by the readiness to grant *restitutio in integrum* to *medici militum*.[126] There were, it seems, military hospitals,[127] but their development for civilians was largely a phenomenon of the Christian Empire.[128]

Modestinus, a late classical jurist, tells us that medical practitioners were exempt from the burden of tutories, as well as of other public duties, and recorded that Antoninus Pius had allowed to the smaller towns of Asia five doctors with exemption from public burdens, to the larger cities seven, and to the largest ten.[129] There was clearly some recognition of what

122 Livy 10.47; Val. Max. 1.8.2.
123 Suet. *Claud*.25; D.40.8.2, Modestinus 6 *reg*; CJ 7.6.1.3 – AD 531.
124 Martial 14.78.
125 Cf. Martial 5.9 and the ninety cold hands – of medical students – on his pulse.
126 D.4.6.33.2, Modestinus *de enucl. casibus*.
127 Davies (1989), ch. x, 'The Roman military medical service', pp. 209–36.
128 Though Celsus *proemium* 65 could refer to those in charge of large hospitals – *qui ampla valetudinaria nutriunt* – but he may be thinking of the East.
129 D.27.1.6.1–4, Modestinus 2 *excus*; h.t.11, Paul *de excus. tutorum*; 50.9.4.2,

made a trained doctor,[130] because we have texts remarking
that a city can withdraw recognition and the consequent
privileges.[131] This seems to mark a definite stage of advance
in medical care. Antoninus Pius' moves may have been uni-
versal, but they were modelled on existing practice in the
eastern provinces, where the cities seem to have employed
doctors long before they were recognised by Rome with privileges.[132] The first certain reference to a medical officer of
health for Rome is not until 368,[133] when there is mention of
senior physicians for each of the regions who are to 'prefer to
minister to the poor honourably rather than to serve the rich
shamefully' – not only an ancient complaint. It may be unlikely
that Rome should lag so far behind the provinces,[134] but it is
very clear that she did not lead. It has even been suggested
that Romans of the Republic and early Empire wanted philosophy, compassion and companionship from a doctor rather
than a cure.[135]

In the City it does not seem safe to run far ahead of the
evidence. For most of our period the upper classes felt superior
to the majority of doctors, who would normally be Greeks, and
frequently slaves or freedmen,[136] while the lower classes seem
to have distrusted them all as quacks.[137] While the social and
professional status of doctors was certainly improving in the
second and third centuries, as seen by the change in their
patients' contract with them from *locatio conductio* to man-

Ulpian de off. curatoris r. p.; 34.1.16.1, Scaevola 18 *dig*: . . . uti publice
(quod medicus erat) salaria ei praestarentur.
130 There was some degree of specialisation; we hear of a *medicus clinicus,
chirurgus, ocularius* – ILS 7812 (= CIL XI 5400) – of a *medicus auricularius*
– ILS 7810 (= VI 8908) – a dentist – Martial 10.56; implicit in Cicero
de leg.2.24.60.
131 D.27.1.6.6, Mod. 2 *excus*, citing Ulpian 4 *de off. proconsulis*; 50.4.11.3,
Modestinus 11 *pandect*, but cf. 50.9.5, Callistratus 2 *de cognit*, where such
withdrawal can only be for good cause.
132 D.34.1.16.1, Scaevola 18 *dig*. shows a woman requesting an official salary
from the local municipality for her freedman – *quod medicus erat*.
133 CTh 13.3.8–9 – AD 368.
134 Below (1953): 49.
135 Scarborough (1969): 113–14.
136 D.38.1.25.2, Julian 65 *dig*.; h.t. 26pr & 27, Alfenus 7 *dig*. & Julian 1 *ex
Minicio*; 40.5.41.6, Scaevola 4 *resp*.
137 Martial 1.47 probably reflects popular opinion:
    Diaulus, ex-physician, / Now works as a mortician.
    What's in a name? / The job's the same.

date,[138] it was not necessarily very high.[139] Their acceptance into the framework of local government may well have been postponed until the Christian Empire.

CIVIL REMEDIES AND PUBLIC HEALTH

The Roman chemical and transport industries were insufficiently developed for them to know many of the risks with which we must live: Chernobyl, Flixborough, Bhopal, Seveso, or simply a lorry shedding its load. But they did recognise the problem in principle. The interdicts generally were used for the well-being as well as the convenience of the public. Servitudes were not necessary to uphold a man's basic right to light, that is, a view of the sky from his windows, and to access to the public street.[140] And the same sort of legal mechanism could, although it did not always, protect a man from his neighbour's fumes or steam.[141] The precise boundaries will, must, always be debatable, but the framework for high density yet civilised living was achieved.[142] One should remember Vitruvius' remark[143] that cornices should be plain and therefore easily dusted in rooms where there were fires or lamps. 'For plasterwork, with its glittering whiteness, takes up the smoke that comes from other buildings as well as from the owner's.' It does not seem that he would have been surprised by the concept of passive smoking.

138 To illustrate the general theme of health there is a text on a mandate to a Ravenna physician to build a *sphaeristerium* – D.17.1.16, Ulpian 31 *ad ed.*
139 As appears from D.50.6.7(6), Tarruntenus Paternus 1 *militarium*, originally concerned specifically with military matters.
140 See ch. 3.
141 D.8.2.13pr, Proculus 2 *ep*; 8.5.17.2, Alfenus 2 *dig.*; cf. Martial 13.32.
142 Cf. D.8.5.8.5,6, Ulpian 17 *ad ed.*
143 Vitruvius 7.3.4.

9

CONTROL OF SERVICES

Services convenient for the population of a city (or other community) can be supplied by the state or the local authority or by private enterprise. Even in the last case there will always be some services that need control, whether for reasons of health or state security or the maintenance of order, and this control may be exercised by central or local government. A modern local authority spends considerable resources in licensing premises or trades, things such as pubs or taxi cabs. Other areas may be subject to state control, instead of, or as well as, local regulation. For example, in Britain agents of central government inspect the local authority schools and, until recently, also inspected those run by private persons, while in some European countries the selling of tobacco is a state monopoly. In Britain theatres are licensed, but for the Romans their link with religion meant that these were places *extra patrimonium*, not run for profit but rather an ostentatious example of 'deficit spending' in the public sphere.[1] We license second-hand dealers but, while these must have existed in Rome[2] – indeed, how else would bath thieves have made a living? – we hear nothing of any control over them. Controls are in fact better evidenced for the cities of the eastern part of the Empire, but there was certainly the power to regulate in Rome what could be regulated in other cities – even if not necessarily the inclination.

Whatever the differences in detail, there were, then as now, various services provided for the benefit of persons living in the City by other persons, working for their private profit, which affected the welfare or the safety of society in general; some

---

1 Cavallaro (1984).
2 Possibly, though they could be private sales, in D. 18.1.45, Marcian 4 *reg*; certainly in D.21.1.37, Ulpian 1 *ad ed. aed. cur.*

control was therefore exercised over these activities. In Rome the principal areas of civic concern seem to have been: markets; bars, eating houses and inns, often together with stables where horses could be hired; the associated trade of prostitution; and crafts and professions.

MARKETS[3]

There appears to have been only one major market in Republican Rome, situated a little to the north of the Forum, probably in the Argiletum.[4] It presumably grew as the Forum itself became more monumental and thus less suitable for ordinary domestic shopping. It seems to have absorbed the *forum piscarium*, and other specialist markets, by a process of development during the earlier second century BC.[5] This market may well have been demolished to make way for the new imperial fora of Caesar and Augustus; at the latest, it would have been destroyed in AD 64. Its restriction, or its disappearance, will explain why Augustus was responsible for the erection of a new market, the Macellum Liviae, which was probably just outside the Esquiline Gate; it was dedicated by Tiberius in 7 BC.[6] Another general provision market, the Macellum Magnum on the Caelian, was dedicated by Nero in 59.[7] These are the only markets we know of,[8] and were presumably the only centres where one could buy meat, game and fish, vegetables and fruit, bread, cheese and sweetmeats, wine and everything else for the table – and other things as well – all in one

---

3 Fronto *ad Marcum* 4.12.4 (Nab. 72) tells us that market stalls were among the places where imperial portraits hung. Thédénat (1904b); Schneider (1928); MacMullen (1970).

4 Varro *LL* 5.145 & 152; Livy 27.11. Anderson (1982).

5 Livy 40.51; 44.16. We hear of the *forum cupedinis*, originally limited to delicacies according to Varro *LL* 5.146, but Festus 42L, backed by Apuleius *Met*.1.24, describes it as a general market. The *forum holitorium* (the vegetable market), just outside the Servian Wall (Nash (1981): 418–23) is mentioned by Tacitus, *Annals* 2.49. Festus 27L speaks of the *forum boarium* where cattle used to be sold. D.1.12.1.11, Ulpian *de off. p. u.* attests the Urban Prefect's control of the *forum suarium*; cf. ILS 7515 & 7516 (= CIL VI 9660; 9631). The *forum vinarium* appears in ILS 7502 (= VI 9182); cf. ILS 7929 (= VI 9189); 7504 (= XI 3156).

6 Dio 55.8; ILS 5592 (= CIL VI 1178).

7 Dio 62(61).18; CIL VI 1648, which mentions an imperial procurator of this market; ILS 7501 (= VI 9183).

8 The *Breviarum* gives only these two.

enclosure.[9] Horace implies that there were other markets,[10] and indeed this seems highly likely, but they were presumably just street stalls, catering to the convenience of a particular quarter. Trajan's Market seems to have been more what we would now call a shopping centre – a group of permanent retail establishments.[11]

The jurisdiction of the curule aediles over sales in the markets is well known.[12] The wiles of horse-copers and slave-dealers were notorious and the buyer needed a degree of protection. Under Tiberius, it seems possible that the Senate could intervene in the affairs of the markets.[13] The Urban Prefect, before he came to have general powers of regulating the City, acquired control over particular markets; he regulated the pig market, and also the provision of other meats.[14] While the Prefect's control was linked to the provision of subsidised foods, it also confirms for us that there continued to be specialised markets, although not whether this specialisation was grounded on custom or on regulation. We know that markets outside Rome needed to be licensed,[15] at least by the third century.

We do not know about the holding of individual stalls or shops. Were they put out to tender? It seems likely, but if so, this might have taken place annually, or every five years. Livy records that M. Fulvius, censor in 179 BC, built his fish market surrounded by shops, which were sold to private persons;[16] it was presumably the use which will have been sold. The legal texts tell us[17] that the sale of bankers' or other booths on public ground is the sale of the right not the freehold, since

9 Horace *Sat.*2.3.227–30; Martial 10.59; Pliny *NH* 18.28.107–8; cf. Seneca's scorn for someone being reluctant to die because he had not tasted all that was in the market – *Ep.*77.17. Richardson (1988): 198–202, gives a helpful description of the main market at Pompeii.
10 Horace *Sat.*1.6.111–12.
11 Anderson (1984): 160–7; MacDonald (1965): 75–93.
12 Impallomeni (1955); most recently, Watson (1987).
13 Suet. *Tib.*34. He proposed 'annonam macelli senatus arbitratu quotannis temperandam'.
14 D.1.12.1.11, Ulpian *de off. p. u*: cura carnis omnis ut iusto pretio praebeatur ad curam praefecturae pertinet, et ideo et forum suarium sub ipsius cura est; sed et ceterorum pecorum sive armentorum quae ad huiusmodi praebitionem spectant ad ipsius curam pertinent. See ch. 10.
15 D.50.11.1, Modestinus 3 *reg*, talks of 'nundinis impetratis a principe'.
16 Livy 40.51.
17 D.18.1.32, Ulpian 44 *ad Sab*: Qui tabernas argentarias vel ceteras quae in solo publico sunt vendit, non solum sed ius vendit, cum istae tabernae publicae sunt quarum usus ad privatos pertinet.

the stalls are public though the use is private. (Ulpian, talking of absconding debtors, classes as keeping himself absent the man who continues to trade in the same forum, if he hides himself behind the pillars or booths.[18]) Could someone's right to a stall or booth be withdrawn? and if so, by whom? In the Republic it seems most likely to have been the aediles. Eventually the Urban Prefect will have exercised such control, but it is not clear when his jurisdiction superseded that of the aediles.

Furthermore, there were standard weights and measures, which could be inspected for accuracy. There may well be a reference to a standard weight in the case where someone lent a buyer over-heavy weights.[19] While, naturally, the title dealing with false reports by surveyors is largely concerned with land, the action available to the aggrieved buyer could be extended to cover inaccuracies over corn or wine or anything else susceptible of measurement.[20] Ulpian thought such actions should be available against both a fraudulent *mensor machinarius* and a clerk who cooked his figures.[21] (One may wonder whether the vigneron who is left with the previous vintage on his hands because the buyer is tardy and who, to make room for the new wine, is allowed to measure out 'per corbem' and to pour away the uncollected wine,[22] is using a particular measure known to the custom of his trade.) We hear of oil being sold with false measures or ones specifically too small.[23] In sales of wine, corn or any other thing, if either seller or buyer falsified the publicly approved measure, he was condemned to a twofold penalty, and fell under Hadrian's sentence of relegation.[24] This sentence is recorded elsewhere as applied specifically to someone who used

18 D.42.4.7.13, Ulpian 59 *ad ed*: eum quoque qui in foro eodem agat, si circa columnas aut stationes se occultet.

19 D.47.2.52.22, Ulpian 37 *ad ed*: Maiora quis pondera tibi commodavit cum emeres ad pondus; . . . non enim ex voluntate venditoris accipis cum erret in pondere.

20 D.11.6.5.2, Ulpian 24 *ad ed*.

21 D.11.6.7.1 & 4, Ulpian 24 *ad ed*. Perhaps such a *mensor* used an unbalanced pair of scales.

22 D.18.6.1.4, Ulpian 28 *ad Sab*.

23 D.19.1.32, Ulpian 11 *ad ed*: Si quis a me oleum quod emisset adhibitis iniquis ponderibus accepisset, ut in modo me falleret, vel emptor circumscriptus sit a venditore ponderibus minoribus . . .

24 D.48.10.32.1, Modestinus 1 *de poenis*: Si venditor mensuras publice probatas vini frumenti vel cuiuslibet rei aut emptor corruperit dolove malo fraudem fecerit, quanti ea res est eius dupli condemnatur; decretoque divi Hadriani praeceptum est in insulam eos relegari qui pondera aut mensuras falsassent.

false measures in connection with the *annona*;[25] Paul too seems
to be referring to grain measures when talking of the penalty
for commodity hoarders.[26]

Weights that are false in themselves, rather than the cheat-
ing involved in their deliberate use, seem sometimes to be
the issue. When someone hired measures and the magistrate
ordered them to be destroyed as false, only the hirer who knew
them to be false was liable to their owner on the contract of
hire; if they proved not to be false, the hirer was liable if it was
through his fault that the magistrate had taken action.[27] There
might be local variations from the imperial standard; the *divi
fratres* enacted that wine merchants could agree on measures
as on prices.[28]

Ammianus[29] reported that the Urban Prefect restored standard weights throughout the Regions in 367–8, and we hear in
the fifth century of *pondera examinata*.[30] The degree of control
needed to enforce such regulations implies an administrative
activity by the aedilician[31] and other authorities that is not
revealed in the legal sources. Further, one must not forget the
existence of various taxes, such as that on the sale of slaves. (In
the Later Empire we know, for example, of the *siliquae*, a sort of
early VAT, and a couple of years later the emperor was referring
to the black economy.[32]) The aediles and their successors would

25 D.47.11.6.2, Ulpian 8 *de off. proconsulis*.
26 D.48.19.37, Paul 1 *sent*: In dardanarios propter falsum mensurarum
modum ob utilitatem popularis annonae pro modo admissi extra ordinem
vindicari placuit.
27 D.19.2.13.8, Ulpian 32 *ad ed*: Si quis mensuras conduxerit easque
magistratus frangi iusserit, si quidem iniquae fuerunt, Sabinus distinguit,
utrum scit conductor an non; si scit, esse ex locato actionem, si minus,
non. Quod si aequae sunt, ita demum eum teneri, si culpa eius id
fecit aedilis.
28 D.18.1.71, Papirius Iustus 1 *const*: Imperatores Antoninus et Verus Augusti
Sextio Varo in haec verba rescripserunt: quibus mensuris aut pretiis
negotiatores vina compararent, in contrahentium potestate esse; neque
enim quisquis cogitur vendere, si aut pretium aut mensura displiceat,
praesertim si nihil contra consuetudinem regionis fiat. It seems possible
that there might be agreement on the use of non-standard weights –
D.4.3.18.3, Paul 11 *ad ed*.
29 Ammianus 27.9.10. ILS 8627 shows the Urban Prefect approving weights
in the earlier third century.
30 Nov. Maj. 7.1.15 – AD 458, cf. Nov. Val. 16.1.2 – AD 445.
31 ILS 8630 (= CIL X 8067); 8632 (= XI 6727); 8634 (= XIV 4124) of first
century AD; earlier, Polybius 3.26.1; Cicero *ad fam*.8.6.5.
32 Nov. Val. 15 – AD 444/5; Nov. Val. 24 – AD 447.

seem likely to have been involved in the collection of these taxes. Until Diocletian, however, control of prices seems highly unlikely, except in the case of state-subsidised foodstuffs.

BARS, EATING-HOUSES AND INNS[33]

That there was a special control over bars, inns and hire stables is most easily illustrated from the existence of the edict *nautae, caupones, stabularii*, which imposed on these persons a liability over and above the normal contract with their customers for goods brought onto their ship or into their premises.[34] There was also a vicarious liability for theft imposed on this group of providers of services; they were liable for their slaves and free employees, and also any permanent residents – *inhabitatores* – though not for ordinary travellers, whom they could not choose.[35]

The legal texts otherwise give us only scattered information on such premises. A resolution of the Senate on what fixtures could not be left as a separate legacy extended not only to houses, but also to various other buildings, including bars or eating houses.[36] One seems to have entered such a place at one's own risk: 'No security is due [for threatened loss] to someone who strolls on my land or washes in my baths or lodges in my inn';[37] it was common practice for an *institor* to run such places for the owner.[38] We have relatively little about administrative control of such establishments; most legal texts would be of relevance rather to the possibly distant and probably respectable

33 Kléberg (1957) still gives the fullest discussion of the various terms and their changing meanings. The general tendency was for the meaning to become pejorative; in general, *tabernae* were bars, *popinae* basic cafés and *cauponae* inns, but *cauponae* went down in the world and *hospitia* became the respectable sorts of hotel.

34 D.4.9 *passim*.

35 D.47.5. unique, Ulpian 38 *ad ed*. It is not clear whether Ulpian meant that by law a traveller could not be turned away: namque viatorem sibi eligere caupo vel stabularius non videtur nec repellere potest iter agentes.

36 D.30.41.8, Ulpian 21 *ad Sab*: non tantum ad aedes sed et ad balinea vel aliud quod aedificium vel porticus sine aedibus vel tabernas vel popinas extenditur. For the wider context, see Demolitions, ch. 3.

37 D.39.2.13.4, Ulpian 53 *ad ed*: Ceterum neque ei qui in meo deambulet neque ei qui in meo lavet vel in mea taberna devertat [de damno infecto] caveri debet. The verb suggests that '*taberna*' is here more than a bar.

38 D.14.3.5.5–7, Ulpian 28 *ad ed*; cf. 17.2.52.15, Ulpian 31 *ad ed*; 47.10.5.5, Ulpian 56 *ad ed*.

owners, but we do learn that stables were likely to be on a city's fringes.[39] We hear about the *instrumenta* that were attached, and a distinction was drawn between the *instrumenta* of a *taberna*, here clearly a bar, and of a *caupona*.[40]

There was control over the foods available in café-bars, which the authorities seem to have preferred to remain drinking shops – did sitting round a table too easily lead to sedition? – for surely fights can more easily start when men are standing up, so public order in the conventional sense is unlikely to be the explanation. Thus we hear that Tiberius ordered the aediles to restrict the foods available in bars and inns, even banning bread.[41] Claudius, presumably before he became emperor, had had tenants who were fined by the aediles for illegally selling cooked food; in revenge he deprived the aediles of their control over the cook-shops.[42] In another account we are told that Claudius abolished taverns and forbade the sale of boiled meats and hot water.[43] Nero forbade boiled food in the taverns, except for vegetables and pea soup,[44] and Vespasian allowed no cooked food save pulses.[45] It is just possible, of course, that these were temporary restrictions; Kléberg has pointed out[46] that all of them are of the first century and do not seem to have been in force later.

Naturally enough, it was the aediles who in the Republic[47] and later exercised control over such establishments.[48] Philostratus expected someone to be inspecting the taverns, or at least keeping an eye on them; he recounts that there was a harpist singing Nero's compositions in the inn where Apollonius was staying, and that failure to listen and to pay the harper could lead to arrest for lèse-majesté.[49] Three centuries later we find the Urban

---

39 D.20.2.4.1, Neratius 1 *membr.* implies this; cf. 50.16.198, Ulpian 2 *de omn. trib*; Petronius *Sat*.79. Kléberg (1957): 49 points out that at Pompeii the stables were sited by the gates; cf. Casson (1974): 205–7.

40 D.33.7.13 and 15pr, Paul 4 *ad Sab* and Pomponius 6 *ad Sab*.

41 Suet. *Tib*.34: dato aedilibus negotio popinas ganeasque usque eo inhibendi ut ne opera quidem pistoria proponi venalia sinerent.

42 Suet. *Claudius* 38.2, but we do not know for how long.

43 Dio 60.6.

44 Suet. *Nero* 16; Dio 61(62).14.

45 Dio 65.10.

46 Kléberg (1957): ch iv.

47 Cicero *ad fam*.8.6.4; Caelius was curule aedile.

48 Suet. *Tib*.34; *Claudius* 38, referred to above. See also local aediles in Apuleius, *Met*.1.24.

49 Philostratus *Apollonius of Tyana* 4.39.

Prefect controlling the bars and eating-houses: 'No wine shop was to open before the fourth hour, nobody was to heat water for the public, the cooked food sellers were not to peddle cooked meat before a fixed time of day, and no respectable person was to be seen eating in public.'[50]

There is very little direct information about *stabularii*, but it seems clear that for reasons of convenience to the travelling public they were often identical with *caupones* or *tabernarii*. The same magistral edicts could deal with them, as also with *nautae*, who may have included those who ferried people short distances in rowing boats (and perhaps pleasure cruisers) as well as those in charge of sea-going ships.[51] Were there controls other than contractual on the hiring of horses? Was there any equivalent to the various terms built into carriage by sea? It seems unlikely, since we hear nothing of any such measures.[52]

Interestingly, in the Later Empire we actually find a few non-pejorative references to inns and stables, suggesting that the authorities had finally acknowledged that there was some real utility in these establishments. *Caupones* could be useful in handling the horses of the *cursus publicus* and other officials when there was special need.[53] And in AD 425 there seems to have been approval for public restaurants.[54]

PROSTITUTION

That bars, eating-houses and inns were not of good reputation is nicely confirmed by the references to bad emperors frequenting such haunts;[55] also those who served therein were exempt from the operation of the legislation criminalising adultery.[56] Other

50 Ammianus 28.4.4: ne taberna vinaria ante horam quattuor aperiretur, neve aquam vulgarium calefaceret quisquam, vel usque ad praestitutum diei spatium lixae coctam proponerent carnem, vel honestus quidam mandens videretur in publico.

51 D.4.9.1.4, Ulpian 14 *ad ed*; see also ch. 6. And Horace – *Sat*.1.5 – was on a barge with sleeping accommodation.

52 The use of horses and vehicles in the City is looked at in ch. 5.

53 CTh 11.10.1 – AD 369; 11.10.2 – AD 370/376.

54 CTh 15.1.53 – AD 425.

55 Seneca *prov*. 5.4; Juvenal 8.158 & 167 & 171 – on consuls; Suet. *Vitellius* 7; Dio 80.13; Tertullian *de fuga* 13; SHA *Hadrian* 16.3–4; *Verus* 4; *Commodus* 2; *Elagabalus* 30.1; *Gallienus passim*; Aurelius Victor 33.56. The truth of such allegations is irrelevant.

56 *PS* 2.26.11.

legal texts explicitly class inn-keeping with running brothels. A brothel-keeper has girls, slave or free, for hire; he is still liable, even if his main source of income is keeping an inn or being in charge of baths.[57] In the context of the lack of *conubium* between senators and certain classes of women, we read: 'We do not call whore only the woman who prostitutes herself in a brothel but also her who is not ashamed to work in a bar or inn; . . . if she sells her body while working in an inn, as many women customarily do, she can be defined as a prostitute.'[58] The same connection was made in another context in a rescript of Severus Alexander which laid down that the sale of a female slave, on terms that she was not to be prostituted, could not be circumvented by employing her in an eating-house in a dual capacity.[59]

If then, the aediles kept a register of prostitutes, as Tacitus' remark indicates,[60] and indeed as seems not unlikely, control of premises used for prostitution would include inns and bars, as well as actual brothels. In the eyes of the authorities there seems to have been no reason to distinguish. It was as improper for an *arbiter* to hear a case in a *popina* as in a brothel, or any other dishonourable place.[61] There is no doubt that there were houses specifically for prostitution;[62] after all Frontinus was indignant at such places being supplied with running water.[63]

As with the *tabernae*, the legal texts concerned with prostitution are often aimed at distant beneficiaries; Ulpian confirmed the legality of rents drawn from brothels, for many respectable

57 D.3.2.4.2, Ulpian 6 *ad ed*.
58 D.23.2.43pr,9, Ulpian 1 *ad l. Iuliam et Papiam*: Palam quaestum facere dicemus non tantum eam quae in lupanario se prostituit, verum etiam si qua (ut adsolet) in taberna cauponia vel qua alia pudori suo non parcit. . . . Si qua cauponam exercens in ea corpora quaestuaria habeat (ut multae adsolent sub praetextu instrumenti cauponii prostitutas mulieres habere) dicendum hanc quoque lenae appellatione contineri. Cf. ILS 7478 (= CIL IX 2689).
59 CJ 4.56.3 – AD 225: Eam quae ita venit ne corpore quaestum faceret, nec in caupona sub specie ministrandi prostitui, ne fraus legi dictae fiat, oportet.
60 Tac. *Annals* 2.85: licentiam stupri apud aedilis vulgaverat.
61 D.4.8.21.11, Ulpian 13 *ad ed*.
62 E.g. Petronius *Sat*.7–8; Martial 1.34; Dio 78.16. The *Breviarum* of the *Curiosum Urbis* gave a total of 46 *lupanaria* for the City, the *Notitia* 45; this suggests that the term implies an establishment on quite a scale.
63 Frontinus *aq*.76, though on grounds of hygiene his indignation seems misplaced.

persons owned property on which such establishments were run.[64] Ulpian also rather neatly pointed out the non-availability of a remedy to recover what had been paid to a prostitute: 'for she behaves immorally in that she is a whore, but she does not receive money immorally, since she is a whore'.[65]

Some stories, dubious as fact because their source is un-reliable, but nevertheless credible as image-building, refer to legislation in this area. Hadrian is said to have forbidden the sale of male or female slaves to brothels (or the gladiatorial schools) without a cause.[66] Severus Alexander forbade the tax from pimps, whores and male prostitutes to be placed in the treasury, but put it directly towards the expenses of repairing various public buildings;[67] as in the case of the markets, the fact of taxes must involve record-keeping and so some control. The same emperor is also alleged at one stage to have ordered female prostitutes, enormous numbers of whom had been arrested, to be enslaved, and to have de-ported male prostitutes.[68] The emperor Tacitus (AD 275–76) forbade brothels within the City, 'but this could not last long'.[69] Later emperors seem also to have made attempts to clean up the City,[70] with equally little success. Jordan held that the oversight of the brothels and the baths passed from the aediles to the curators of the Regions at some stage in the Principate, and finally to the Urban Prefect.[71] The link with bars and inns seems inherently likely, the more so because such places were frequently scenes of gambling, another sphere of aedilician jurisdiction which will be considered under low life.[72]

---

64 D.5.3.27.1, Ulpian 15 *ad ed*: pensiones . . . licet a lupanario perceptae sunt; nam et in multorum honestorum virorum praediis lupanaria exercentur.

65 D.12.5.4.3, Ulpian 26 *ad ed*: illam enim turpiter facere, quod sit meretrix, non turpiter accipere, cum sit meretrix.

66 SHA *Hadrian* 18; confirmed to some degree by Severus Alexander's legislation in CJ 4.56.1 – AD 223.

67 SHA *Sev. Alex.*24: lenonum vectigal et meretricum et exsoletorum.

68 SHA ibid., 34.

69 SHA *Tacitus* 10: quod quidem diu tenere non potuit.

70 *Coll.* 5.3.1–2, especially concerned with homosexuals; CTh 15.8.2 – AD 428; Nov Th 18 – AD 439; CJ 11.41.6 & 7 – AD 428 & 457/67. We also find concern for fallen women – CJ 5.5.7 – AD 454 (= Nov. Marcian 4); Nov. J. 14 – AD 535.

71 Jordan (1871–1907) II 69–70.

72 Ch. 13.

CONTROLS OVER TRADES AND PROFESSIONS

Certain persons were disqualified from public office, or from various public functions, by reason of the trade or profession they practised. We hear of auctioneers and undertakers, those condemned in a *bonae fidei* action, sworn gladiators, bankrupts, calumniators, those discharged with ignomy from the army, prostitutes (male), *lanistae*, actors and pimps.[73] For this to be effective, a register seems more likely than mere notoriety.

We know that from the early Empire there was a general control over *collegia* framed in a resolution of the Senate (ILS 7212). (This is not in itself relevant to this chapter's theme, though it will be looked at briefly under sedition on pp. 199–200.) This too suggests that 'police' records were kept on a considerable scale in the offices of the relevant magistrates or officials. Callistratus wrote that the members – the full members – of certain colleges and guilds, which had the right of assembly, also had immunity from various public burdens because of their public utility; he specified the *fabri*.[74] *Collegia* of other workers also received privileges, among them the fishermen and divers of the Tiber.[75] Most prominent, not surprisingly, are the guilds connected with the *annona*, the subsidised food supplies.[76] A 'corporate state' did not fully emerge, even in the Later Empire, but Severus Alexander is said to have established *corpora* of wine merchants, greengrocers, cobblers, and other trades.[77] The progressive growth of controls in matters affecting the stability of society, whether in the *annona* or the fuelling of the baths,[78] was already well under way.

Dealing with what we would call the professions, where there was power to appoint, to pay, and to dismiss, one must assume that some regulation of qualification for the job and performance in it was normal, or at least possible. I can hardly, simply by calling myself a philosopher, demand an exemption from certain taxes, and even the claim of a rhetorician will have

73 FIRA i 13 (p.140ff) *tab. Heracleensis*, vv. 104, 110–23; D.3.2.1, Julian 1 *ad ed* gives a very similar list.

74 D.50.6.6.12, Callistratus 1 *de cognit.* – *faber* here probably means master builder; Antoninus Pius had imposed certain limitations on their privileges. Generally, see Waltzing (1895–1900).

75 ILS 7266 (= CIL VI 1872); see ch. 6.

76 See ch. 10.

77 SHA *Sev. Alex*.33.

78 Sirks (1984):677; cf. Symmachus *Rel*.44; see also MacMullen (1976).

had to be based on more than his self-evident skill. For example, when in AD 6 all foreigners except doctors and teachers were expelled from Rome because of the corn shortage,[79] there must have been some way of certifying these categories. In so far as this was certainly a municipal matter in the cities of the Eastern Empire, it seems reasonable to treat it as part of local government in Rome.

The central legal text relating to the definition of the liberal professions is a discussion by Ulpian of the jurisdiction of provincial governors concerning those who claimed rewards as *honoraria*, not as *merces*.[80] (In the second and third centuries, the degree of control over education was probably more advanced in the Eastern Empire than at Rome,[81] as with medical care.) Teachers of the liberal arts, that is, rhetoric, grammar, geometry, fell into the category of claimants for *honoraria*; so, by this period, did doctors, whether oculists, dentists, or other specialists, but not those who cured by charms and incantations. Philosophers were told that they should spurn material reward;[82] Pliny talks of a philosophy teacher in Prusa claiming exemption from jury service.[83] On rather different grounds law professors too were not to claim rewards.[84] Ulpian was careful to exclude from this extraordinary jurisdiction the claims of *opifices* and *artifices*. Their usefulness was recognised by the granting to certain trades of exemption from the more burdensome *munera*.[85] There must have been some public recognition of what made a doctor[86] or a professor[87] (who, like publicly appointed doctors, could be removed from their posts for inefficiency[88]). Vespasian established teachers of both Latin and Greek in Rome, paid

---

79 Dio 55.26.
80 D.50.13.1, Ulpian 8 *de omnibus tribunalibus*.
81 Philostratus *Lives of the Sophists* 8.580; 10.589; 13.594; 16.596; 33.627.
82 Also stressed in D.50.5.8.4, Papinian *1 resp*: etenim vere philosophantes pecuniam contemnunt, cuius retinendae cupidine fictam adseverationem detegunt.
83 Pliny *Ep*. 10.58.
84 D.15.13.1.5, Ulpian 8 *de omnibus tribunalibus*. Cf. D.27.1.6.5, Modestinus 2 *excus*.
85 D.50.6.7, Tarruntenus Paternus 1 *militarium*.
86 See ch. 8.
87 D.27.1.6.1–4, Modestinus 2 *excus*; 50.13.1pr and 6, Ulpian 8 *de omn. trib*.
88 CJ 10.53(52).2 – Gordian: Grammaticos seu oratores decreto ordinis probatos, si non se utiles studentibus praebeant, denuo ab eodem ordine reprobari posse incognitum non est.

from the public treasury;[89] immunity from billeting is said in one text to have been granted to grammarians, orators, doctors and philosophers by Vespasian and Hadrian.[90] All this assumes some official way of distinguishing these persons.

As for lawyers, the courts themselves exercised control; someone could be forbidden to practise in the courts, permanently or temporarily.[91] The exercise of jurisdiction seems to have included control over the professionals – *advocati, causidici* – employed there; the Urban Prefect had powers to ban unworthy persons from the practice of a profession (including advocacy) or a business.[92] This leads us to the problem of how and where practitioners acquired their qualifications. How far were there law-schools in our period[93]? The usual view taken is that aspiring jurists attached themselves to the circle of an accepted jurist and learned by watching (and perhaps devilling). There were probably privately-run and profit-making establishments teaching law for the notary, the attorney, the law shop on the corner where the humbler citizen might get his will made out or the terms of a contract drawn up.[94] There may well have been no controls on their output. But what about the teaching that we hear of through Aulus Gellius? He recorded a particular case when there was debate about the possibility of raising an action before the praetor against a serving quaestor; there was enquiry on the point in many of the regular places at Rome where instruction or legal opinions are publicly given.[95] The question was resolved in the affirmative after reference to Varro's *Antiquitates Rerum Humanarum*, produced by Gellius, which held that even a curule aedile could be so cited by a private citizen since he lacked powers of summons or arrest, and 'all came to agree with the opinion of Varro'.[96] This certainly sounds like some sort of formal teaching, but there is nothing

89 Dio 65.12.
90 D.50.4.18.30, Arcadius Charisius *de muneribus civilibus*. Cf. *Inst.* 1.25.15.
91 D.48.19.9, Ulpian 10 *de off. proconsulis*; cf. 3.1.6.1, Ulpian 6 *ad ed*; h. t.8, Papinian 2 *quaest.*
92 D.1.12.1.13, Ulpian *de off. p. u.* Similarly there was power to bar merchants who had offended in the matter of the grain supply from pursuing their trade – D.47.11.6pr, Ulpian 8 *de off. proconsulis*.
93 Liebs (1987).
94 Juvenal's sort of lawyer.
95 Gellius 13.13.1: in plerisque Romae stationibus ius publice docentium aut respondentium.
96 Gellius 13.13.6.

to show whether there was any element of public control; it would not, however, be unlikely, in view of the use of the term 'publice'.[97]

We cannot clearly make out the framework of control, but official appointments were unlikely to have been made without some objective criteria, and the recognition of *collegia* was undoubtedly a matter of law. The variety of cases which emerges does suggest an underlying system of record-keeping which must have applied quite generally, but did not normally interest either lawyers or historians.

97 Tellegen (1989): 64–9 is a recent discussion.

10

FEEDING THE CITY

Religion, though it probably helped to make life interesting with its processions and other displays, as well as occasional free banquets, was not the opium of the masses at Rome. The traditional pacifiers of the Roman people were food, subsidised or free, and amusements (particularly at the Circus and in the theatre and amphitheatre). Once Rome had grown to huge dimensions, ensuring that the population was adequately fed was just as much an essential part of community life as the provision of a water supply;[1] political stability, social need, and the display of wealth were intertwined. Bread, or rather the grain from which both bread and porridge were made, was the vital calorific food of the ancient Mediterranean world. Organised social welfare, though restricted, must have been considerably more efficient for its beneficiaries than any reliance by clients on their patrons for *sportulae*. Not that there was ever any notion that the state had sole responsibility for feeding the citizen population; public and private interest ran together, and the state intervened, in Republic and Empire alike, when the need was great. However, the treatment of these areas will be relatively brief, because they were very much under imperial control.[2]

THE PROCUREMENT OF GRAIN

An interest in importing adequate supplies of grain was already apparent in the second century BC. It was a concern wider

---

1 Consider the importance of the harvest in Eastern European countries in current circumstances.
2 There is an enormous literature. The most important modern books are (alphabetically): Garnsey (1988); Herz (1988); Pavis d'Escurac (1976). Rickman (1980); Sirks (1991b); Virlouvet (1985). Van Berchem (1939) is older but still useful.

144

than that for the City – most obviously it also applied to Rome's armies – but it was there most concentrated. C. Gracchus introduced the enduring concept of a permanent government concern with a sufficient and cheap supply of grain, the staple of the Roman diet, but even before his time we hear of occasional official interventions in the victualling of Rome. In so far as military needs were paramount, the consuls and praetors, as the magistrates with *imperium*, were naturally concerned with food supplies, but the aediles too had their role in the *cura urbis*. Thus in 203 and 201 BC the aediles had grain from Spain and Africa to distribute at a low price – by neighbourhood (*vicatim*), at least in 203.[3] The *porticus Aemiliana* was built by the aediles of 193 BC, and the trading quarter – the Emporium – developed,[4] and another portico was built in the area by the curule aediles of the following year.[5] In 189 BC the aediles were fining those merchants who hoarded grain,[6] but this is the only recorded Republican case of prosecution for manipulation of the grain supply. We do not hear of the aediles making grain available at subsidised prices in years of food shortage; free distributions by prominent politicians were rare.

While there was a growth in the population of the City – and of other Italian towns – at the end of the second century, there seems to have been some decline in grain-growing in central Italy,[7] where olives, vines and cattle were more profitably raised, and hence arose the policy of tithing the produce of Sicily and Sardinia. The Sicilian authorities brought the corn to the ports; offers were made by private merchants, who would often ship public and private grain together. The creation of the province of Africa in 146 BC meant that there was a new source of private as well as taxed corn. It seems likely that the authorisation for the procurement of grain, whether the tithe that was due as tax from Sicily and Sardinia, or the

---

3 Livy 30.26; 31.4; cf. Cicero *de off*.2.17.58. They sold African grain even more cheaply in 200 and Sicilian in 196 (Livy 31.50; 33.42).

4 Livy 35.10.

5 Livy 35.41.

6 Livy 38.35; Plautus *Captivi*, 492ff, may refer to some Roman statute on this offence.

7 See Garnsey (1988): 190f, on this decline having been much exaggerated; he quite agrees that the contribution of Italy to the feeding of Rome did as a proportionate share decrease markedly, but general urban expansion was taking place in Italy at the time.

compulsory purchase of grain over and above this tithe which was needed from time to time, was the task of the consuls or praetors, or the Senate; the merchants did the actual buying and transporting, and the aediles saw to it that the Senate's wishes were carried out once the grain arrived in Rome.[8] The bulk of it is likely to have been released at the market price after public needs had been met, either the ordinary needs of the state or the recurrent problems of food shortage. C. Gracchus' measures were almost certainly designed as much to stabilise the market for the growers as to win votes for himself, or to check the use of private distribution by other ambitious politicians.[9]

C. Gracchus was probably the first to build public *horrea* to store grain for distribution – the *frumentationes*.[10] It is possible, of course, that there was no state interest in the storage of grain, as opposed to its procurement, before the first free distributions which followed Clodius' legislation in 58 BC.[11] This seems rather unlikely, however, in view of the importance of victualling the City. A surplus economy, one capable of supporting a great city as Rome already was in the second century BC,[12] needed to store its surplus, and traders needed facilities at the dockside; nevertheless, most *horrea* in the Later Republic were privately owned, although they could, and probably did, rent out storage space for state grain. Alzon thinks that just as the State used private *horrea* for some of its needs, so it let out space in public *horrea* to private persons[13] – in the Empire it might be for the *praefectus annonae* (Prefect of the Grain Supply) to decide if there was free space.

Pirates were a severe threat to the supplies to the City from

8 Rickman (1980): 36.
9 Pavis d'Escurac (1976): 5–6. Cf. Cicero *pro Plancio* 26.64, of his own sending grain to Rome when quaestor in Sicily; Pliny *NH* 18.4.16 on the aedile of 74 BC who distributed cheap grain in a crisis.
10 Plut. *C. Gracchus* 6.
11 Asconius, in Pison., OCT p. 8; *Schol. Bob.* (Stangl p. 132); Cicero *pro Sestio* 25.55.
12 The population of Rome in 130 BC is estimated by Brunt (1971) and accepted by Garnsey (1988): 191, at around 375,000, thus needing 8·5 to 11 million *modii* of grain a year.
13 Alzon (1965): 15, and 304–6; cf. D.20.4.21.1, Scaevola 27 *dig*. Alzon also makes the point that the use of private law for the predominantly public *horrea* is significant as indicating that the grain supply was not 'nationalised' in the Principate.

the late 100s BC, the period of the Sicilian slave revolts and the consequent disruption in the production of grain; in the 70s – a decade when there was war in Spain and in the East against Mithridates and, from 73 BC, the Spartacus rebellion – matters were worse. Pirates seem even to have plundered Ostia in 68 BC,[14] which led to Pompey's special commission (bitterly opposed by most of the Senate) the following year to clear the seas of them. Pompey's second commission, a five-year *cura annonae* granted him in 57 BC,[15] was perhaps an exercise in restoring confidence (though it too was opposed by the *optimates*) rather than an attempt to replace improvisation by system; still, he granted Roman citizenship to those provincials who served the *annona* for a number of years, and granted other privileges of some sort to the ship-owners and grain merchants of Rome (and Puteoli).[16] The aediles continued to have the normal responsibility, although the problems involved were becoming too complex for them. 18 million *modii* of wheat (or more) were needed each year for public distribution after Clodius' *lex frumentaria* of 58 BC, though in normal years some two-thirds of this came in as tithe from Sicily, Sardinia and Africa. A few years later Julius Caesar tried another solution, with the creation of two new aedileships, the *aediles cereales*, whose only function was to deal with the corn supply.[17]

After the long-drawn crisis caused by nearly twenty years of civil war, Egypt, captured by Augustus in 30 BC, could supply all that was needed for the subsidised supplies to the *plebs frumentaria*, that is, the 12 million *modii* needed for the 200,000 recipients (which was probably the official number in 2 BC);[18] indeed, during the early Empire, Egypt provided up to one-third of all Rome's need for grain. Nevertheless, as has been made very clear, private supplies, from Italy as well as from farther afield, far outweighed the corn supplied through the intervention of the state.[19] In the crisis of 22 BC Augustus

14 Dio 36.22.
15 Cicero *ad Att*.4.1.7; Livy *per*.104; Plut. *Pomp*.49–50.
16 Cicero *pro Balbo* 18.41; *pro Scauro* 19.43; *ad fam*.13.75 & 79.
17 Suet. *Julius* 41; Dio 43.51; D.1.2.2.32, Pomponius *enchiridion*.
18 Josephus *BJ* 2.383–5; *Ep. de Caes*.1.6.
19 Pavis d'Escurac (1976): 253f; Sirks (1984): 20–1; the economic importance of independent ship-masters and corn merchants is also stressed by Herz (1988).

restored stability of prices and so calmed public anxiety about grain imports simply by the exercise of his *auctoritas*.[20] Following hunger in successive years, Augustus gave charge of the procurement, as well as the provision, of grain to consulars in AD 6 and 7;[21] it was only some time after AD 8, but during his reign,[22] that the prefecture of the grain supply was established. His general concern for the fleet, and the maintenance of peaceful seas, was also largely in the interests of the supply (from all sources) of grain and other essential goods to the City. (This explains the political importance of the defeat of Sextus Pompey in 36 BC.[23])

The *praefectus annonae* was a permanent official, the delegate of the emperor, who ranked third of all the equestrian officials, inferior only to the Prefect of Egypt and the Praetorian Prefect(s).[24] (During the third century, since routines were well established and most grain came from imperial estates, the post declined in importance, and under Constantine[25] it became subordinate to the Urban Prefect, but senatorial.) This *cura* of the grain supply was to last; it came to involve dealings with the warehouse-keepers and the bakers as well as the corn-merchants and the shippers, but it was primarily concerned with procurement.[26] The prefect must have been kept informed of what was happening in the corn-growing provinces, where there seems to have been a shift, noticeable by the later first century, from *ager publicus*, farmed by *publicani*, to imperial estates run by imperial officials. Some provinces were primarily concerned with feeding the armies; ease of transport to the City was a normal consideration, except in crises as after the Great Fire when grain was brought from Moesia.[27]

In the earlier first century the *praefectus annonae* seems to have paid those shippers who had been chartered, and to

---

20 Herz (1988): 360f has commented on the political and ideological nature of Augustus' dictatorial empowerment.
21 Dio 55.26; 55.31.
22 Tac. *Annals* 1.7.
23 *RG* 25.1 and Brunt and Moore (1967): 66.
24 D.1.2.2.33, Pomponius *enchiridion*.
25 Sidonius Apollinaris *Ep*.1.10.
26 Sirks (1984): 12; he is particularly concerned with relations with the shippers.
27 ILS 986 (= CIL XIV 3608).

have bought additional supplies as needed;[28] he may have kept a record of other imports. Both Claudius and Nero were concerned to prevent crises, and so we find privileges for shippers linked to the size of their ships and the frequency of their sailings,[29] which must have been matters of record, presumably by registration with the *praefectus annonae*. (We possibly have traces of investigators at Ostia checking whether a Latin had actually put a sizeable ship into service in the grain trade.[30]) Gaius tells us that Claudius gave full citizenship to a Junian Latin who built a sizeable sea-going ship and employed it for six years in the grain trade.[31] Trajan and Hadrian began to think in corporate terms for the supply of victuals to Rome, which included the role of the bakers,[32] and by the later second century serving the *annona* was acknowledged as a possible ground for exemption from *munera publica*.[33] Independent corn-merchants, however, continued to flourish[34] and ship-owners were free to ply their trade outwith the demands of the *annona*.[35] Membership of a *collegium* was what proved a man's right to certain immunities,[36] but it was still individuals who made contracts with the state.

Roman retailers seem to have bought indifferently from public granaries, from private granaries, and from ships at the docks. The *praefectus annonae* organised the supply for the *frumentationes* but sold any surplus public grain on the open market. Prices were held level and, if possible, low, but the interests of the farmers and the merchants were taken into account as well as those of the populace.[37] Gracchus' fixed price of six and one-third *asses* a *modius* will have been lower than the usual prices, but those will have fluctuated and on occasion dropped below it. Tiberius in AD 19 subsidised the

28 D.14.1.1.18, Ulpian 28 *ad ed.*
29 Tac. *Annals* 13.51.
30 CIL XIV supp. 4319, as interpreted by Meiggs (1973): 301.
31 G. 1.32c; Ulp. *Reg.* 3.6.
32 G.1.34; FV 233–5; Aurelius Victor 13.5; ILS 7269 (= CIL VI 1002).
33 D.50.5.3, Scaevola 3 *reg*; 50.6.6.3 & 6, Callistratus 1 *de cognit.*
34 E.g. ILS 3696 (= CIL XIV 2852); ILS 6987 (= III 14165); SHA *Sev. Alex.*33.
35 Though Rickman (1980): 130, quotes Hunt and Edgar, *Select Papyri* (1932) no.113, to show that Alexandrian shippers at least required a dimissory document before they were allowed to leave Italy after discharging their grain.
36 E.g. D.50.5.10.1, Paul 1 *sent*, referring to the *corpus mensorum frumenti*; 50.6.6.12, Callistratus 1 *de cognit.*
37 Suet. *Aug.*42.3.

grain merchants after fixing the price.[38] It is not clear if, when Nero forced the price down,[39] this was a return to 'normal' or the setting of an artificially low level. Pricing must normally have relied, not on decrees of the Senate or emperor,[40] but on the release onto the market of reserves of corn, or the supply of stocks at specially low prices. We hear, however, of attempts to check speculators.[41]

The quaestor stationed during the Republic at Ostia had in the third century BC been concerned with the fleet as a naval force, fighting the Carthaginians; by the end of the second century his office was clearly focused on dealing with the arrival of the grain supplies. It was an onerous post, but one which did not attract glamorous rewards. It seems to have involved supervising the reception, storage and trans-shipment of the corn.[42] Under Augustus its importance was clearly marked when Tiberius was sent to be Ostian quaestor in 23–22 BC during the crisis in the supply of corn which led Augustus to take on the *cura annonae*.[43] However, after Claudius had finished the new harbour, the quaestor was replaced by officials directly subordinate to the *praefectus annonae*, the *procurator annonae Ostis* and the *procurator portus*.[44] Puteoli seems to have remained important, both for trans-shipping Egyptian corn to Ostia and Rome and as a place for import in its own right.[45] Procurement thereafter was essentially a matter of increasing imperial control.

The fisc drew up contracts for the shipment of fiscal goods (primarily grain for the distributions) during the first and second centuries AD and even later, when the *munus navicularium* had already been introduced.... From the end of the second century on, shipments for the fisc were carried out in fulfilment of the *munus navicularium*, yet this did not

38 Tac. *Annals* 2.87.
39 Tac. *Annals* 15.39.
40 Tac. *Annals* 6.13; Suet. *Tib.*34.
41 D.47.11.6 pr, Ulpian 8 *de off. proconsulis*; 48.12 *passim*; 48.19.37, Paul 1 *sent.*
42 Cicero *pro Murena* 8.18; Seneca *brev. vitae* 18–19; ILS 6171 (= CIL XIV 3603); cf. D.48.2.13, Marcian 1 *de pub. iud.*
43 *RG* 5; Velleius 2.94.3; Suet. *Tib.*8. Chandler (1978) thinks that Tiberius did hold this quaestorship, but Badian (1974) maintains the contrary.
44 Suet. *Claud.*24.2; Dio 60.24.3; ILS 1534 (= CIL VI 8470). Cf. Castagnoli (1980); Houston (1980).
45 Seneca *Ep.*77.1–2; Frederiksen (1984), ch. 14; Rickman (1980) Appendix 5.

preclude other shipments being effected on a contractual basis.[46]

Indeed, in the fourth century the price fixed for Ostian and fiscal bread is suggestive of other sources of supply, as the existence of Tiber boats to be requisitioned implies the survival of private enterprise.[47]

THE DISTRIBUTION OF GRAIN

The *lex Sempronia* of 123 BC provided a monthly allowance of corn, sold at a subsidised rate from a given location.[48] Gracchus envisaged it as the duty of the state to provide regular distributions of cheap corn to all citizens, though there may have been restrictions of age and sex, residence, and free birth; overall limitations on the number of recipients came later. In either 103 or 100 BC Saturninus had tried to fix a price which seems to have been considerably lower than the Gracchan one, but his bill probably never became law. A *lex Octavia* may have reduced the numbers eligible, or the amount of the ration, or increased the price, or all of these; its date is unknown, although it is nowadays generally reckoned to have been passed in the 90s. Cicero spoke approvingly of it.[49] The subsidised distributions were probably abolished by Sulla, but restored, perhaps by the *lex Aemilia* of 78 BC, perhaps by the *lex Terentia Cassia* of 73 BC; a monthly limit of 5 *modii* – sufficient for two but not enough for three – for each entitled citizen was set; the latter law imposed on the praetor the duty to requisition grain, perhaps for only 40,000 citizens.[50] Cato's grain law, the *lex Porcia* of 62 BC, keeping the Gracchan price of six and one-third *asses* for each *modius*, seems to have given grain to some 200,000 persons, perhaps doubling the number of recipients.[51]

In 58 BC Clodius brought about free distributions,[52] to an

---

46 Sirks (1991b): 404.
47 CTh 14.19.1 – AD 398; 14.21.1 – AD 364. For the *annona* in the Later Empire, see, as well as Sirks (1991b) also Tengström (1974) and Herz (1988).
48 Cicero *pro Sestio* 25.55 & 48.103; Livy *per.*60; Velleius 2.6.3; Plutarch *C.Gracchus* 5; Appian *BC* 1.3.21.
49 Cicero *de off.*2.21.72.
50 Sallust *Hist.*3.48.19. The number eligible suggests that the *lex Octavia* rather than the *lex Sempronia* was the model.
51 Marshall (1985): 97.
52 *Schol. Bob.* (Stangl: 132).

unknown number, but possibly to all citizens, including freed-men; although he did not widen eligibility, it was alleged (and maybe with truth) that he thus encouraged the drift to the City of the rural poor,[53] and perhaps also the incidence of manu-missions.[54] We do not know about the mechanics of distribu-tion, but there may be a link with another law passed by Clodius in that year, lifting the ban on *collegia*, for it is possible that their services were used.[55] Free distributions made the grain much more useful to the poor, who had anyway to meet milling and baking charges before they could eat their grain;[56] they thus still needed employment. (The public works programmes of the Principate may have been partly designed to permit the buying of supplementary grain by plebeian families;[57] this was also probably one of the reasons for the giving of imperial lar-gesses.) Clodius seems, however, to have given so much control to Cloelius (or Sextus Clodius), a private individual concerned with his own profit,[58] that the organisation virtually collapsed. Pompey was therefore given a five years' *cura annonae* in 57 BC, to bring stability. Apart from his measures to ensure an adequate supply, he may have revised the lists of those eligible to receive free grain; he is said to have organised a register of newly made freedmen who were not yet on the census lists,[59] which surely must have been used for this purpose. Such a revision was certainly undertaken by Julius Caesar who, in 46 BC, held a special census (*recensus*) by neighbourhoods using the services of the *domini insularum*; this excluded the informally manumitted, non-residents, and others. He reduced the number of recipients by more than half, fixing their number at 150,000, with replacements coming in from a waiting list by lot under the supervision of the praetor[60] and the *aediles cereales*. Caesar

---

53 E.g. Varro *RR* 2 Intro.3.
54 Scholiast on Persius 5.73; DH 4.24.5.
55 Nicolet (1980): 195.
56 Baking was not possible in an apartment in an *insula*; such rooms seem normally to have lacked chimneys, and certainly did not have ovens.
57 See ch. 2.
58 Cicero *de domo* 10.25.
59 Dio 39.24. This blacklist may have had a precedent; the early sections of the *tabula Heracleensis* may be concerned with a similar blacklist of those who professed themselves until recently to have been Italian citizens – Nicolet (1980): 198–9.
60 Suet. *Julius* 41; Dio 43.21.

also tried to reduce the population of the City by colonisation,[61] and he may have added subsidised oil to the grain.[62]

Largesse by great men had certainly not been ended by Gracchus (Agrippa as aedile distributed olive oil and salt to all[63]). Augustus himself in 23 BC distributed twelve rations – *frumentationes* – to each member of the Roman *plebs*, at least 250,000 on each occasion, from grain bought with his own money.[64] Such measures, however, were not adequate in the long term. In 22 BC there was a crisis when the Tiber flooded and there was plague in Italy. The people appealed to Augustus to take charge;[65] he did not take a new power, but rather accepted a new responsibility.[66] Following a policy of 'co-operation not confrontation',[67] he appointed praetorian senators as *praefecti frumenti dandi*[68] (also sometimes known as *curatores frumenti*) to handle the distribution – there were four of them in 18 BC[69] – while the aediles continued to be responsible for the supply.

In 5 BC Augustus issued a largesse to the urban plebs, of whom there were then 320,000 eligible members. In 2 BC there was another special census by neighbourhoods which left a list of perhaps 200,000 recipients of free grain,[70] or maybe fewer. By this stage senators and equestrians were excluded, perhaps in law as well as in practice;[71] otherwise, citizenship was in itself a cause of eligibility for the lists, provided the (male) citizen was near-adult and permanently resident,[72] but the *lex Fufia Caninia* of the same year, restricting manumissions by will, may well have been relevant to eligibility. Certainly the number of possible mouths could be a problem. In the food crisis of AD 6 we hear that Augustus was concerned to try to reduce the City population; all foreigners, save physicians and teachers, were expelled, gladiators and slaves up for sale

61 Suet. *Julius* 42.
62 Dio 43.21.
63 Dio 49.43.
64 *RG* 15.1.
65 *RG* 5; Dio 54.1.3 & 4; also, Velleius 2.89; Suet. *Aug*.52.
66 Pavis d'Escurac (1976): 13–14.
67 Herz (1988): 360f; and *privilegia* were to be used to encourage this co-operation.
68 Suet. *Aug*.37; Frontinus *aq*.100; Dio 54.1.4; *RG* 5.
69 *RG* 18; Dio 54.17. Cf. *RG* 15.4; Suet. *Aug*.40.
70 *RG* 15; Pliny *Pan*.25; Dio 76.1.1.
71 D.32.35pr, Scaevola 17 *dig*.
72 Cicero *pro Archia* 4.9; Seneca *de ben*.4.28.2.

were banished to a distance of 100 miles, Augustus himself and others who had to stay in Rome sent many of their retinue away, while senators were freely permitted to leave Rome and the courts were closed.[73] He also appointed consulars to oversee the supply and sale of the corn dole;[74] his intention may have been to double the ration, still of 5 *modii*,[75] and halve the recipients, since Augustus himself gave as much again to those who were entitled. In AD 7 the food shortage reappeared towards the end of the year, and two consulars were appointed again as commissioners of the grain supply, with lictors.[76] These crises seem at least partly due to the German wars which only ended in AD 11. Peace in the north and the appointment of the *praefectus annonae* to co-ordinate the supply mark something of a new beginning, but the *praefecti frumenti dandi*[77] continued to oversee the distribution.

There is no evidence from this period for any single distribution centre;[78] the Temple of the Nymphs, where certain records of the censors were held,[79] is, according to Nicolet, sited within the *porticus Minucia frumentaria* of the Empire, which was built perhaps under Claudius (who would have remembered the Minucian tradition of generosity with grain) but there seems to have been another portico of the same name in the Republic, surrounding the temples of the Largo Argentina.[80] The *horrea* themselves may have been the sites of the distributions, or some convenient *porticus*; the date and place were probably announced to all recipients simultaneously. *Tesserae* as tickets of entitlement were certainly in use under Augustus,[81] and maybe earlier. Those on the lists seem to have held a permanent ticket as sign of entitlement – and indeed of free status – and to have

73 Suet. *Aug*.42.3; Dio 55.22.3; 55.26; 55.28.1.
74 Dio 55.31.4.
75 Brunt and Moore (1967): 59.
76 Dio 55.31. At this stage Augustus was presumably thinking of establishing a (relatively) independent *cura*, as for water or public works.
77 Rostovtzeff [Roztowzew] (1912): 176f.
78 Indeed, as Rickman (1980): 185, points out, the language of the *tabula Heracleensis* – FIRA i 13 (p.140ff) v. 15 – *if* this is relevant – makes it plain that the time and place were to be announced.
79 Cicero, *pro Milone* 27.73. Nicolet (1976).
80 Velleius 2.8.3; seemingly repaired by Domitian – *Chron. ann. 354*, p. 189. The Regionaries list both a *frumentaria* and a *vetus*. See Nicolet (1976), and (1980): 199f.
81 Suet. *Aug*.40.

received temporary ones which were handed over in return for the ration of grain.

THE OPERATION OF THE *CURA ANNONAE* AT ROME

Tiberius made it clear that feeding the capital was an imperial concern,[82] though much of the time left in the hands of private enterprise. Claudius too remedied a shortage of corn in 41,[83] by supporting the market from the imperial resources, and again in 51, when fifteen days' subsistence was all that remained in store, he persuaded the shippers to put to sea in winter;[84] he also encouraged the grain trade by granting full citizenship to Junian Latins who engaged in it on a large scale, while citizens were exempt from the penalties of the *lex Papia Poppaea* and gained the *ius liberorum*.[85] When work on the new harbour at Ostia began, it was natural to send a procurator there, and there seems to be no political element in the withdrawal of the Ostian quaestor. Nero made regulations for the export of corn from the provinces and gave privileges to the shippers;[86] there was a special form of *locatio* for *navicularii*. He also, after the Great Fire, imposed a maximum price (the low one of 3 sesterces a *modius*) on grain in the market, while the distributions of wheat were suspended;[87] his aim was presumably to benefit all the inhabitants of the City, not just the *plebs frumentaria*. Trajan similarly gave citizenship to a Latin who built a mill grinding at least 100 bushels of corn a day and operated it for three years.[88] The *mensores frumentarii*, who checked the quantities of incoming grain, were relieved of the burden of tutory by Marcus Aurelius and Commodus in a rescript to the Prefect of the Grain Supply; this applied only to the City *mensores*, not in the provinces.[89] In a passage of the Vatican Fragments we

82 Tac. *Annals* 2.87; 3.54.6–8; 15.36. Cf. *Annals* 4.6.6; 6.13.2; Velleius 2.126.3; Suet. *Tib*.34.1.
83 Seneca *de brev. vitae* 18.
84 Suet. *Claud.* 18; cf. Tac. *Annals* 12.43; *Acts of the Apostles* ch. 27–8; D.45.1.122.1, Scaevola 28 *dig.*
85 Suet. *Claud*.19; G.1.32c; Ulpian *Reg*.3.6. Cf. Sirks (1980).
86 Tac. *Annals* 13.51, but cf. D.27.1.17.6, Callistratus 4 *de cogn.*
87 Dio 62.18. They were probably functioning again before his death, certainly under Titus – ILS 6045 (= CIL VI 943).
88 G. 1.32c & 34.
89 D.27.1.26, Paul *de excus*; 50.5.10.1, Paul 1 *sent.*

read that master bakers in Rome were excused from tutories by Trajan, and that this was put into effect by their registration with the Prefect of the Grain Supply; this was later extended by Hadrian and then Caracalla to cover release even from being tutor to their colleagues' children.[90] Oil-merchants and shippers who had the greater part of their property tied up in the *annona* were privileged with five years' exemption from other civic burdens.[91] Pork butchers, with two-thirds of their capital tied up in the state-subsidised supply system, were granted immunity by Severus and Caracalla; they were registered with the Urban Prefect, who controlled the meat markets.[92] Trades connected with the *annona* received privileges, and were submitted to controls, earlier than, for example, the guild of actors,[93] but the co-operation of private enterprise and public service inevitably tended toward a licensing system.

What was needed was 'to maintain a steady and fairly low price for corn in the open market. . . . The job of the *princeps* and his delegate, the *praefectus annonae*, was not that of running what was more or less a state owned monopoly but, as the sources precisely state,[94] exercising a *cura* over a free market, attempting to coordinate supplies and plan ahead to avoid famines'.[95] 'The role of the *praefectus annonae* was . . . purely local in its aims and yet empire-wide in attempting to satisfy those aims.'[96] Distribution remained no part of his duties until 331;[97] the *praefectus annonae* continued, however, to exercise a considerable jurisdiction in civil cases concerning the food markets. He was based in Rome, because of its importance, and watched over the long-term storage of grain and the markets in oil as well as corn.[98] He may have become concerned with all

90 FV 233–5, probably, despite the different ascription, identical with D.27.1.46, Paul *de cognit*; FV 234 explains that this privilege was not given to Ostian bakers.
91 D.50.4.5, Scaevola 1 *reg.*
92 FV 236; see ch. 10.
93 CJ 11.41.4 – AD 394.
94 E.g. Tac. *Annals* 3.54.6–8.
95 Rickman (1971): 310.
96 Rickman (1980): 92.
97 Chastagnol (1960): 57, 62.
98 Dio 52.24.6 in the Maecenas speech, makes this point; Chastagnol (1960): 55, holds that the *praefectus annonae* was not concerned with wine or meat (which were directly controlled by the Urban Prefect) but only with corn and oil; Pavis d'Escurac agrees (1976): 201. ILS 1342 & 1340 (= CIL VI 1620 & 1625) are clear indications of the prefect's involvement with

supplies to the City, but it is more likely that the Urban Prefect had that overall responsibility.[99] It is of imperial doings that the literary sources speak.

Wine was important, though the most drastic measure we actually hear of is Domitian's (unenforced) edict forbidding the planting of new vineyards in Italy and ordering the destruction of provincial vineyards.[100] Antoninus Pius is said to have relieved a shortage of wine, oil and wheat by making free distributions at his own expense.[101] Septimius Severus is said to have instituted the distribution of free oil,[102] while Severus Alexander was concerned with the price of meat, as was Aurelian, who subsidised wine as well as issuing bread, oil and pork.[103] Aurelian also changed the form of the grain distribution to rations of bread.[104]

The *praefectus annonae* had an *officium*,[105] which may have been located close to the temple of Ceres. His deputy in the first century is called *adiutor*;[106] in the later second century we find a sub-prefect.[107] The transformation of the prefect's office into the *fiscus frumentarius* seems to date from the Flavians; it had *tabularii* in charge of the records, a *libellis* who dealt with claims, *dispensatores* or pay clerks and an actor *a frumento*.[108] The title *a frumento* probably refers to the office staff of the *praefectus annonae* rather than of the *praefecti frumenti dandi*. The *praefecti frumenti dandi* (a post normally held by unambitious senators) had their own staff, secretaries, copy clerks, orderlies and criers, to aid them in the administration of their office, which took up some three months of the year.[109]

By the reign of Claudius at the latest the headquarters of the grain distribution was at the *porticus Minucia* in the Campus

olive oil from the mid-second century; see Pavis d'Escurac (1976): 188–97; Panciera (1980).

99 D.1.12.1.11, Ulpian *de off. p. u.*

100 Suet. *Dom.*7; see Tchernia (1986): 221–33.

101 SHA *Ant. Pius* 8.

102 SHA *Sept. Sev.* 18 & 23 – though daily issues seem unlikely, and quite unnecessary; Aurelius Victor 41.19–20.

103 SHA *Sev. Alex.*26; *Aurelian* 35, 47 & 48; Aurelius Victor 35.7. Sirks (1991b) section 160 deals with *vina fiscalia*.

104 SHA *Aurelian* 35.

105 E.g. ILS 1705 (= CIL VI 8473).

106 ILS 1535 (= CIL VI 8470) – a freedman of Pallas.

107 ILS 1412 (= CIL V 8659); see also 1359 (= X 7584), 1370 (= III 1464).

108 ILS 1540 (= CIL VI 544), 1540a (= VI 634), 1541–45 (= VI 8474–7).

109 Frontinus *aq.*100–1.

Martius. The portico was divided into arcades, with *ostia* or gates – probably 45 – in each, designed for distributing the tokens (or possibly even the grain itself). Each arcade had a group allocated to it; engraved, and therefore permanent, lists, set out by tribe or by *vicus* (with the former slightly more probable[110]) were posted there.[111] Entitlement to the public corn seems to have been proved by the *tesserae*; these were alienable and heritable,[112] but presumably, as Rickman holds,[113] any change of ownership had to be registered so that the lists of recipients could be adjusted. It is clear that, if there had been simultaneous distribution of the ration, a single issuing centre would have been impossible. If the entitlement was spread throughout the month, using the differentiated entrances of the *porticus Minucia*,[114] groups need be only some 200 strong and there would be no physical problem. However, when bread replaced grain, this, while easier for the recipients, must have caused organisational difficulties, since issues of bread would need to be more than monthly – at least weekly, if not more frequently, depending on the type of bread baked.

The *praefecti frumenti dandi* seem to have survived until the mid-third century; they are perhaps to be identified with the *praefecti Miniciae* found under the Severi,[115] but by this time they had probably been brought under the *praefectus annonae*. The *procurator Augusti ad Minuciam* is first evidenced under Trajan.[116] Under Commodus or Septimius Severus there appeared a consular *curator aquarum et Miniciae*;[117] it seems possible that the distribution of water and grain was then amalgamated. It was also under Commodus that the African fleet was organised as a semi-public body, that huge warehouses

---

110 Mommsen vs Hirschfeld; Hirschfeld (1870): 92 – who cites there the Mommsen view.
111 Nicolet (1980): 197.
112 D.5.1.52.1, Ulpian 6 *fideicomm*; 31.49.1, Paul 5 *ad l. Iuliam et Papiam*; 31.87pr, Paul 14 *resp*.
113 Rickman (1980), Appendix 8.
114 E.g. ILS 6069–71 (= CIL VI 10223–5).
115 ILS 1110 (= CIL VIII 12442) – a late second-century *praefectus Miniciae* – the spelling had changed.
116 ILS 2728 (= CIL XI 5669).
117 ILS 1128 (= CIL V 7783) refers to one who had been consul in 191; ILS 1186 & 1191 (= XIV 3902 & VI 1532) are of the mid-third century. The office is last heard of in 328, after having been held by Mavortius Lollianus – ILS 1223 (= X 4752). See Rickman (1980), Appendix 10; Hirschfeld (1870): 63–7.

were built at Ostia, and that the fall of Cleander was attributable to the failure of the corn supply.[118] It seems to have been a period, like the mid-first century, when reorganisation was in the air. A few years later Septimius Severus added oil to the grain distributions, but its supply was somewhat irregular,[119] though the distributions seem to have been re-established by Aurelian. His measures, like those of Severus Alexander, under whom it is clear that shipping as exercised for the government within the framework of the collegia was no longer contracted for but had become a *munus*,[120] seem attested by their existence in the fourth century. In the context of local government they also seem to be a desperate attempt to provide for a contented citizenry in difficult times.

118 SHA *Commodus* 17.7.
119 SHA *Sept. Sev.*18; ILS 1403 (= CIL II 1180) records a man, probably based at Rome, dealing with Spanish and African oil – see Rodriguez-Almeida (1980); cf. Panciera (1980).
120 Sirks (1984): 8; 73–5.

11

SHOWS AND SPECTACLES

The importance of television in providing cheap – and sometimes nourishing – entertainment, particularly for the poor, should stop us moralising against 'circuses', even if we find the particular form some of the Roman entertainments took revolting. In the first place, it is clear that, even had they wanted to, the Roman urban masses could not have spent their days in idleness at the races, the theatre or at other shows. Just after the Social War, at the start of the period considered in this book, there were 57 days of games, taking up approximately three separate weeks in April, one in July, a fortnight in September and another in November.[1] These regular, public games were part of the religion of the state, commemorating triumphs and the averting of disasters. On the same grounds, further sessions were added by Sulla and then by Julius Caesar; the tendency to establish regular festivals to celebrate imperial occasions had led by AD 354 to there being a total of 177 days on which public games took place. (The modern office worker in Britain has over 130 free days in the year.)

While 'games' is the literal and customary translation of the Latin 'ludi', it is potentially misleading. The majority of the days of public games were devoted to theatrical performances – *ludi scaenici* – often with chariot racing, which was much more expensive to put on, as the climax on the last day; gladiatorial fights, known technically as *munera*, were generally not part of the regular public games. 'So on 56 of the 77 days of regular public games at the time of Augustus, on 101 out of 177 days in the mid-third [*sic*] century AD, any Roman who could secure

---

1 This chapter owes much to Balsdon (1969), ch. viii 'Holidays at Home: Public Entertainment', here at p. 246.

a seat sought his entertainment in the theatre; on seventeen in Augustus' time, on sixty-six in the fourth century, he sought it in the Circus'.[2] While the Circus Maximus could probably hold 150,000 or so spectators,[3] the three theatres together only seated between 25,000 and 28,000, and it seems possible that only one theatre was used at a time; we are specifically told of a play being given twice in a day, which suggests this was somewhat unusual. On the other hand, Suetonius, admiring Augustus' lavish and splendid shows, said that sometimes players were performing throughout the City and on many stages.[4] The amphitheatre, now known as the Colosseum, in which gladiatorial and wild beast shows came to be concentrated, could hold some 50,000.[5] Only a small proportion of the population – except on racedays – could, therefore, be amusing itself in this way, and such entertainment was by no means available every day, though the emperors did put on extraordinary shows to mark particular events.

Special *ludi*, vowed by a general, might be put on at his own expense, using his booty, but the normal public games were funded from the *aerarium* on the authorisation of the Senate; ambitious magistrates used their own resources to make their games more memorable.[6] In the Republic the aediles were usually responsible for presiding over and organising the games. This task was transferred to the college of praetors in 22 BC, still with the basic funding from the *aerarium*; no one praetor was allowed to spend more than another.[7] In 20 BC, however, we hear of games given by the aediles on their own initiative.[8] In 13 BC, again on the occasion of Augustus' birthday, the Senate authorised the son of the praetor to give games in the Circus.[9] Nerva abolished many horse-races, and some other spectacles, to reduce expenditure.[10] Antoninus Pius too is said to have imposed limits to expenditure on the gladiatiorial games;[11]

2 ibid. 248.
3 Humphrey (1986): 126.
4 Suet. *Aug*.43: Fecitque nonnumquam etiam vicatim ac pluribus scaenis per omnium linguarum histriones ...
5 Balsdon (1969): 268.
6 On the costs of *ludi*, see Cavallaro (1984).
7 Dio 54.2.
8 Dio 54.8: horse-races and a slaughter of wild animals.
9 Dio 54.26.
10 Dio 68.2.
11 SHA *Ant. Pius* 12.

Marcus Aurelius, who was well known for disliking the spectacles (but he did leave instructions, when he went away from Rome, about who should provide them) imposed such limits in considerable detail.[12] The general supervision of public order at the games as elsewhere came to be in the jurisdiction of the Urban Prefect, but the praetor in charge of a particular show had summary powers over the performers.[13]

THE THEATRE

Theatrical shows were the main feature of the public games; they were dedicated to the gods by someone holding public office. Until nearly the end of the Republic they took place in temporary wooden structures. Pompey built the first permanent, stone theatre; its opening saw a wild beast show, gymnastics, and musical contests.[14] There followed those of Balbus and of Marcellus, dedicated in 13 BC and 11 BC.[15] But, as mentioned above, we hear of theatrical shows under Augustus which must have been performed in temporary theatres.[16] Trajan seems to have built another, but it disappeared in the reign of Hadrian.[17]

The shows took various forms – tragedies, comedies, farces or pantomimes – and in our terms seem to have ranged from straight drama to musicals and cabaret. Roman dramatic writing, which owed much to the Greeks, flourished from the mid-third to the end of the second century BC, but by the end of the Republic new plays for performance had almost stopped being written; nearly all the plays Cicero mentions in his letters were revivals, and the popularity of straight drama was clearly fading.[18] Pantomime, roughly comparable to our ballet, was enormously popular from Augustus' time on, and so was mime. Mime was more like a musical or a variety show; the script, more often in prose than verse, could be improvised,

---

12 FIRA i 49 (p.294ff) *SC de sumptibus ludorum gladiatorum minuendis*; SHA *M. Ant. Aurelius* 11 & 23.
13 Tac. *Annals* 1.77; 13.28; D.1.12.1.12, Ulpian *de off. p. u.*
14 Livy *ep.*48.23; Val. Max.2.4.1; Pliny *NH* 8.20.53; Plut. *Pomp.*52; Tac. *Annals* 14.20; Dio 39.38.
15 Suet. *Aug.*29.5; Dio 54.25; Pliny *NH* 8.25.65.
16 Suet. *Aug.*43.
17 SHA *Hadrian* 9.
18 Balsdon (1969): 273f.

and was frequently accompanied by music and songs. Mime was performed by a troupe of actors under an *archimimus,* and was perhaps even more disreputable as an occupation than other forms of acting.[19] It was often highly topical, and seems to have been subject to no prior censorship, though there was a risk of arbitrary punishment.[20] We hear too of puppeteers, conjurors, acrobats, jugglers and clowns.[21] There were also public readings at the theatre.[22]

Music on its own – concerts – seems to have played a very small part in Roman entertainment; the Odeum, erected by Domitian,[23] was not a large building. Concerts were not given as part of the public games.[24]

THE CIRCUS

Horse-racing, particularly in the form of chariot-racing, seems to have been an early passion of the Romans, for the construction of the Circus Maximus as a racecourse is alleged by Livy[25] to date from the time of the kings. It was used not only for the chariot-races but also for other forms of horse-racing, such as the gymkhana-like riding of the *desultores,*[26] and even for foot races. A second racecourse, the Circus Flaminius, was dedicated around 221 BC.[27] In the first century AD the *circus Gaii et Neronis* was constructed in the Vatican area.[28] The Circus Maximus was also used for ritual manoeuvres, comparable probably to our

---

19 *PS* 5.26.2; D.3.2.1, Julian 1 *ad ed*; 3.2.2.5, Ulpian 6 *ad ed*; cf. 3.2.3, Gaius 1 *ad ed. prov*; 3.2.4pr-1, Ulpian 6 *ad ed*; 48.5.11.2, Papinian 2 *de adulteriis*; 48.5.25 (24)pr, Macer 1 *pub. iud*; Martial 3.86; see also ch. 13, on offences against public order.
20 For example, the comic actor Datus, referring to the deaths of Nero's parents, sang 'Good-bye, father; good-bye, mother' accompanied by gestures of eating and swimming in an Atellan farce; for which he was banished – Suet. *Nero* 39.
21 Horace *Sat.*2.7.82; Seneca *Ep.*45.8; Petronius *Sat.*53; Martial 9.38; Quintilian 10.7.11. And see Gaheis (1927).
22 Gellius 18.5.2.
23 Suet. *Dom.*5.
24 Laurence Keppie informs me that Augustus' Mausoleum was used, first as a bull-ring, then as a concert-hall down to the 1930s.
25 DH 3.68; Livy 1.35.8–9; cf. Livy 8.20.2; Varro *LL* 5.153.
26 Cicero *pro Murena* 57; DH 7.73.2; Livy 44.9.4; D.19.5.20pr, Ulpian 32 *ad ed.*
27 Varro *LL* 5.154; Livy *ep.*20.
28 Pliny *NH* 36.15.74; Suet. *Claud.*21.2; Tac. *Annals* 14.14.

tattoos, such as the equestrian Game of Troy, undertaken by boys of good family.[29]

Horse-racing continued to be a passion; Pliny the Elder tells us of a fan's self-immolation at the funeral, soon after 77 BC, of the Red charioteer, Felix.[30] The emperors were nearly all enthusiastic racegoers.[31] Measures might be taken, presumably in the City as well as the provinces, against fans who got out of hand, the 'lads'; these could include banning them from attendance, as well as more severe penalties.[32] In the Later Empire Ammianus Marcellinus commented disapprovingly on the Roman enthusiasm for the races,[33] and the riots arising from the rivalry between the Greens and the Blues in Constantinople are well known. Such races formed part of early Roman religious ritual,[34] but by the Late Republic the organisation into the two teams of the Whites and the Reds[35] was a secular affair – slightly odd to us in that it does not seem to have attracted organised gambling; the Romans did not have bookmakers, or off-course betting.[36] Nevertheless, the religious element remained, and was stressed by Tertullian.[37] These races were classed as *ludi* and were provided free to the populace by the relevant magistrates at specific festivals spread throughout the year.

In the Republic and early Empire private persons hired out the horses, chariots, drivers and grooms, etc, to the producers of the games, the *editores ludorum*, that is the magistrates who were required to give games. These persons were the *domini*

29 E.g. Suet. *Julius* 39.2; *Aug.*43; Dio 51.22; Suet. *Claudius* 21.
30 Pliny *NH* 7.53.186.
31 Vitellius and Caracalla were Blues supporters, while Caligula, Nero, Domitian, Verus, Commodus and Elagabalus were all fans of the Greens.
32 D.48.19.28.3, Callistratus 6 *de cognit.*; cf. Tac. *Annals* 14.17: at Pompeii, around AD 59, after a riot at a gladiatorial spectacle, such *munera* were forbidden for ten years, certain *collegia* were dissolved, and those held to be the ringleaders of the riot were exiled.
33 Ammianus 14.6.25–6; 28.4.29–31.
34 DH 7.72–3; Livy 2.36; 25.12.14; Ovid *Amores* 3.2.
35 Reds and Whites may be older, as Tertullian alleges (*de spectaculis* 9), but Greens and Blues may well be almost as old, particularly as neither Suetonius nor Tertullian ascribes an originator to them, and both were interested in such things. See Cameron (1976): 56–61.
36 Though we hear of an *eques* from Volterra who used a carrier swallow to send the *quadriga* results back home by tying a coloured string to its leg – Pliny *NH* 10.34.71; cf. Petronius *Sat.*70; Juvenal 11.201; Tertullian *de spectaculis* 16, for some other cases of private betting. It was in general prohibited – D.11.5.2.1, Paul 19 *ad ed.*
37 Tertullian *de spectaculis* 4, and *passim*.

factionum, clearly co-operating rather than competing,[38] for they were in the sport as a business. They seem usually to have bred their own horses specially for racing; this may explain why Augustus gave the senatorial order permission to breed horses for profit so that they were not at the mercy of such contractors.[39] In the late second century and the early third, it is clear that horses and drivers were still in the private sector; Marcus Aurelius forbade manumission arising from the clamour of the crowd.[40]

This system, monopolistic but akin to the traditional public tender, had given way to imperial provision by the fourth century at the latest. By that time magistrates could in effect no longer hire horses from any source outside the imperial munificence, since any successful ones were to remain in the service of the factions;[41] it would not have been worth anyone's while to contract for such a service, at least in Rome and, in any case, buying suitable animals was no easy matter.[42] The factions had seemingly become dependent on imperial horses, and their administration was no longer by entrepreneurs but by managers, who sometimes at least were themselves charioteers.[43] In the fifth century the managers are firmly part of the imperial bureacracy.[44] (The pairing of the four factions was certainly not immutable; it is likely that four 'stables' were simply easier to run.[45])

The Romans seem never to have been very interested in athletic contests, the mainstay of Greek games, except for boxing and all-in wrestling (*pancration*), which were popular as spectator sports.[46] Augustus introduced 'Greek' games to Rome, but they then lapsed until Nero revived them in 60 and 65, with

---

38 Suet. *Nero* 22, when the *domini* began to refuse to hire out their teams for less than the whole day.

39 Dio 55.10, of 2 BC.

40 D.40.9.17pr, Paul *de libertatibus;* cf. Dio 69.16.3.

41 CTh 15.7.6 – AD 381.

42 Symmachus *Ep.*4.58 & 60; 7.48, concerning his son's praetorian games of 401.

43 ILS 5296–7 (= CIL VI 10058, 10060).

44 CTh 8.7.22 – AD 426.

45 Caligula had the Circus decorated in Red and Green – Suet. *Caligula* 18; Diocles seems to have raced for all four colours, ILS 5287 (= CIL VI 10048); ILS 5298 (= VI 10057) shows someone in the employ of Green and Blue.

46 E.g. Horace *Ep.*2.1.186; DH 7.73.3; Ovid *Tr.*4.6.31; Suet. *Aug.*45.2; *Caligula* 18.1; *Nero* 45.1.

poetry and music competitions as well as amateur athletics.[47] There was a Stadium for such contests in the Campus Martius, put up by Domitian and restored by Severus Alexander;[48] its site is the modern Piazza Navona. Otherwise, athletics of various sorts were simply practised without official organisation on the Campus Martius.[49] Even in the East, interest in athletics seems to have faded quite away by the fourth century, and the gymnasium disappeared. Most exercise enjoyed by amateurs seems, after the building of the imperial *thermae*, to have taken place in the *palaestra*.

GLADIATORIAL GAMES

Gladiatorial games, *munera* as opposed to *ludi*,[50] also had religious origins, linked with funereal sacrifices, but these again were becoming secularised by the late Republic. In the Republic these games were theoretically private matters; when Julius Caesar put on 320 pairs of fighters in 65 BC, it was in memory of his father, dead twenty years before. The first *munera* in the public games were given at the Cerialia in 42 BC, when the aediles substituted gladiatorial fighting for the chariot races on the last day.[51] But *munera* normally remained separate from the *ludi*; they were frequently linked with hunting games, *venationes*. They were primarily occasional events; even in the fourth century calendar only ten days of the festival year were devoted to them, all in December.

Augustus put on only eight gladiatorial shows during his reign, though their scale was lavish.[52] As early as 22 BC the Senate's permission was needed if anyone other than the emperor wished to put on *munera* at the public games, and this was

47 *RG* 22.1; Suet. *Aug*.43; *Nero* 12.
48 Suet. *Dom*.5; SHA *Sev. Alex*.24.3.
49 E.g. D.9.2.9.4, Ulpian 18 *ad ed.* on javelin-throwing *'in campo'* and Aquilian liability. Most of the Campus Martius was built over, but there seem to have been open spaces still on the northern fringes, near Augustus' Mausoleum and the Tiber.
50 *Munera* in this sense were originally the burdens incumbent on an heir; the use of the term became blended with the burdens of a magistrate, although the commonest legal meaning is of the burdens incumbent on a citizen by reason of his citizenship – D. 50.4, *passim*. SHA *Sev. Alex.* 43 implies that *munera* was by then – actually the fourth century – the term for all games.
51 Dio 47.40.6.
52 *RG* 22.1.

not to be more than twice a year or with more than 60 pairs of fighters.[53] Private persons who wished to give gladiatorial games in Rome needed special permission, and presumably good cause.[54] The emperors thus controlled this form of entertainment, though, from Claudius' time on, it was usually paid for by the quaestors collectively before they entered office.[55] The giver of the *munus*, the patron, contracted with a *lanista* for the supply of gladiators, animals, attendants such as the Mercuries who dragged away dead bodies or the boys who brushed the sand to hide the blood, and so on.[56]

Gladiators were trained in special schools, of which in the Empire there were four, all in the neighbourhood of the Colosseum, as the *amphitheatrum Flavium* was later nicknamed. There were always doubts about the wisdom of bringing highly trained but unreliable armed men into the capital,[57] and the emperors were clearly determined to exercise effective control over them. When there was famine in Rome in AD 6, the gladiators, among others, were banished from the City.[58] Gladiators included free men, professional fighters, as well as prisoners of war and condemned criminals.[59] Hadrian forbade slaves to be sent to the gladiatorial schools without a cause.[60] There were prohibitions on persons of the upper classes appearing as gladiators, or on the stage, though these were not always observed.[61] Senators and equestrians were forbidden to fight as gladiators as early as 38 BC;[62] in 200 AD we find women being forbidden to fight in single combat.[63]

53 Dio 54.2; cf. Suet. *Tib*.34.1.
54 D.35.1.36pr, Marcellus *lib. sing. resp*; cf. Tac. *Hist*.2.95.
55 Tac. *Annals* 11.22.3; 13.5.1; Suet. *Dom*.4.1; SHA *Sev. Alex*.43.3.
56 G. 3.146; FIRA i 49 (p.294ff) SC *de sumptibus ludorum*; Quintilian 8.3.34 describes *munerarius* as a word invented by Augustus. See Guarino (1985); Prichard (1959).
57 Cicero *Cat*.II 12.26.
58 Dio 55.26.
59 For the first see, e.g. Suet. *Tib*.7 or *Claudius* 21; for the last FIRA i 49 (p.294ff) SC *de sumptibus ludorum* v. 12 or D.48.19.8.11, Ulpian 9 *de off. proconsulis*. Marcus Aurelius' senatusconsult also deals (v.11) with the free professionals' share of the fees – very like modern footballers.
60 SHA *Hadrian* 18.
61 Suet. *Caligula* 18; *Nero* 12; Fronto *ad Marcum* 5.22–3 (Nab. 82); Dio 53.31; 55.10; 67.13.
62 Suet. *Tib*.35; Dio 48.43; 54.2; Augustus had forbidden equestrians to take part – Suet. *Aug*.43.
63 Dio 76.16; see Suet. *Dom*.4 for women taking part in gladiatorial shows.

These shows were originally put on in the Forum or some similar public open space; the *lex Julia municipalis* allowed those celebrating games to make use of public spaces as necessary, with (temporary) stages, platforms and scaffolding.[64] They became centred in the Colosseum built by Vespasian and his sons.[65] An earlier amphitheatre, that of Statilius Taurus, which was dedicated in 29 BC, seems to have been partially stone built,[66] but it was burned in the Great Fire of 64, and so presumably was Nero's wooden one.[67] (It is likely that the technology of setting up a mock sea battle was too expensive and too complicated to be attractive on a regular basis, so *naumachia* sites seem always to have been ephemeral.)

ANIMALS ON SHOW

The amphitheatre was also suitable for the hunting games which had already become popular in the Late Republic and were to turn into large-scale animal massacres under the Empire.[68] Amphitheatres, unlike a forum, were designed to separate participants from spectators; for the same reason, from the last century BC, the Circus Maximus was used for spectacles involving wild animals.[69] Not all shows involved the killing of the animals; there were some simple displays,[70] but they seem to have aroused less attention. The tendency was to combine them with the gladiatorial games; condemnation to the beasts became an economical form of the aggravated death penalty.[71] Polycarp was condemned by the Asiarch to the fire, not the beasts, only because the days of the animal games were past.[72] It must have been a very real problem to keep the animals alive and in con-

64 FIRA i 13 (p.140ff) *tab. Heracleensis*, vv. 77–9; there is a reference to such scaffolding in an account of a formal entry by Nero into Rome – Tac. *Annals* 14.13.
65 Suet. *Vesp*.9.1; *Titus* 7.3.
66 Dio 51.23.1.
67 Tac. *Annals* 13.31.1; Suet. *Nero* 12.1.
68 Pliny *NH* 8.20.53; 8.24.64. They were banished from the City by Tiberius, but clearly not for long – Dio 58.1.
69 *RG* 22: I gave *venationes* twenty-six times 'in Circo aut in Foro aut in amphitheatris'; Pliny *NH* 8.20.53; Gellius 5.14.5–8.
70 E.g. Suet. *Aug*.43.
71 D.48.19.8.11, Ulpian 9 *de off. proconsulis*; 48.19. 31pr, Modestinus 3 *de poenis*.
72 ACM *Mart. Polycarpi* 12.

dition,[73] let alone ready to attack when faced with an arena full of people, noise and strange smells.

The magistrates giving the games had in the Republic been responsible for the provision of the animals; hence Marcus Caelius Rufus' passionate pleas to Cicero for panthers.[74] The emperors took over much of this task; consequently there were staging-post zoos outside Rome.[75] Hadrian, for example, is alleged to have put 1,000 wild beasts into the arena.[76] But the magistrates still played a role; we hear of the praetors providing games in AD 39,[77] and also that in 212 it was the senators who furnished many wild beasts, while Caracalla had bought only a few.[78] The enforcement of responsibility for harm caused by any wild animals which escaped was through the edict of the curule aediles, who were often themselves responsible for shows.[79] It seems likely that the Urban Prefect acquired this jurisdiction when he became responsible for the 'disciplina spectaculorum'.[80]

AUDIENCE CONTROL

As has been said, the overall control of spectacles became the province of the Urban Prefect, and indeed remained so as long as there were such things at Rome.[81] Safety as such, despite the disastrous collapse of the (wooden) amphitheatre at Fidenae in AD 27,[82] does not seem to have been much regarded. It has been remarked that it is baffling that we hear of no injuries to spectators from ill-aimed spears or arrows, particularly in the hunting games. There was only a (usually) dry ditch, and

73 Suet. *Caligula* 27; see Jennison (1937).
74 Cicero *ad fam.*8.2; 8.4; 8.9; 8.8.
75 There was a *vivarium* outside the Porta Praenestina – ILS 2091 (= CIL VI 130). The imperial herd of elephants, supervised by a procurator *ad elephantos*, was kept near Ardea from the time of Augustus, or perhaps even from that of Caesar – ILS 1578 (= VI 8583); Juvenal 12.102–10; Aelian *De natura animalium* 2.11. Varro *RR* 3.13 describes a secure enclosure for game.
76 SHA *Hadrian* 7.
77 Dio 59.14; they were compelled by Caligula to follow old custom.
78 Dio 78.10.
79 See ch. 13.
80 D.1.12.1.12, Ulpian *de off. p. u*; see also ch. 12 on the policing of shows.
81 Cassiodorus *Variae* 6.4.6–7; 7.10 deals with the *tribunus voluptatum* who exercised a subordinate responsibility.
82 Tac. *Annals* 4.62–3.

perhaps netting, to separate the customers from the animals.[83] Access and evacuation – the problems of the simultaneous movement of large numbers of people – were dealt with largely by the architect; stairs and gangways were more lavishly provided than in many modern equivalents, but standing in the aisles seems to have been permitted. We hear, however, of distinguished spectators, equestrians, being crushed to death at the quinquennial games of 65.[84] There were tunnels under the arena for the use of gladiators, wild animals, and attendants.[85]

Awnings, manned by sailors from the fleet, provided shelter from sun and showers at the theatre and amphitheatre; we know nothing of what happened on a day of steady, heavy rain, or snow. Traffic control of some kind may not have been necessary in the neighbourhood of a spectacle or show when there was so little private transport; those who were allowed wheeled transport in the City may well have sent their vehicles away. However, we do hear of persons, two of senatorial rank, being crushed to death in the crowds coming to witness a *naumachia*.[86] The provision of snacks, cushions and similar items seems to have been entirely an affair of private enterprise. Water was laid on by permission, as we hear from Frontinus,[87] but nothing is said about sanitary arrangements – modern male Glaswegians unconcernedly urinate against the walls or down the terracing. The internal management of these buildings came to be an imperial concern, often using procurators with conventional office staff.[88] They presumably saw to the clearing up after a show as well as to the preparations.

The one area in this field which seems to have interested the public, and so we hear about it, was seating. Seats seem to have been free, though a ticket was necessary for admission.[89] Anyone could attend, free or slave, male or female, except for Augustus' prohibition on women watching athletics;[90] to be

---

83 DH 3.68.
84 Tac. *Annals* 16.5. After the collapse at Fidenae, the Senate decreed that no building work on such a structure should take place until the foundations had been approved – *Annals* 4.63.
85 Archaeological remains, e.g. at Trier, or the Colosseum.
86 Suet. *Julius* 39.4.
87 Frontinus *aq*.97.
88 E.g. ILS 5155 (= CIL VI 10163); 5268 (= VI 10088).
89 This is true, for example, of attendance at many BBC concerts.
90 Suet. *Aug*.44.

turned away was grounds for an action for *iniuria*, defamation.[91] However, it seems that those who came without a toga, or otherwise improperly dressed, would have to sit in the gods at the theatre, and stand on the roof over the women's gallery at the Colosseum. This is probably where slaves were expected to go, but it would not have been possible, even had it been desired, to refuse them admission.[92] Seats for men and women were not segregated at the Circus. Women, however, traditionally sat apart from men at the theatre; Augustus emphasised the loss of the private character of the gladiatorial shows – private *munera* could hardly be subject to state regulation – when he laid down that there too women should sit apart in the upper rows.[93]

Senators had had privileged seats at the theatre from the mid-Republic, and Augustus extended this to the Circus;[94] Later, this privilege was extended to the amphitheatre. The equestrian order had had reserved rows of seats at the theatre since the *lex Roscia*,[95] and they had special seats of some kind at the Circus too from AD 5, if not earlier.[96] We are told that in AD 41, after Claudius' restoration of the Circus, while the senators, the knights and the populace had traditionally sat apart, specific sections were now assigned to the upper classes,[97] which could include distinguished foreign guests.[98] The upper classes could, however, dress informally and sit elsewhere; we hear from Martial of people being expelled from the better seats by the ushers for improper dress.[99] We find this discrimination between the orders echoed in the municipal laws; for example, the *lex Ursonensis* laid down that municipal pontiffs

91 D.47.10.13.7, Ulpian 57 *ad ed.*
92 Rawson (1987).
93 Suet. *Aug.*44. His whole concept of an ordered society is revealed at the theatre, with places assigned to all by rank and status.
94 Suet. *Aug.*44. Cf. Asconius *in Cornel*.61 (Stangl p.55), where it is said that seats for senators were first made separate by order of the censors at the *ludi romani* given in 194 BC by the curule aediles, C. Atilius Serranus and L. Scribonius Libo.
95 Plut. *Cicero* 13.
96 Dio 55.2.
97 Tac. *Annals* 15.32; Suet. *Nero* 11; Dio 60.7. But Tacitus could find himself sitting beside an *eques*, and one who asked if he came from Rome or the provinces – Pliny *Ep.*9.23.
98 Suet. *Claudius* 25, despite *Aug.*44.
99 Martial 5.8. Caligula had relaxed some of the regulations, and permitted senators the use of cushions and hats – Dio 59.7, but the toga was still worn at the start of the second century – Juvenal 11.204.

171

and augurs were to be assigned seats among the decurions –
the fourteen rows; other sections of the law provided formal
rules about the allocation of seats at the *ludi circenses* and at
the theatre.[100]

100 FIRA i 21 (p.177ff) *lex Ursonensis* c.66; cc.125–7; cf. *JRS 76* (1986, 147ff)
   lex Irnitana Tab.IXA <ch.81>.

12

THE FORCES OF LAW
AND ORDER

When dealing with the problem of law and order in ancient Rome, one must remember the words of Jones:

> there is no reason to believe that crime *was* efficiently repressed . . . . The system had been satisfactory for a small town such as Rome once was. . . . If in a huge city it no longer worked, it may have been tolerated by inertia; after all, the British government in similar circumstances for generations tolerated a judicial system which failed to suppress widespread violent crime in London.[1]

Football hooligans or hopelessly unemployed rioters can cause considerable damage in communities which do have trained police forces and a multiplicity of courts. Most people in modern Britain would, I think, hold that we do live in a society in which it is generally safe to walk in the streets (even though journalists can always find frightened old people who dare not go out after dark). The evidence seems to suggest that the Romans during most of our period felt the same; our literary sources, upper-class sources, of course, view unpleasant incidents as exceptions to normality.

Despite the brawlings of rival gangs, Cicero was never happy to be long away from Rome, as his letters reveal; Juvenal's laments on the wickedness of city life were written by someone who clearly had no intention of living elsewhere; Pliny the Younger in his letters never casts doubt on the civilised nature of urban life. It was indeed in some ways a much rougher society than ours. Cicero applauded assassination,[2] and Dio

1 Jones (1972): 19.
2 E.g. Cicero *ad fam*.9.14; 12.1; *ad Att*.14.4.

records the Senate voting in AD 32 that senators should be searched for hidden daggers.[3] Roman attitudes to law and order, like pre-anaesthetic views of pain, may have had a different starting-point from ours; nevertheless they do not seem objectively so very different.

There are two principal questions to ask: what were the forces at the disposal of the authorities for the maintenance of law and order – with the subsidiary question of what resources were available to those forces? – and what behaviour was regularly seen as needing to be repressed, even when not specifically criminal? The first question, the subject of this chapter, needs separate treatment for the Republic and the Principate.

REPUBLICAN MEASURES[4]

Once the Principate is reached, the forces available to the authorities in charge of the capital were considerable, but earlier there seems to have been no significantly sized body of men reserved for this purpose. The legions might be used in Rome on occasion, but such use was normally unconstitutional, indicating civil commotion if not full-scale civil war; the special regulations for a triumph, which allowed armed troops across the *pomerium* into the City, make clear this contrast.

The authorities in the Republic were technically the consuls, except when the dictatorship was revived, but it was the Senate which developed the process which culminated in the *SC ultimum*, a declaration of a state of emergency. The consuls, by virtue of their *imperium*, had powers of life and death over all citizens, subject to *provocatio*, and over all non-citizens without legal restraint; they were, however, not much concerned with daily petty crime.[5] The jurisdiction of the Urban Praetor was normally civil (though this included the delicts of assault and theft) but since he too held *imperium* he had huge residual power; he was not limited to private law.[6] The role of the

---

3 Dio 58.18; though Tac. *Annals* 4.21, perhaps ironically, describes a charge, of AD 24, of entering the Senate wearing a sword as too dreadful to be true.
4 Echols (1958); Nippel (1984).
5 Despite Cicero *in Pisonem* 11.26.
6 FIRA i 30 (p.240f) *SC de Bacchanalibus*, vv. 15–21, laid down that permission to hold meetings of more than five persons or for senators to attend such meetings must be sought from the urban praetor.

aediles was humbler. They had no *imperium*, and though we find them prosecuting a range of crimes[7] – mostly connected with the *cura urbis* – in major matters of law and order they seem to have acted at the behest of the Senate. For minor affairs there were inferior magistrates who had a more specifically repressive function, the *triumviri capitales*.

The *triumviri* or *tresviri capitales* were members of the college of minor magistrates known, clumsily, as the vigintisexvirate, and later the vigintivirate.[8] They appear to be identical with the *tresviri nocturni* who played a part in fire control and had charge of, at least for that purpose, a gang of slaves.[9] The *tresviri* were clearly proper magistrates, though minor ones. In the *lex Latina tabulae Bantinae* and again in the *lex Acilia*[10] they are listed, together with the *IIIviri agris dandeis adsignandeis*, as magistrates of the Roman people, after the plebeian tribunes and the quaestors, and the higher magistrates. They had a jurisdiction of their own[11] as well as providing an executive force for higher magistrates. Cicero said of their particular task: 'let them see to the imprisonment of the guilty, let them inflict capital punishment . . . let them do whatever the senate demands'.[12] They were normally young men hopeful of a senatorial career, for which this was the first step on the civilian ladder. Auxiliary to them were pro-magistrates, ranking perhaps with scribes: 'And because it was unsuitable for magistrates to be concerned with public matters during the evening hours, a board of five men was established, for this side and beyond the Tiber, who could act as pro-magistrates'.[13] These *quinqueviri* are mentioned as concerned with law and order early in the second century BC,[14] and may have been appointed by the aediles.[15]

A romantic case, but one that illustrates the chain of command, is the famous story of the woman 'condemned for killing someone freeborn whom the praetor handed over to the triumvir to be put to death in the prison. She was lodged there, but

---

7 Dignös (1962); Bauman (1974).
8 See Mommsen (1887): II 592–610; de Martino (1972–5): III 279; IV 632–3.
9 D.1.15.1, Paul *de off. praef. vig.*
10 FIRA i 6 (p.82ff) v. 15; FIRA i 7 (p.84ff) vv. 2 & 22.
11 FIRA i 2 (p.80), *lex Papiria*.
12 Cicero *de leg.*3.3.6.
13 D.1.2.2.31, Pomponius *enchiridion*. See ch. 1, the divisions of the City.
14 Livy 39.14.10, on the Bacchanalian affair of 186 BC.
15 Mommsen's suggested emendation to D 1.2.2.33.

the gaoler in charge, moved by compassion, did not strangle her at once.' He compromised, however, by not feeding her and by searching her daughter, who was permitted to visit, for forbidden food; to his surprise she did not starve, and his curiosity eventually discovered that the daughter was feeding the mother with her own milk. So the gaoler reported this 'to the triumvir, the triumvir to the praetor, the praetor to the panel of judges', and she obtained a pardon[16] – the variant of this story of *caritas romana* has the daughter feeding her father. While this story smacks of the pious pelican, that is not grounds for total disbelief of the circumstantial details.

The most fruitful source for the activities of the triumvirs is Plautus, who is considerably earlier than our period, but there is no reason to think that their functions changed significantly. They seem to have been the authorities to whom one reported a crime: 'I shall report your name to the *tresviri*.' 'Why?' 'Because you carry a knife.' 'But I'm a cook.'[17] This links with Cicero's tale of how, after the disappearance of Asuvius, his freedman and friends bring a suspect – the man in whose house he was last seen – before the *tresviri*.[18] The clearest account comes from Asconius:

> The plebeian tribunes led one of the *triumviri capitales* to the Rostra and inquired of him whether he had arrested Galata, Milo's slave, in the act of murder. He replied that he had been taken as a runaway while sleeping in a wine shop and brought before him.[19]

Who then actually arrested the sleeper? Someone under the orders of the *triumviri*, such as a *praeco* or *viator*? Or the tavern keeper (unlikely, but not impossible)? Nevertheless, triumviral responsibility is attested; he might have arrested the slave, and Galata was brought before him.

Although they might be held responsible to tribunes, aediles or praetors, or of course to the consuls, the *tresviri* nevertheless seem to act on their own initiative within their own narrow sphere of jurisdiction, and to have had powers of *coercitio*.

---

16 Val. Max. 5.4.7.
17 Plautus *Aulul*.416ff; cf. *Asin*.130–2: Ex hoc loco Ibo ego ad tres viros vostraque ibi nomina Faxo erunt.
18 Cicero *pro Cluentio* 13.38.
19 Asconius *in Milonian*. OCT p.37.

Plautus has a slave worrying: 'What shall I do if the *tresviri* lock me up in prison?';[20] he is wandering around by himself at night, without any authorisation, and if he is arrested he fears a beating in the morning, from eight strong men. Was eight the number of men on patrol? or the total attached to the *tresviri* (but that seems rather small for a *familia publica*)? or their headquarters staff? The 'eight' seems the sort of reference meant to be taken by an audience. Cicero referred obliquely[21] to the *columna Maenia* (not very far from the prison) as their *statio*, and this was amplified by Pseudo-Asconius: 'for instance, thieves and worthless slaves are customarily punished by the *tresviri capitales* at the Maenian Column'.[22] This presumably refers to thieves caught in the act, or in the attempt, and to types whom it would be farcical to sue by an *actio furti*. Horace also referred[23] to a beating administered by the *tresviri* in a context which suggests that it was for being a vagabond – without visible means of support – rather than for any specific offence, for his upstart has made good, which would be somewhat unlikely (even in Horace's satirical context) if he had a formal conviction.

As well as inflicting corporal punishment on their own authority, the *tresviri* may have had powers to imprison, even citizens. There is no mention of any preceding trial or of intervention by a higher magistrate in the cases of either the poet and dramatist Naevius or C. Cornelius. Naevius 'was thrown into prison by the triumvirs for his constant abuse and mocking of the leading men of Rome';[24] of course, his link with the stage may have put him in the class of disreputables.[25] Cornelius was accused of the *stuprum* of a freeborn boy and his defence, that the boy was a whore, was clearly not believed by the tribunes since they refused their *auxilium* to him; in consequence, after C. Pescennius, *triumvir capitalis*,

---

20 Plautus *Amph*.155ff.
21 Cicero *div. in Caec.*16.50.
22 Pseudo-Ascon. *in div.*50 (Stangl, p.201): velut fures et servos nequam qui apud iiiviros capitales ad columnam Maeniam puniri solent.
23 Horace *Epod.*4.11: Sectus flagellis hic triumviralibus Praeconis ad fastidium. 'This creature, once flogged with the magistrates' lash, till the crier himself was sickened' (tr. W. G. Shepherd, Penguin, 1983), though the crier's function at a flogging is obscure – perhaps counting the strokes?
24 Gellius 3.3.15.
25 See ch. 13, and ch. 11, footnote 18; furthermore, the story is that the Metelli were ill-disposed towards him – Mattingly (1960).

had confined him in the public gaol, 'he was constrained to die in prison'.[26] A more difficult passage is that from Valerius Maximus recording that 'Alexander, suspected of having killed a Roman knight, was tortured six times without confessing. But then he did confess, was condemned by the judges, and was crucified by L. Calpurnius, the triumvir'.[27] It is not possible that in the Republic a slave had appeared before the judges of a standing jury court,[28] still less before the assembly, and the wording seems very odd for domestic jurisdiction; perhaps the *iudices* are the *tresviri* sitting as a college, alone or with a *consilium*. Their normal responsibility for executions was as subordinates.

Indeed, Cicero[29] stressed the partial authority, the auxiliary function of the *tresviri*. Probably, like the quaestors, their original functions were solely auxiliary, perhaps to the Urban Praetor since the Papirian Law gave him supervision of their election by the people.[30] And though the explicit references to the *tresviri* are not very numerous, there are many more to the use of prison as a place of restraint or of execution where the presence and sphere of office of the *tresviri* are implied. Fairly frequently we find them leading people off to prison, and sometimes executing them there, at the behest of higher magistrates or of the Senate.

In the aftermath of the Catilinarian conspiracy Cicero 'ordered the triumvirs to make ready what was necessary for the executions. He himself, with his escort around him, led Lentulus to the prison. . . . Lentulus was lowered down and the triumvirs ordered him strangled by the noose.'[31] There are many other examples, for instance, in 60 BC Pompey put the consul Metellus Celer in prison[32] and the Senate ordered numbers to prison in 53 BC;[33] Rufus Egnatius 'being thrust into the prison with his accomplices in crime, died a death worthy of his life'.[34] The

26 Val. Max. 6.1.10, probably of the late fourth century BC.
27 Val. Max. 8.4.2.
28 Robinson (1981). And the episode probably took place long before the creation of the jury courts.
29 Cicero *de leg*.3.3.6.
30 La Rosa (1957).
31 Sallust *Cat*.55, referring to them as 'vindices rerum capitalium'.
32 Dio 37.50.
33 Dio 40.45.
34 Velleius 2.91.4.

officers in charge of the prison[35] were the *triumviri*. They can
be presumed to have given the actual order for executions,
although from the *caritas romana* story they do not seem always
to have been present (but there was no political interest in
that case, or they would doubtless have been more careful).
Naturally they did not themselves carry out executions; they
were often future senators. That was a task for the *carnifex*, a
man so polluted that he was not supposed to enter the Forum
or to live within the *pomerium*, according to Cicero.[36]

As already pointed out, it seems quite likely that there was a
patrol, whether of public slaves or free men, which picked up
Galata.[37] Even if the *triumviri* called on volunteers for guarding all the gates of Rome in 186 BC,[38] they had a gang for
fighting fires;[39] they must also have had an office staff, and
maybe *apparitores* for the rough work. Alexander, as we have
seen, was tortured six times before he was crucified,[40] perhaps by the same eight lusty fellows whom Sosia feared.[41]
From Horace[42] we know they had a *praeco* on their staff;
inscriptions record *viatores* for the *triumviri capitales* as well
as for the *quattuorviri viis in urbe purgandis* (and the *decemviri
slitibus iudicandis*).[43] But how big a staff they had must remain
obscure.

Other magistrates of course had their lictors or *apparitores* who
could be used in the maintenance of order,[44] but the essentially
personal nature of their services[45] means that they were not
likely to be of great use for daily law enforcement. When the

35 The old *carcer* with its lower chamber which alone, strictly, was the
    Tullianum, and the *lautumiae*, the former quarries on the Capitoline,
    named after the infamous Syracusan quarries, used to hold the captive
    Athenians – Varro *LL* 5.151.
36 Cicero *pro Rab*.5.15; note that it was a *servus publicus* who was sent to
    kill Marius – Val. Max. 2.10.6.
37 Asconius *in Milonian*. OCT p.37.
38 Livy 39.17.5.
39 D.1.15.1, Paul, *de off. praef. vig*, where there is mention of a *familia publica*
    stationed round the wall and gates of Rome.
40 Val. Max. 8.4.2.
41 Plautus *Amph*.159–60.
42 Horace *Epod*.4.11, cited above.
43 ILS 1929–30 (= CIL VI 1936, 466); 1909 (= X 5917).
44 E.g. Val. Max. 8.1.3 *absoluti*: Lictor igitur et carcer ante oculos observabantur.
    A tribune should have used his *viator*, not a client, to lock up the consul in
    91 BC – Val. Max. 9.5.2.
45 Jones (1949b).

scale or nature of a crime, or threatened crime, led the consuls
to intervene, they had their lictors, but this was not a significant
force.[46] Cicero at the time of the Catiline affair simply ordered
Cethegus, Lentulus and the others into house arrest in the care
of the praetors; he had an escort of senators and young men
when he conducted the arrested men to the prison, for there
was clearly no suitable official force of adequate numbers to
overawe a crowd if it should turn nasty.[47] This is how the
Republic was meant to function. It is reminiscent of Juvenal's
nostalgic remark: 'the happy era which . . . saw Rome content
with one prison'.[48] We learn a little about crowd control in just
one episode; to arm themselves, Tiberius Gracchus and his
friends broke in pieces the spear shafts with which the *viatores*
held back the crowds;[49] it is clear from the tone that the spears
were normally used not as pointed weapons but as staves.

Our look at the forces available to the authorities for the
maintenance of law and order in the Republic leads therefore
to the conclusion that for the riff-raff there were the *tresviri* as
a sort of cross between justices of the peace (with the powers
they had in Tudor England) and police superintendents, but
that for major public disorder there was no remedy, if only
because to bring in the legions was itself a further breach of
order; the armed gangs of the *populares* were met by the armed
gangs of the *optimates* – 'and I am wounded by this *apparitor* of
Clodius'.[50] The magistrates could theoretically maintain law and
order but, once anyone of standing ceased to play by the rules,
the remaining magistrates did not have the men, though they
had the notional powers, to repress him. There were powers
to flog and imprison the petty thief, the drunk, the runaway
slave, and the more flagrant subverters of the public order, but
the *tresviri* will have had their hands more than full with a city
the size of Rome in the last century BC. We shall consider in the
next chapter the kind of behaviour they repressed in the context
of Republic and Principate together.

46 Val. Max. 9.7.1, on the occasion in 100 BC when a mob broke into the
   prison.
47 Plutarch *Cicero* 22. Plutarch adds that the City was overjoyed, not so much
   at the suppression of the conspiracy as because it was done so quietly and
   without disturbance.
48 Juvenal 3.312–14.
49 Plutarch *T. Gracchus* 19.
50 Asconius *in Milonian*. OCT p.41.

THE FORCES IN ROME UNDER THE EMPIRE

In imperial Rome the picture is quite different. A very considerable number of military or quasi-military bodies were stationed
actually in the City, but they had several distinct functions: the
protection of the emperor and his family, the maintenance of
order in the capital, and the prevention or suppression of fires.[51]
(The *vigiles*, or night watch, are usually distinguishable, but
unfortunately our sources all too frequently refer without further specification to 'soldiers', and it is by no means always
clear from the context whether Praetorians or Urban cohorts
are meant.) 'Rome had her own peculiar forces, namely three
Urban and nine Praetorian cohorts', says Tacitus.[52]

A fourth reason for the presence of various and miscellaneous
troops in and near the City was simply that Rome was the general headquarters of the army until the fourth century. Most of
the troops in this category were quartered in a transit camp, the
castra peregrina on the Caelian; they included the *frumentarii*,[53]
deputati, *supernumerarii*, and *evocati*, as well as transient legionary and auxiliary officers and men.[54] There was also the *castra
Misenatium* for the sailors who were needed for *naumachiae* and
who were also in charge of the awnings at the Colosseum,[55]
and were no doubt used for other tasks where nimbleness
and ropes were required. The *equites singulares* – whose predecessors under Augustus and the other Julio-Claudians were the
Germani or *Batavi*[56] – were a personal bodyguard, Household
Cavalry, recruited from the fiercer shores of the Empire, and
loyal to the person of the emperor not the concept of Rome. They
can be found, once, employed against the rioting populace,[57] but
this was not their proper office and from the point of view of the
normal maintenance of order in the City they can be ignored.

---

51 Watson (1969), pp. 13 and 16–21.
52 Tac. *Annals* 4.5: quamquam insideret urbem proprius miles, tres urbanae,
   novem praetorianae cohortes . . .
53 Sinnigen (1962) deals with the beginnings of their 'secret police' functions.
54 Dio 52.24; Ashby and Reynolds (1923); Reynolds (1923).
55 SHA *Commodus* 15.
56 Augustus is said to have dismissed his *Germani* on receiving the news
   of Varus' defeat – Suet. *Aug.*49 – but there were German bodyguards
   there to riot on the death of Caligula – Dio 59.30. See Speidel (1965).
57 Herodian 1.12.5–9, in AD 190, when the Urban cohorts came to the rescue
   of the populace.

The three bodies the sources tell us most about are the Praetorian cohorts, the Urban cohorts, and the *vigiles* or Night Watch.[58]
A praetorian guard was the perquisite of every general under
the Republican constitution, and the imperial Praetorians' first
role was that of bodyguard;[59] when the Greek writers speak of
somatophulakes they could mean either the *equites singulares* or
the Praetorians (who were more properly *hoi doruphoroi*). For
example, Dio ascribes to Augustus twenty-five legions, exclu-
sive of Praetorians and Urban cohorts, auxiliaries and sailors,
and then says that in AD 5 he had 10,000 *somatophulakes* organised in ten cohorts and 6,000 *phrouroi* or watchmen organised in
four cohorts.[60] There are further problems about numbers and
dates, but it is clear that there is room for confusion.

Linked with the prime role of the Praetorians as bodyguards,
accompanying the emperor when he campaigned,[61] is their extension into being a ceremonial body;[62] they could also provide
special detachments in war or peace,[63] and they guarded other
members of the imperial family.[64] They were available for crowd
control and so, during rioting,[65] they could be used like the
nineteenth-century British militia or the twentieth-century American National Guard, but the Praetorians were essentially fully
armed, fully trained, full-time professional troops. They were
probably established in their new form in 27 BC,[66] although
Praetorian Prefects were first appointed only in 2 BC;[67] before
that the cohorts had been, traditionally, under the direct command
of the emperor as their general. Augustus had troops in Rome,
partly for his own security and partly for that of the City, but
he never kept more than three cohorts at a time in the City, and
these were dispersed, while the other cohorts were quartered in

58 On the Praetorians, see Durry (1938) and Passerini (1939); on the
   Urban cohorts, Freis (1965, 1967); on the *vigiles*, Reynolds (1926), and
   more recently, though still unpublished, Rainbird (1976). See also von
   Domaszewski (1967).
59 Tac. *Annals* 12.69; *Hist*.1.29; Suet. *Otho* 6; cf. Martial 10.48.
60 Dio 55.24 (though the cohort sizes are those of his own day).
61 Dio 76.6; 79.37; ILS 2089 (= CIL VI 2464); CIL VIII 21021.
62 As in the state visit of AD 66 – Dio 62(63).4 'when the entire City had
   been decorated with lights and garlands'; cf. the triumph over Caractacus
   – Tac. *Annals* 12.36.
63 In war, Dio 55.10a; Zosimus 1.50–3. In peace, Pliny *NH* 6.35.181.
64 Tac. *Annals* 13.18; Dio 57.4; 61.8.
65 Tac. *Annals* 13.48; 14.61 probably refers to the Praetorians; cf. 16.27.
66 Dio 53.11.
67 Dio 55.10.10.

nearby Italian towns.[68] On the death of Augustus there were nine cohorts of Praetorians. The number of cohorts was increased and cut back, and then settled at ten from Domitian onwards.

Their commanders, the Praetorian Prefects (sometimes two but sometimes only one), were of equestrian status, from an administrative as much as a military background; they developed wider functions than the command of a bodyguard largely for the simple reason that they were physically so often close to the emperors. (Eventually when they exercised a jurisdiction *vice sacra*, their authority was specifically excluded from Rome and a 100-mile radius round the City, within which the jurisdiction of the Urban Prefect ran;[69] this demarcation was fixed at some time between the reigns of Marcus Aurelius and Caracalla, most likely under Severus.) They and their cohorts were never really part of the local government structure.

One of the chief distinctions between the Urban cohorts and the Praetorians was the difference in their commanders. The Urban Prefect was a proper magistrate[70] and always a senator, with the toga as his official dress;[71] the purpose of the Urban cohorts was to enable him to carry out his functions: 'to repress the servile elements and the insolence, unless overawed, of disorderly citizens'.[72]

> Keeping the peace among the populace and maintaining order at public shows are regarded as belonging to the Urban Prefect's supervisory function; indeed, he has a duty to station soldiers on guard duty to preserve peace among the populace, and to keep him informed of what is going on and where.[73]

He was, therefore, the man specifically charged with the maintenance of law and order in the City, and also of gathering intelligence, and he was given the force with which to do so. After the death of Gaius Caligula, some in the Senate seem to have hoped to restore the Republic; they entrusted the City to

68 Suet. *Aug*.49.
69 D.1.11.1, Arcadius Charisius *de off* .*p*. *p*.
70 D.1.2.2.33, Pomponius *enchiridion*; 2.4.2, Ulpian 5 *ad ed*. See Vitucci (1956).
71 He was usually consular – Dio 79.14; Rutilius Namatianus (himself Urban Prefect c. AD 414) 1.468.
72 Tac. *Annals* 6.11; the creation of this office is a little obscure, as Tacitus explains.
73 D.1.12.1.12, Ulpian *de off. p. u.*

the Urban cohorts, with whom, for a while, they threatened to attack Claudius and the Praetorians.[74]

The Urban cohorts were certainly created under Augustus; the weight of the evidence seems to favour an earlier rather than a later date. In particular, the argument from the continuous numeration of the cohorts – Praetorians I to IX and Urban cohorts X to XII – strongly suggests that Augustus thought of the two bodies together.[75] What is quite certain is the existence of both bodies in AD 14, for in his will Augustus left the Praetorians 1000 HS each, the Urban cohorts 500,[76] and 300 each to the legionaries. Further Urban cohorts were created under the Julio-Claudians[77] (and cut back under Vespasian[78]). But the extra cohorts seem mostly to have been stationed outside the City; when we calculate the forces available in Rome itself, it is normally only three or four Urban cohorts and no more than nine or ten cohorts of Praetorians. For policing purposes, we are dealing with a fairly stable number.

The *praefectus vigilum*, the Prefect of the Night Watch,[79] was subordinate to the Urban Prefect; he was an equestrian official appointed by the emperor, not technically a magistrate.[80] The forces under his command were inferior to the other City cohorts, since they had their origins in a gang of slaves. Their organisation was para-military but they were recruited from

74 Josephus *AJ* 19.188; *BJ* 2.204–8; cf. Suet. *Claudius* 10.
75 Freis (1965): 1126; nevertheless, it is a little strange that, if the Urban cohorts were already in being in 19 BC, the Senate would have voted a bodyguard for the consul – Dio 54.10. This episode has been held to have been the cause of their formation – von Premerstein (1937): 135–7. Mario Mazza, in Talamanca (1979): 534, thinks that the first commander of the Urban cohorts may have been Statilius Taurus in 16 BC. Another possible date for their creation is AD 5 – Dio 55.24.6; an alternative is AD 13, when Piso became the first regular Urban Prefect, as Cadoux (1959): 153 holds.
76 Tac. *Annals* 1.8; Suet. *Aug.*101; Dio 56.32.
77 There was a XIII at Lyon, XV and XVI for Ostia and Puteoli under Claudius, XVII at Carthage, a XIV must be presumed, and Tacitus (*Hist.*1.64) indicates an XVIII – Freis (1965): 1129–31.
78 The Ostia and Puteoli cohorts were disbanded and *vigiles* took their place at Ostia, while the Lyon cohort was reconstructed as I Flavia Urbana and remained independent; we find XIII in Carthage and X, XI, XII and also XIV (dating probably from Domitian, anyway from between 76 and Trajan) in Rome – Durry (1938): 13 & 16. Under Constantine there were only three, X-XII; XIV was probably suppressed by Aurelian.
79 See ch. 7.
80 D.1.2.2.33, Pomponius *enchiridion*.

freedmen[81] and the urban proletariat. The *vigiles* were given their final form, with seven cohorts and seven centuries in each, in AD 6.[82] They were not normally concerned with problems of law and order, though they could be called upon in emergency;[83] they were fully occupied with their fire-fighting duties.[84] The only strictly military use, after Augustus,[85] of the *vigiles* – although they were listed, along with the sailors from the fleet and the gladiators, as a force to be reckoned with in AD 41[86] – was in the troubled year of AD 69 when Flavius Sabinus, the Urban Prefect, took command of them for the fighting in Rome.[87]

The question of the numbers stationed in Rome is related to that of the size of the cohort. The original complement of both Praetorian and Urban cohorts was probably 500 men;[88] it seems unlikely, when Augustus was introducing a novelty by establishing a permanent armed force or forces within the City, that he would make it harder for the conservatives to accept by setting them up in more than legionary force.[89] Under Severus, that number was increased to 1,500 or possibly 1,000.[90] Severus wanted a stronger police presence, and by this time

81 Suet. *Aug*.25; Dio 55.26. ILS 2163 (= CIL VI 220) shows recruitment from the freeborn in Severan times.
82 Strabo 5.3.7; Suet. *Aug*.25; Dio 55.26; D.1.15.1, Paul *de off. praef. vig.*
83 In AD 31, when Sejanus' downfall was being engineered, they replaced the Praetorians guarding the Senate House – Dio 58.9 & 12.
84 Rainbird (1976) ch. 4.
85 Suet. *Aug*.25. He twice sent contingents of *vigiles* to the wars – in Illyricum and on the Rhine. But they did not count fully as veterans – D.27.1.8.4, Modestinus 3 *excus*. – although they did have the right to make a military will – D.37.13.1.1, Ulpian 45 *ad ed.*
86 Josephus *AJ* 19.253.
87 Josephus *BJ* 4.645; Tac. *Hist*.3.64, when the anti-Vitellian party pointed out that the Urban Prefect had his own Urban cohorts and could also rely on their slaves and on the *vigiles*, and *Hist*.3.69, when the Urban Prefect confined *omnisque miles urbanus* and the *vigiles* to barracks.
88 Freis (1967): 38–42, dismisses Josephus (*BJ* 2.373) as unreliable, Tacitus (*Hist*.2.93) as talking only of the civil wars of 69, and Dio (55.24) as thinking of his own time.
89 Webster (1979): 114, gives 480 – 10 *contubernia* of 8 men to each century, with 6 centuries to a cohort – as the effective strength of a legionary cohort.
90 Freis follows the implication in Herodian (3.13.4) in thinking that the Praetorians and *vigiles* went from 500 to 1000, and the Urban cohorts from 500 to 1500 under Severus – Dio 55.24; so too Birley (1969): 64. Keppie (1984): 188, thinks that the size of the cohort in both Praetorian and Urban forces was 1000 men from AD 69. Campbell (1984): 4, holds that the military cohorts dated from Domitian.

the Praetorians were being employed away from Rome quite regularly.

Recruitment of the Urban cohorts (as originally of the Praetorians) was always from within Italy, right up to the time of their disappearance in the early fourth century.[91] (Both were always an elite; while the Praetorians were paid most and served only for sixteen years, the Urban cohorts were paid more than legionaries and served only twenty years, compared to the legionary twenty-five.) Both Praetorians and Urban cohorts were originally billeted through the City – that is, those of them who were not stationed outside Rome – but under Tiberius the dispersed cohorts of the Praetorians were brought together into barracks, on the grounds that orders could more efficiently be given and the troops be under better discipline.[94] The *castra Praetoria* was outside the City on the north-east, a little to the east of the *porta Collina*; Aurelian built its perimeter into his wall.[93] It was the permanent home of the Praetorians from AD 23 or so;[94] it is generally presumed that the Urban cohorts were from this time on quartered in the same barracks,[95] until Aurelian moved them.

There has been argument about who controlled these various forces. Clearly the immediate command of the *vigiles* pertained to the Prefect of the Night Watch, but it has been held that he was subordinate to the Praetorian Prefect as well as the Urban Prefect.[96] This seems impossible: first, because it is made quite plain in the legal texts that the Prefect of the Night Watch was responsible to the Urban Prefect,[97] and second, the function

---

91 ILS 722 (= CIL VI 1156), the latest inscription to mention the Urban cohorts, records, between 317 & 327, 'a tribune of the three urban cohorts and the pig market'; CTh 4.13.3 – AD 321 mentions 'urbani milites'. The Praetorians were disbanded in 312 (Aurelius Victor, *de Caes*.40.24–5); Sinnigen (1957): 88–94, thinks that the Urban cohorts went at the same time, though Chastagnol (1960): 255, places their dissolution later in the century, between 357 and 384.

92 Tac. *Annals* 4.2; Suet. *Tib*.37; Dio 57.19.

93 Aurelian also built a separate *castra Urbana* at the *Forum Suarium* (*Chron. ann. 354*, p. 148); there may be a link with the distribution of pork to the populace, under the control of the Urban Prefect. ILS 2091 (= CIL VI 130) tells us that the two corps were still quartered together in 241.

94 Dio 57.19 refers to AD 20.

95 It should, perhaps, be stressed that units under different commanders may occupy the same base; the Emperor could give orders to both bodies of men.

96 E.g. Durry (1938): 20.

97 D.1.15.4, Ulpian *de off. p. u.*

of the *vigiles* was specific, and of no interest to the Praetorian Prefect.

It has been rather more widely held that the command of the Urban cohorts was in the second century taken from the Urban Prefect and given to the Praetorian Prefect and then restored in the third century.[98] This claim is relevant to whether the keeping of order really was under direct imperial control or whether it was left to the Urban Prefect as a matter of *prima facie* local government. The evidence adduced for the Praetorian Prefect's command seems solely epigraphic, based primarily on one particular inscription[99] and also on the joint issue of diplomata to the Praetorians and the Urban cohorts.[100] The absence of the Urban Prefect in the diplomata is not really remarkable since it is accompanied by the absence of the Praetorian Prefect; moreover, it was the emperor, as commander-in-chief, who granted privileges to his veterans. For the inscriptions there are arguments and counter-arguments;[101] the difficult case of ILS 2012 may be explained quite simply as a loyal dedication from all those attached to the *castra Praetoria*, in order of seniority. At no stage was the Urban Prefect ever based there, whereas the Praetorian Prefect as a military commander was; the tribunes of the Urban cohorts were military men, and so presumably living with their troops. The *equites singulares* under their tribune were under the overall command of the Praetorian Prefect but they are not listed in this inscription for the simple reason that they were quartered elsewhere – like the Urban Prefect. The literary[102] and legal evidence seems to me decisive in the absence of some new overwhelming testimony from an inscription.

But the strongest argument of all is the simple constitutional position of the Urban Prefect as an independent magistrate with *iurisdictio* and therefore *coercitio*, whose function, his *provincia*, was quite specifically to restrain, by force if necessary, the

98 Durry (1938): 15 & 166f; von Domaszewski (1967): 16–17.
99 ILS 2012 (= CIL VI 1009).
100 E.g. ILS 1993 (= CIL III p.853).
101 ILS 2117 (= CIL IX 1617) of AD 146 seems fairly clinching for the Urban Prefect's command: a decurion from Beneventum 'militavit in coh. I [?XI] urb ad latus tribunor., fuit secutor, optio valetudi., optio carcaris [sic], singularis, benefic. tribuni, a quaestionib. factus per Annium Verum praef. urbis, et tessarius, optio, signif., fisci curator, optio ab act., cornicul. trib., benef. Valeri Asiatici praet. [sic] urb., missus ab imp. Hadriano Aug. [AD 134]'.
102 E.g. Statius *Silv.*1.4.9–16.

servile population and the excesses of the mob.[103] The nature
of this function is confirmed by the literary evidence of the first,
second and third centuries.[104] It is inconceivable that this force
was taken away from him; it is even more inconceivable that it
should have been taken away from him and given to the Praetorian Prefect without adverse comment from the literary sources
which are predominantly senatorial and anti-Praetorian. The
only odd situation is connected with the fall of Sejanus, when
Tiberius quite clearly was unable to trust the Praetorians; it
is not, however, clear why he used the *vigiles* rather than the
Urban cohorts, unless it was for the tactical reason that they were
quartered separately, outside the camp, and so their movements
would not cause an alert[105] – but anyway this took place far
earlier than any supposed date of control by the Praetorian
Prefect of the Urban cohorts.

JURISDICTION: THE URBAN PREFECT
AND OTHERS

The creation of this new 'police' force by Augustus did not mean
the immediate supersession of the old authorities, but they do
fade away. The vigintisexvirate, reduced under Augustus to the
vigintivirate,[106] continued to provide for most the first step in a
public career,[107] but the *tresviri capitales* lost their fire-fighting
responsibilities to the *praefectus vigilum*[108] and their repressive
duties are rarely mentioned. Horace's upstart must (from the
poet's date of death) have been flogged by the *tresviri* before
the establishment of the *vigiles*, and probably of the Urban
cohorts. Tacitus, however, talking of Domitian, records that
'to the triumvirs was delegated the duty of burning in the
Comitium and the Forum the masterpieces of famous men'.[109]
The aediles too did not at once lose their police functions; Dio
records them rather than the *tresviri* as being responsible for

103 Tac. *Annals* 6.11; D.1.12.1.12, Ulpian *de off. p. u.*
104 Velleius 2.98.1; Statius *Silv.* 1.4; e.g. Martial 2.17; Juvenal 13.157ff.
105 Dio 58.9; and Macro, who was about to take command of the Praetorians,
    was a former *praefectus vigilum*.
106 Dio 54.26.
107 Tac. *Annals* 3.29; Dio 60.5.8; SHA *Didius* 1.
108 D.1.15.1, Paul *de off. praef. vig.*
109 Tac. *Agricola* 2.

the burning of Cremutius Cordus' books in AD 25.[110] We are
told that their powers were restricted in 56,[111] and indeed the
other references to their jurisdiction during the Principate fall
more under Control of Services in the *cura urbis*. Street crime
seems to have become the province of the Urban Prefect, and
of his subordinate, the Prefect of the Night Watch.

The Prefect of the Night Watch had duties additional to
his fire-fighting responsibilities, though the latter included
the power to punish with a beating – or to let off with a
warning – those who carelessly allowed a fire to start. He had
jurisdiction over 'fire-setters, house-breakers, thieves, robbers,
resetters, unless the offender is so wicked or so notorious that
he is to be remitted to the Urban Prefect'.[112] He was ordered,
moreover, to send to the Urban Prefect men proved to have set
fires deliberately;[113] such a crime within the City was seen as
particularly atrocious.[114] House-breakers frequented tenement
blocks and warehouses, and their custodians could be punished
for negligence; even imperial slaves were not immune from
being put to the question by the Prefect of the Night Watch if
the warehouses in their care had been broken into.[115] He also
had jurisdiction over the changing-room attendants at the baths
and concerning any dishonest dealings with bathers' clothes.[116]
It seems likely that the burglars and house-breakers were the
kind of criminals who would readily be met on the regular
nightly patrols of the *vigiles*; perhaps the specific concern with
thieving at the baths was linked with their access to a water
supply which might regularly bring patrols of *vigiles* there.
The regular patrols would also seem to explain why Severus
required the Prefect to search out fugitive slaves and return
them to their owners. Runaway slaves, who were not collected
by their owners, were sold off by the Prefect.[117]

We hear elsewhere of the jurisdiction over thieves. A slave,

---

110 Tac. *Annals* 4.35; Dio 57.24.
111 Tac. *Annals* 13.28; the penalties they could impose were reduced.
112 D.1.15.3.1, Paul *de off. praef. vig.*
113 D.1.15.4, Ulpian *de off. p. u.*
114 *PS* 5.20.1–5. The reason was certainly not lest he should be judge in his
own cause; Roman magistrates and officials regularly exercised jurisdiction
in their own spheres of administration.
115 Cf. D.19.2.56, Paul *de off. praef. vig.*
116 D.1.15.3.1–2 & 5, Paul *de off. praef. vig.*
117 *PS* 1.6a.6 – through his office staff.

suspected of theft, was handed over to be put to the question, on the understanding that he should be returned to his owner if innocent; the victim of the theft handed the slave over to the Prefect of the Night Watch as if he had been caught in the act, and the Prefect had him executed.[118] One who brought a thief before the Prefect of the Night Watch (or a provincial governor) must choose what level of reparation he was seeking, because of the risk of torture to the thief.[119] There is also the curious case of the fullers, heard by successive Prefects, which took place over the period 226–44. They were probably defending themselves against the claims of the fisc; there is no certain agreement as to the grounds for the jurisdiction of the Prefect of the Night Watch, although both prefect and fullers needed access to plentiful supplies of water.[120]

The Urban Prefect himself had, by Ulpian's day, jurisdiction over all criminal matters whatsoever within the City and in Italy (or within a 100-mile radius from Rome).[121] His jurisdiction specifically included hearing slaves who had sought asylum from their owners, and the complaints of patrons against their freedmen – both matters likely to touch the concept of public order.[122] Similarly, he had explicit jurisdiction over cases arising from the interdicts *quod vi aut clam* or *unde vi*, for such force was defined as that which affected the rule of law and public order.[123] For much the same reasons, he had jurisdiction over money-lenders and bankers,[124] since their dealings affected public confidence. During the second century, incidentally, the repression of the Christians became a recorded part of the Urban Prefect's duties, whether based primarily on his duty to suppress illegal societies,[125] or on his general care for the City and its ancient customs. Along with his power to deport to an island (a penalty for the upper classes) or to send to the mines

---

118 D.12.4.15, Pomponius 22 *ad Sab*; the text does not throw doubt on the Prefect's competence, but is concerned with the remedy available to the slave's owner against the victim of the theft.
119 D.47.2.57(56).1, Julian 22 *dig*.
120 CIL VI 266 or FIRA iii 165 (p.510ff). See also Mommsen (1887) II 1058; de Robertis (1982).
121 D.1.12.1pr & 4, Ulpian *de off. p. u*; e.g. h.t.1.5, idem.
122 D.1.12.1.1–2 & 8 & 10, idem.
123 D.1.12.1.6, idem.
124 D.1.12.1.9, idem; h.t.2, Paul *de off. p. u*.
125 D.1.12.1.14, Ulpian *de off. p. u*.

(one for the lower orders), he could sentence people to death.[126] Naturally he had the power to ban people from the City and, perhaps more practically, from attending the shows.[127] His jurisdiction continued in the Later Empire,[128] unaffected by the disbandment of the Urban cohorts in the fourth century.

THE TOOLS OF LAW AND ORDER

Recognisable uniforms must have been useful in maintaining order on the streets; arresting people for the commission of statutory crimes was not, as we have said, a normal function of the Roman state. We also know, from inscriptions and reliefs, that the soldiers of the Urban cohorts normally carried a sword and a short knife, and one or two objects of more doubtful purpose.[129] Pertinax forbade[130] the Praetorians to carry axes, or to strike innocent passers-by. The *vigiles'* equipment was designed for fire-fighting, but those members of the corps who served on the staff of the Prefect presumably had available *fustes* and *flagella* and the necessary implements to interrogate slaves.[131] But more important than the formal equipment with which the City-based corps were armed must have been their discipline. This certainly could break down, as in 189[132] and 238,[133] but normally it must have overawed a mob, particularly since the Praetorians had mounted squadrons[134] and modern mounted police are usually very effective at crowd control.

Discipline was imposed through the military organisation of the three corps. In both Praetorian and Urban cohorts and in the *vigiles* we find, below the centurionate,[135] a *commentariensis*[136]

126 D.1.12.1.3 & 10, idem; ACM *Mart. S. Justini et al* 1 & 5; *Mart. SS. Ptolemaei* and *Lucii* 16.
127 D.1.12.1.13, Ulpian *de off. p. u.* Cf. ch. 9.
128 CTh 9.40.5 – AD 364 addressed to Symmachus; Symmachus *Ep.*10.36, referring to a treason trial; Cassiodorus *Var.* 4.23; Nov. J. 13.1.2 – AD 535.
129 See the illustration of an *urbanus* in D & S V, 603.
130 Herodian 2.4.1.
131 D. 1.15.3.1–2; h.t.4, Paul *de off. praef. vig.*
132 Dio 73.13; Herodian 1.12–13. See Whittaker (1964).
133 Herodian 7.11–12; SHA *Max. et Balb.* 9–10.
134 ILS 2053–5 (= CIL IX 3573, VI 2672, VI 2601); ILS 2081. Keppie (1984): 188, holds that the *equites singulares Augusti* acted as the Praetorians' cavalry arm; Grosso (1966): 902, remarks on the confusion between *equites singulares* and mounted Praetorians.
135 Breeze (1974).
136 ILS 2073 (Praetorians); ILS 2157 (= CIL VI 1058) (*vigiles*); CIL VI 8402.

who held a senior post subordinate only to the *cornicularius*. We know from Lydus[137] that in the Later Empire the *commentariensis* was the official in charge of criminal proceedings; it was his duty to see to the arrest and safe-keeping of the accused, his production before the Prefect, the correct recording of the proceedings, the questioning of the accused under torture, and the carrying out of the sentence on conviction. There were at that period *applicitarii* to do the actual arresting, *clavicularii* to guard, and *lictores* to torture; the death stroke was probably also their function.

These duties must also have been performed during the Principate – except in the case of condemnation to the beasts, when it appears that it was the job of the gladiators to finish off the condemned[138] – and it is tempting to think that they were already the executive responsibility of the *commentariensis*. The Digest texts point this way; *speculatores*, *optiones* and *commentarienses* are all in a position to rob the condemned.[139] Further, there are references in the Acts of the Christian Martyrs to the *commentariensis*, among others, being involved, for example, in bringing Crispina before the tribunal[140]; it is, however, usually unspecified *beneficiarii* (roughly, senior sergeants or warrant officers) who carry out these tasks, and they are mostly – in the nature of things, since most of these trials took place outwith Rome – from the office staff of a provincial governor.

The other member of the office staff in the prefectures who seems to have been concerned particularly with law and order is the *a quaestionibus* or *quaestionarius*. He existed in all three corps, and ranked as a *beneficiarius* in the Praetorians[141] and *vigiles*,[142] although in the Urban cohorts he seems merely an *immunis* (or junior NCO).[143] The *quaestionarius'* job must have been the supervision of interrogations, which in the case of slaves and, increasingly from the mid-second century, of *humiliores*, were under torture. The imperial rescripts on this topic suggest that simple brutality was not required, though it must often have

137 Lydus *de mag*.3.16.
138 ACM *Passio SS. Perpetuae et Felicitatis* 21.6: Exinde iam exanimis prosternitur cum ceteris ad iugulationem solito loco.
139 D.48.20.6, Ulpian 10 *de off. proconsulis*.
140 ACM *Passio S. Crispinae* 1.1; 3.1
141 ILS 2145 (= CIL VI 2755); 2146 (= IX 1617) does not give the corps.
142 ILS 2157 (= CIL VI 1058), twice.
143 ILS 2115 (= CIL VI 2880).

been present: 'It is stated in imperial enactments that reliance should not always be placed on torture – but not never, either', for some are so tough 'that the truth can in no way be squeezed out of them' while others can be induced to say anything.[144]

But was the *quaestionarius* also the officer in charge of external investigation, door-to-door enquiries? We know that these must have existed to some degree; we hear once of the Emperor Tiberius investigating the scene personally and deciding that there had indeed been a crime.[145] It was the responsibility of the Prefect of the Night Watch 'to search out fugitives', and the notion of investigation seems implicit in Varro: 'Quaestors [are named] from "quaerere", to inquire, who investigate [the use of] public monies and illegal doings, which the *tresviri capitales* investigate nowadays.'[146] There was also clearly security work, or political espionage.[147] While any detective work undertaken was probably rudimentary, it seems that one might hope to get help from the authorities in recovering property, and surely a patrol would follow a trail of blood and make inquiries at the house or inn into which it disappeared.[148]

Ranking definitely below the *commentariensis* and the *quaestionarius* there was on the prefecture staffs another job, that of the *optio carceris*,[149] which clearly was the charge of the prison; it is not, however, certain whether this was the unit's own prison, the 'glass-house', or a prison used for offenders from the general public. We also find in the reign of Valerian an *optio custodiarum* with at least one *clavicularius* under him.[150] (In the provinces, it is certain that legionary as well as municipal prisons sometimes held civilians.[151]) Ptolemaeus is said to have been arrested by a 'hekatontarchos' and held a long while in prison before he was brought before the Urban Prefect;[152] this could have been the Carcer on the lower slopes of the Capitoline, but where the appearance seems to have followed rapidly on the arrest, as with

144 D.48.18.1.23, Ulpian 8 *de off. proconsulis*.
145 Tac. *Annals* 4.22.
146 Varro *LL* 5.81.
147 Philostratus *Apollonius of Tyana* 4.43; Tertullian *de fuga* 13.5; Eusebius *HE* 5.18.6.
148 Apuleius, *Met.* 3.3; cf. Davies (1989), ch. 8, 'The investigation of some crimes in Roman Egypt', pp.175–85.
149 ILS 2117, cited above; ILS 2126.
150 CIL III 15190–1.
151 ACM *Passio SS Perpetuae et Felicitatis* 7.9.
152 ACM *Mart. Ptolemei et Lucii* 11–12; Eusebius *HE* 4.17.

Justin and his companions,[153] the Urban cohorts' own prison or guardhouse seems possible.

The argument for the existence of other prisons in Rome than the traditional one set into the Capitoline is supported by the thought that an increase in policing usually leads to an increase in the discovery of criminals – whether of crime too is a much-argued point – so we could expect to find more need after the establishment of the Urban cohorts; there is also Juvenal's lament for the happy days when one prison sufficed the City.[154] On balance then I think we can detect specific officers of law and order in the office staffs of the prefectures. This view is reinforced by the many references in the Acts of the Christian Martyrs to the *officia* of the provincial governors conducting the persecutions, and this includes both clerical and executive staff, though usually not precisely specified.

Equipment included weapons and horses – I believe that in India police boots were found to be very effective against bare or sandalled feet, and Juvenal attests[155] the same in Rome – which allowed order to be enforced. Discipline, which meant an organisation with a staff, represented order. The third element in the law and order enforcement process was a place of safe custody, whether for drunks (not many of them, it seems) or those condemned to death. Vitruvius put the town planner's view: the prison should be close to the Forum, the Curia and other such public places.[156] This rule certainly applied to the Carcer, reputedly built under King Ancus, described vividly by Sallust, and apparently still in use in the fourth century AD.[157] It was a proper part of the administration, as is witnessed by the existence of prison rations, in the Republic[158] as well as in the Principate.[159] In the Republic it was the normal place for executing people,[160] at least those of status, unless they deserved to be hurled from the Tarpeian Rock,[161] which seems

153 ACM *Mart. Justini et al.*
154 Juvenal 3.312–14.
155 Juvenal 16.24–5.
156 Vitruvius 5.2.1.
157 Sallust *Cat.*55; Livy 1.33.8; Ammianus 28.1.57.
158 Sallust *e hist. frag.*3.48.19.
159 ACM *Passio Montani et Lucii* 6.5; cf. *Passio S. Perpetuae* 17.1 for the condemned person's last meal.
160 Livy 34.44; Val. Max. 5.4.7; 9.12.6; Tac. *Annals* 3.51.
161 Tac. *Annals* 6.19 records such an execution for incest of a man who owned large properties in Spain.

largely reserved for criminals of the lower orders (and must have been messy). In the Empire there was an increasing tendency to condemn people to the beasts or to fight as gladiators, or simply to execute them at a spectacle.

The final question in this section is probably unanswerable: what did an *urbanus* or a detachment from the Urban cohorts (and in what force did they patrol?) say when someone was arrested? Did the arresting officer cite his authority as must, in theory, a modern policeman, or did he simply tell the suspect to come along? And, while we know that the Roman system of criminal prosecution was a private process, with individual citizens laying informations, how far was this true of street crime? There was of course the legal simplification of the unity of person between the arresting authority and the jurisdictional office; much street crime was presumably dealt with by *coercitio*, by repression not by due process with a trial.

But when the offence did not fall within the jurisdiction of the arresting authority, for example, when the Prefect of the Night Watch arrested someone for deliberate fire-setting, did the Prefect (or the sub-prefect) or the tribune or centurion or even the *optio* concerned submit a *libellus* to the Urban Prefect? Was he technically a *delator*? The only hint that I have found to confirm this view is the report in Tacitus: 'Celsus, tribune of an urban cohort, although among the informers in the case, released Appius and Claudius from their peril [by his evidence]',[162] but this may merely be private enterprise. It is also possible that when the *triumviri capitales* are heard of before the aediles, their appearance may be as accusers rather than as witnesses.[163] Delators, informers, are represented as private citizens, but then, for the majority of offences in England and Wales, the accusation is still formally made by a policeman in private guise. Probably, in view of Roman distinctions of rank, it would be inconceivable for an ordinary soldier to charge one of the *honestiores*, but a tribune would be himself an *honestior*; and with *humiliores* it may be that *coercitio* often sufficed. Plautus' slave says he will have no chance to defend himself;[164] how widely was this true? Did a man on his own have to be able to refer to some patron to guarantee his *bona fides*?

---

162 Tac. *Annals* 6.9.
163 Asconius *in Milonian*. OCT p.37.
164 Plautus *Amph.* 155ff.

13

PUBLIC ORDER

This chapter is not concerned with violence as a political weapon, violence organised by the upper classes, but rather with the have-nots whom any sophisticated government represses, whether in 57 BC or AD 139, or even the 1990s. What sort of behaviour was unacceptable enough for someone to be arrested? What class of person could be arrested? How often were arrests made? Accusations of murder, of adultery, of forgery, still less of treason, are not of concern here; by presumption of law everyone knows that these are crimes and refrains from committing them. What sort of behaviour would be brought to the Urban Prefect's attention? Would there then have been immediate *coercitio*, that is, administrative discipline by the prefect or tribune, or might a charge have been formulated? The frequency of a particular disorder could lead to its explicit criminalisation.[1] Resolutions of the Senate, rather than statute or even edict, might suitably condemn such behaviour.

VIOLENCE AND SEDITION

The first, and most obvious, instance of such behaviour was riot and public violence (not necessarily *vis publica*, which was a technical term). In the Republic there was little to check this and, as Lintott has pointed out,[2] the worst offenders were those whose duty it was to deal with such offences. Despite Augustus' establishment of the Urban cohorts (and the Praetorians and *vigiles*), our sources tend to present him as quelling disturbances

---

1 E.g. shepherds taking to banditry – CTh 9.30.2 & 5 – AD 364 & 399; CTh 9.31.1 – AD 409; cf. Cicero *pro Cluentio* 59.161; Fronto *ad Marcum* 2.12 (Nab. 35).
2 Lintott (1968): 4; 204–5.

by himself, though Suetonius does tell us that the prevalence of footpads led to the stationing of soldiers in the localities, and that the factions of the *collegiati* led to their suppression;[3] that last measure had previously been taken in 64 BC. There is a rather fine passage in SHA *Thirty Pretenders* about the causes of riot among the Egyptians:

> for merely because a greeting was omitted, or a place in the baths refused, or meat and vegetables withheld, or on account of the boots of slaves (when a slave of the curator of Alexandria was killed by a soldier for asserting his sandals better than the soldier's), or some other such thing, they have broken out into riots so dangerous that troops have been armed to quell them.[4]

Roman riots are not recorded as having started through omitted greetings, nor indeed in the baths – though refusal of a place there might give rise to an action for iniuria – but they did start in the circus and the theatre; above all, failures in the food supply provided occasions for tumult.

Under Tiberius there were riots in the theatre,[5] and trouble about the corn supply on at least one occasion found expression there.[6] Claudius once had to run from an infuriated mob and he only escaped 'through the throng of soldiers',[7] here presumably the Praetorians. Under Nero there were also disorders in the circus, some of which he is said to have encouraged; he is reported as having forbidden 'soldiers' to be present at the theatre[8] and this seems to have aggravated matters; they were, however, back on duty within months. These were presumably the Urban cohorts, judging from Tacitus' description of them as the cohort customarily on guard at the games,[9] since it was one of the Urban Prefect's duties to maintain order at the various spectacles;[10] to this end, indeed, he had power to refuse admission to those who had misbehaved, a power shared

3 Suet. *Aug*.32.
4 SHA *Tyr.Trig*.22.
5 Tac. *Annals* 1.77.
6 Tac. *Annals* 6.13.
7 Tac. *Annals* 12.43; Suet. *Claud*.18.
8 Dio 61.8.
9 Tac. *Annals* 13.24–5: statio cohortis adsidere ludis solita demovetur.
10 D.1.12.1.12, Ulpian *de off. p. u.*

by provincial governors.[11] There is another reference in Tacitus to 'soldiers' at the theatre in Nero's time; he tells us that they stood beside the blocks of seats to act as claqueurs, spurring on the audience's applause.[12] This sounds a more suitable task for a bodyguard than for the Urban cohorts, but under a whimsical sovereign like Nero one cannot be sure.

The civil wars of 69 fall outside the problems of day-to-day administration. The emperors from Nerva to Marcus Aurelius seem largely to have managed to avoid riot, but we get a severe outbreak, concerned with the food supply, under Commodus in 189/190, when the Praetorians and the Urban cohorts were on different sides.[13] A serious outbreak of violence in 223 was actually caused by the Praetorians, who murdered their Prefect, Ulpian.[14] Major riots in 238 had gladiators being released from their barracks and, with the people, attacking the *castra Praetoria*.[15] And there seems to have been a really serious outbreak of rioting connected with Aurelian's reform of the currency.[16] The role of Rome's *proprius miles* in all this should have been clear, but it was not.

Second, there was behaviour which would presumably have fallen under the Julian Acts on *vis publica* or *privata*,[17] committed by persons one could describe as muggers. Juvenal expressed the imagined fears of one carrying even a few valuables if he went out by night, afraid of the robber, trembling at shadows, where the empty-handed traveller could whistle at the

11 D.1.12.1.13, ibid.; 48.19.28.3, Callistratus 6 *de cognit.*
12 Tac. *Annals* 16.5: per cuneos stabant. This way of stationing the security forces doubtless explains the fate of the unfortunate spectator whose chance remark led to his prompt death in the arena – Suet. *Dom.*10.
13 Dio 73.13; Herodian 1.12; cf. Dio 74.13.
14 Dio 80.2 (Loeb p. 481). *Turba* is defined by Ulpian himself in D.47.8.4.3, 56 *ad ed*, citing Labeo; two can make a brawl, but a mob consists of ten or so persons at least.
15 Herodian 7.11–12; SHA *Maximin.*20, also in *Max. & Balb.*10.
16 Eutropius 9.14; SHA *Aurelian* 38.
17 D.48.6 and 48.7. The distinction between the two offences is not entirely clear in our sources. *Vis publica* covered going armed in public or having an armed gang, even without further action, as well as offences of violence such as rape; it also included abuse of power by a magistrate or official – 48.6.7, Ulpian *de off. proconsulis*. *Vis privata* included violence by unarmed gangs, other offences of violence, and self-help where one should have used due process of law. The praetor also issued interdicts *de vi* and *de vi armata*, and here, at least, sticks and stones were interpreted as arms – D.43.16.3.2, Ulpian 69 *ad ed.*

brigand;[18] even after getting home there were burglars to be feared.[19] In another poem he talked about crimes of sacrilege;[20] when a statue was found scraped of its gilding or a temple robbed of its chalices, surely there must have been an investigation. Suetonius, Tacitus and Dio all referred to Nero's mohock habits, and the bad example they set.[21]

Third, there is sedition that has not yet broken out into violence, secret or foreign rites, and illegal *collegia*. The boundary here between what was prohibited and what was tolerated was not always at all clear in law.[22] In the Republic there had presumably been rumours about the Bacchanals before an information was laid that could lead to action being taken.[23] In 139 BC the Peregrine Praetor banished astrologers from the City and from Italy for exciting shallow minds to their own profit.[24] The cult of Isis was not in itself forbidden, but the Senate ordered the demolition of the newly constructed temple and, because no-one dared lay hand on the work, the consul himself seized an axe and inflicted the first blow.[25] One wonders if the *tresviri* had reported that matters were getting somewhat out of hand in Isis-worship.

Among foreign cults in the Principate the Jews and the Christians seem to have been the chief objects of suspicion, but the 'Egyptians' were in trouble in 21 BC[26] and Agrippa, acting under his *cura urbis*, forbade their rites to be practised within a mile of the City. They were in disfavour again around AD 18, when the Jews were also involved. Four thousand Egyptians and Jews, those who were freedmen, were sent off to repress brigands in the notoriously unhealthy island of Sardinia; the others were to leave Italy, unless they abandoned their unholy worship by a given date.[27] The Jews and the Egyptians are recorded by Suetonius also as having been repressed by Tiberius,[28] and Claudius later expelled them from

18 Juvenal 10.19–22.
19 Juvenal 3.302–5.
20 Juvenal 13.147–53.
21 Tac. *Annals* 13.25; Suet. *Nero* 26; Dio 61.8–9.
22 D.47.22.1 & 3, Marcian 3 *inst.* & 2 *iud. publ.*
23 Livy 39.8–19; Val. Max. 1.3.1; Bauman (1990).
24 Val. Max. 1.3.3.
25 Val. Max. 1.3.4.
26 Dio 54.6.
27 Tac. *Annals* 2.85.
28 Suet. *Tib.*36.

Rome for creating disturbances.[29]

The persecution of the Christians is a topic on which much has been written,[30] but it must be remembered that it was not systematic. The legal basis for the harsh measures recorded remains largely unclear, although it is a fact that non-citizens were always liable to *coercitio* and that there seems to have been a constitutional convention, stemming from the city-state concept, that undesirables could be kept from Rome, even if not convicted of anything, by the Senate and later by the emperor.[31] Ulpian is cited as writing that those discharged with ignominy from the urban cohorts are obviously exempt from tutories, since they are not allowed to enter the City, whereas the normal ex-soldier with a dishonourable discharge did not have exemption.[32] We find in the Martyrdom of Ptolemaeus that Lucius joined him in his martyrdom because he protested to the Urban Prefect, Q. Lollius Urbicus, that 'he has not been convicted of adultery, fornication, murder, clothes-stealing, robbery, or of any crime whatsoever' and then admitted that he too was a Christian.[33] The Urban Prefect was formally responsible, at latest from Septimius Severus' time but probably earlier, for hearing accusations against those alleged to have joined illegal societies.[34] *Collegia* were always regarded with suspicion; they were restricted by Augustus and more severely by Hadrian (but it is not evident that this was the usual legal ground for persecuting Christians[35]).

UNDESIRABLES

Attitudes towards Christianity and other alien religions are perhaps illuminated by looking at the Roman treatment of astrologers, philosophers, *mathematici*, and other such.[36] (Diocletian referred

---

29 Suet. *Claud*.25.
30 In the first place, Pliny *Ep*.10.96–7; see also Barnes (1968): 32–50.
31 Cf. D.48.22.13, Paul; Dio 37.9 records that in 65 BC resident aliens were banished from the City, but apparently through a law passed on the proposal of a plebeian tribune.
32 D.27.1.8.9 & 5, Modestinus 3 *excus*.
33 ACM *Mart. Ptolemei et Lucii*.
34 D.1.12.1.14, Ulpian *de off. p. u.*
35 Despite Mayer-Maly (1956). In ACM *Mart. Justini et al*.3, the Urban Prefect asks Justin where the Christians meet, but does not pursue the issue.
36 E.g. Cramer (1954); MacMullen (1966).

to 'the damnable art of mathematics';[37] there was in the ancient world no clear distinction between astronomy and astrology.) They might be connected with foreign cults, their beliefs might be of foreign origin, and this was clearly an important argument against them: they were not Roman, they had ideas – and might be expected to spread them. (They might also of course, under the developed law of the Empire, be treasonable if they started forecasting the emperor's length of life or the identity of the next emperor.) But Romans of standing were interested in philosophy, and that meant Greek philosophy, and many too, including emperors, were interested in astrology and whether their fate was in themselves or in their stars. So these classes of person were not precisely on the wrong side of the law; they were tolerated, except when external circumstances suggested that they should not be.[38]

In 33 BC Agrippa, as aedile, expelled the astrologers and charlatans;[39] there may also have been a link with the fact that Antony's base was in the East. Under Tiberius there was another purge;[40] a resolution of the Senate was passed expelling *mathematici* and *magi* from Italy, and some were executed;[41] a legal source, though a late one, tells us that, under a Senate resolution of AD 17, *mathematici*, Chaldeans, *arioli*, and such like were interdicted from fire and water and their property confiscated, but if they were non-citizens they were put to death.[42] At that time – though not later – it was agreed that it was not their knowledge, their skill, which was being penalised but its profession; and nearly all the subsequent emperors forbade anyone to involve himself in any way.[43]

Tacitus records of AD 52 that the astrologers were banished from Italy by a fierce but fleeting resolution of the Senate;[44] their associates were punished.[45] 'Nero was opposed to philosophy,

37 CJ 9.18.2 – AD 294.
38 Compare the report of Dio 55.26 that in AD 6 the gladiators and the slaves up for sale in the City were removed to a distance of 100 miles because of the severe famine; clearly there was no idea of permanent removal.
39 Dio 49.43.
40 Suet. *Tib.*63.
41 Tac. *Annals* 2.32.
42 *Coll.*15.2.1, confirmed by Dio 57.15.
43 *Coll.*15.2.2–3.
44 Tac. *Annals* 12.52: de mathematicis Italia pellendis factum senatus-consultum atrox et inritum.
45 Dio 61(60).33.

because he suspected its devotees of being addicted to magic and of being diviners in disguise; and at last the philosopher's mantle brought its wearers before the law courts';[46] Musonius was imprisoned, and was later encountered, having been condemned to forced labour in chains, digging Nero's canal across the Isthmus.[47] Nero took his departure for Greece in 66 only 'after issuing a proclamation that no-one should teach philosophy in public at Rome'.[48] Vitellius, in his brief reign, issued an edict forbidding astrologers to remain in Italy after 1 October 69,[49] and he executed some at least of those who stayed in the City.[50] In his turn Vespasian banished the astrologers from Rome, even though he was himself in the habit of consulting the best of them; he exiled the philosophers soon after.[51] Under Domitian there was further persecution of both groups.[52]

The attitude of the authorities is clear: both that such groups could be repressed, and that these prohibitions or persecutions, even when accompanied by severe penalties, were never intended as serious attempts to root out such people for good. They were measures taken when there was a particular danger to an emperor or a swell of hostility from public opinion. Thus Antoninus Pius took measures against trouble-makers in *Gallia Lugdunensis*, and Marcus Aurelius relegated an unwise prophet to an island.[53] It was a grey area in which people seem often to have been punished for what they might do rather than for what they had in fact done; 'sus' laws, repression based on mere suspicion, are not unique. And if provincial troops kept lists of undesirables, including Christians,[54] it seems safe to assume that similar lists were kept by the Prefect of the Night Watch or the Urban Prefect.

There were other groups too who were on occasion found undesirable or unpopular – or even too popular; these, however, seem distinct, because there was nothing secret or mysterious about them. Into this category come, above all, the actors,

46 Philostratus *Apollonius of Tyana* 4.35.
47 Philostratus *Apollonius of Tyana* 5.19.
48 Philostratus *Apollonius of Tyana* 4.47.
49 Dio 65(64).1.
50 Suet. *Vit.*14.
51 Dio 66(65).9 & 13.
52 Suet. *Dom.*10; Dio 67.13; Philostratus *Apollonius of Tyana* 7.4.
53 *Coll.* 15.2.4–5.
54 Tertullian *de fuga* 13.

although it could also include other public figures such as gladiators or charioteers, and even such innocents as the Greek tradesmen whose right to return to the City was expressly stated in 440.[55] Dealing with the actors could pose something of a problem, for they were popular with many of the emperors and extremely popular with the crowd. The only way in the Empire that public opinion could readily be shown was at the spectacles[56] – the theatre, the amphitheatre, the circus – and so the leading figures at these venues were dangerous as a focus, even though it must have been rare for any of them to have political ambitions.[57] We are told[58] that actors, like judgement debtors and those who had been confined to prison, were not protected by the Julian Act on *vis publica*, which protected citizens and other subjects too from arbitrary ill-treatment by those in office, because their behaviour was often *contra disciplinam publicam*.

Augustus was particularly fond of the theatre, as opposed to other forms of games, and he specifically gave actors the protection of the law; this however did not stop him dealing severely with actors who overstepped the mark.[59] Tacitus tells us that the Senate met early in Tiberius' reign and largely confirmed the actors' immunity from arbitrary flogging by magistrates.[60] This happy state of affairs did not last long; after a case of bloodshed at the theatre, Tiberius relegated not only the actors but also their prominent fans – *capita factionum*.[61] This episode seems distinct from the expulsion of actors from Rome for debauching the women and stirring up tumults.[62] (It seems to have been during such a time that, in AD 27, disaster occurred with the collapse of the new amphitheatre at Fidenae,[63] five miles out of the City and so licit even when performances in Rome were

55 *Nov. Val.*5; explicitly, they worked too hard and provided 'unfair' competition in the eyes of the native shop-keepers; there are modern analogies.
56 E.g. Cameron (1976). Cf. Dio's description – 76(75).4 – of a demonstration at the races where he was present.
57 SHA *Elag.*12 – twice; Dio 78.21.
58 PS 5.26.2; D.3.2.1, Julian 1 *ad ed*; 3.2.2.5, Ulpian 6 *ad ed*; cf. 3.2.3, Gaius *ad ed. prov*; 3.2.4pr-1, Ulpian 6 *ad ed*; 48.5.11.2, Papinian 2 *de adulteriis*; 48.5.25(24)pr, Macer 1 *pub.iud.*
59 Suet. *Aug.*45.
60 Tac. *Annals* 1.77.
61 Suet. *Tib.*37.
62 Dio 57.21; cf. Juvenal 6.64–6.
63 Tac. *Annals* 4.62–3; the Globe in Southwark was similarly outside the jurisdiction of the City of London.

forbidden.[64]) One of Caligula's first acts was to recall them.[65] In spite of his fondness for such diversions, Nero was eventually driven to expel actors from Italy, although clearly they were fairly soon recalled.[66] Domitian first forbade actors to appear in public;[67] later he expelled them, though Nerva recalled them.[68] Trajan recalled them after he had earlier sent them away[69] – it was clearly not a matter of contrasting attitudes taken by 'good' and 'bad' emperors, since even Commodus banished them.[70] And, as a coda, we also hear of a resolution of the Senate which ordered deportation to an island for anyone who composed a rude song affecting someone's reputation, or any other sort of lampoon[71] – shades of Naevius!

LOW LIFE

Then there were the people on the seamier side of society. Any security force will keep an eye on brothels, gambling-houses and sources of alcohol; any presumption of innocence for people concerned in running such places is weaker than normal.[72] Gambling was illegal,[73] for most of the year at least,[74] but, as with the street bookmakers more recently, no very serious effort seems to have been made to check it. Juvenal talks of men coming to the gaming tables not simply with purses but with whole treasure chests.[75] From Martial we hear how, betrayed by the sweet noise of the dice-box, the sodden gambler, just dragged from the back-street eating-house, asks mercy from the aedile; we learn too of the man who, at Saturnalia, is not fearfully watching for the aedile when

---

64 Though Tacitus, *Annals* 4.14, says that in AD 23 the actors were expelled from Italy, not just the City.
65 Dio 59.2; clearly they were still there under Claudius – Dio 60.7.
66 Tac. *Annals* 13.25 of AD 56; 14.21 of AD 60.
67 Suet. *Dom*.7.
68 Pliny *Pan*.46.2.
69 Pliny *Pan*.46.2; Dio 68.10 – he was particularly attached to the panto-mimes.
70 SHA *Comm*.3.
71 *PS* 5.4.15: : Qui carmen famosum in iniuriam alicuius vel alia quaelibet cantica quo agnosci possit composuerit, . . . in insulam deportatur.
72 E.g. *infames*, such as brothel-keepers, in D.3.2.4.2, Ulpian 6 *ad ed*; cf. the tavern wench who is below the law – CJ 9.9.28 – AD 326.
73 Horace refers to 'dice forbidden by statute' – *Odes* 3.24. 58; D.11.5.2.1, Paul 19 *ad ed*. See Kurylowicz (1985).
74 Suet. *Aug*.71.
75 Juvenal 1.88–90.

shaking the dice-box.[76] And there is Fronto's story of a certain censor who forbade dicing since the music which came from the gaming houses tempted him to dance.[77] Justinian was to restrict gambling because it led to blasphemy.[78]

Besides these there were the genuine petty criminals, since we must give the benefit of the doubt to the keepers of disreputable but not illegal establishments. We can look back from 395:

> Very many persons institute suits concerning a slave addicted to flight, a theft – manifest or not manifest, concerning an animal that has been seized, a slave, or thing moveable or moving, or property seized by force, or concerning the boundaries of small parcels of land, or concerning small cottages; and then they disturb your court under the guise of a criminal action. . . . Also cases relating to the theft of an animal are brought before you. Since therefore it is an indignity to your authority for you to judge these slight and very petty matters, We decree that only those criminal cases shall be heard by Your Sincerity which the worthy and deserved horror of a criminal inscription has covered.[79]

A familiar distinction is being drawn between solemn and summary procedure; in matters suitable for the latter there is a (realistic) lack of clarity about the frontiers of the criminal law. An inscription[80] leaves it unclear whether this enactment was dealing with the Praetorian Prefect's or the Urban Prefect's jurisdiction; the court of the Prefect of the Night Watch would probably have been more suitable. From the substantive side we hear of offences against *bonos mores*, for instance, when a person showers another with excrement, smears him with mud and filth, defiles waters, water pipes and reservoirs, or pollutes anything to the detriment of the public,[81] or again that an action

---

76 Martial 5.84: Et blando male proditus fritillo, Arcana modo raptus e popina, Aedilem rogat udus aleator; 14.1.3: Nec timet aedilem moto spectare fritillo.
77 Fronto *ad Marcum de or.*10.10 (Nab. 155).
78 CJ 3.43.1 & 2 – AD 529.
79 CTh 2.1.8 – AD 395.
80 ILS 792 (= CIL X 1692).
81 D.47.11.1.1, Paul 5 *sent*: veluti si quis fimo corrupto aliquem perfuderit, caeno luto oblinierit, aquas spurcaverit, fistulas lacus quidve aliud ad iniuriam publicam contaminaverit.

is given, proportionate to the offence, against itinerants who carry snakes around with them and produce them to the fear and hurt of anyone.[82]

Particular sorts of thief are specified in the legal texts: cut-purses, and pickpockets who slip into others' lodgings with a view to theft,[83] bath thieves and dishonest clothes-minders,[84] house-breakers and resetters,[85] most of whom we know fell under the jurisdiction of the Prefect of the Night Watch. A further special sort of thief was the thief of himself, the fugitive slave.[86] Like other automotive property, he might be merely a wanderer, but he was to be sought out, arrested, punished, and restored to his owner or, if that was not possible, sold off.[87] Labour-hungry employers were not to take him in and conceal him. Jurisdiction over fugitives also pertained to the Prefect of the Night Watch.[88]

The literary evidence records the occasional campaign against undesirables in the City; Herodian tells us that Rome was purged under Macrinus of criminals and informers, and also that the mob was hostile to Maximus (emperor with Balbinus) because as Urban Prefect he had been strict with the unstable rabble of the lower orders.[89]

CONTROL OF ANIMALS

A further problem related to law and order is the control of animals, whether dirty dogs or beasts more strange and savage. This was effected through the edict of the curule aediles,[90] themselves responsible for shows and spectacles as well as more mundane aspects of the *cura urbis*, which placed responsibility

---

82 D.47.11.11, Paul 1 *sent*: In circulatores, qui serpentes circumferent et proponunt, si cui ob eorum metum damnum datum est, pro modo admissi actio dabitur.
83 D.47.11.7, Ulpian 9 *de off. proconsulis: saccularii* and *derectarii*.
84 D.47.17.1, Ulpian 8 *de off. proconsulis*; 1.15.3.5, Paul *de off. praef. vig: fures balnearii* and *capsarii*.
85 D.47.18.1, Ulpian 8 *de off. proconsulis*; h.t.2, Paul *de off. praef. vig*; 47.16.1, Marcian 2 *pub. iud*; 1.15.3.1 & 2, Paul *de off. praef. vig: effractores* and *receptatores*.
86 E.g. D.47.2.61(60), Africanus 7 *quaest*.
87 Asconius *in Milonianum*, OCT p. 37; *PS* 1.6a.3–4 & 6.
88 D.1.15.4, Ulpian *de off. p. u*; cf. Suet. *Aug.32*.
89 Herodian 5.2.2; 7.10.6.
90 FIRA i 66 (p.391f); *Inst*. 4.9.1.

on the keepers of dogs as well as of wild animals – and there will have been many wild animals. Nobody was to keep a boar, wolf, bear, panther, lion, or dog, in a place where people commonly passed by in such a way that allowed anyone to be hurt. There was a fine if a free person was killed, reparation if he were injured, and double damages in case of other harm to property, including slaves. This was clearly a matter of public policy. In the ordinary way a man could not be responsible for a wild animal once it had escaped from his control, since he no longer had any right in it, but obviously the ever-increasing traffic in dangerous beasts made police measures necessary. (It seems likely that the Urban Prefect acquired this jurisdiction after he had become responsible for the 'disciplina spectaculorum'.)

The animals were brought to Rome in enormous numbers to be slaughtered at the games; while on the journey, there must have inevitably been night encampments close to the road – *qua volgo iter fiet*. In Rome itself some will have been kept in cages in the lower levels of the Colosseum, but that would presumably only house the beasts for the next day's show. Where were the others? There were certainly some special areas in the suburbs outside the City, for we know of a *vivarium* outside the *porta Praenestina*.[91] Further, there is the additional problem of whom one sued in case of injury or damage, for usually the animals were imported by magistrates or the emperor; one assumes that it was the head keeper who was held responsible – perhaps noxally.[92] But my guess is that a person who actually found a bear loose in the park probably screamed for the Urban cohorts. Quite likely, just as modern police do not like the risks of rounding up stray dogs, they would be slow in coming; perhaps gladiators might be sent by the contractor or official in charge of the entertainment.

Dogs were presumably a problem that people expected their slaves to deal with. We do hear of wolves coming into Rome in 23 BC and again in 16 BC, when people were killed;[93] in AD 211 two wolves were found on the Capitol, one of which was killed in the Forum and the other, later, outside the *pomerium*.[94] Wolves

---

91 ILS 2091 (= CIL VI 130); see also the other references in ch.11.
92 However, for a lower magistrate being sued, see Gellius 13.13, discussed in ch. 9.
93 Dio 53.33; 54.19.
94 Dio 78.1.

could have come down from the Abruzzi hills or they could have escaped from captivity; a household might well have weapons, hunting weapons, adequate for dealing with a wolf, but a lion would have posed more problems.

There was another legal control on animals which did not apply to wild beasts; there the aedilician edict remained in force. The owner of a domestic animal was normally liable for any damage it caused, through *pauperies*, which derived from the Twelve Tables. It applied where the loss was through the fault of no man.[95] There is some argument about what was meant by the damage having to be caused *'contra naturam'* – it is clear that one could not poke a bull with a stick and then sue the owner successfully – but then as now cats seem not to have been within anyone's responsibility.

'PUBLIC DISCIPLINE'

There seems to have been a gradual move away from the simple exercise of reactive *coercitio* by triumvir or aedile or praetor. As the City grew in the last two centuries of the Republic, and as public violence increased, effective policing must have become more difficult. Along with the establishment of a standing military force in the Urban cohorts, supplemented on occasion by the Praetorians, there was introduced a law, the *lex Julia de vi*, to control the exercise of authority and to prevent its abuse. Yet we find, probably increasingly, an extension of the class of infamous person not protected by the Julian Act,[96] the kind of person you could lawfully kill if you caught him in the act of adultery with your wife – such as a pimp, an actor or a performer on the stage as dancer or singer, or someone condemned in criminal proceedings.[97] The virtuous poor could be harassed with impunity in practice; some members of society lacked even the theoretical protection of the law. The concept of *disciplina publica* was invented to justify this, and was thereafter extended.

Behaviour *contra publicam disciplinam* was a reasonably obvious concept to the Romans of the later Principate, though its

95 *Inst.*4.9pr; D.9.1.*passim.*
96 *PS* 5.26.2, which excluded those who did anything *contra disciplinam publicam.*
97 D.48.5.25(24)pr, Macer 1 [*iud.*]*pub.*

boundaries are not entirely clear. For instance, illegal exactions by tax-farmers were to be repaid two- or three-fold and a criminal penalty also imposed; 'the one measure is demanded by the interests of private individuals, the other by the need for strong public discipline'. Irenarchs were in charge of public discipline and the regulation of behaviour. Caracalla laid down that where someone had made an immoral grant *contra disciplinam temporum meorum*, there was no right of recovery. Gordian held that the discipline of his time did not allow people to make dubious compromises with the fisc. Constantine too was concerned that governors should have a care for public discipline and the injuries suffered by the poorer classes.[98] In the local government of the City, we find the concept aimed at law and order, order rather than justice.

98 D.39.4.9.5, Paul 5 *sent*; 50.4.18.7, Arcadius Charisius *de muneribus civilibus*; CJ 4.7.2 – AD 215; 2.17.2 – AD 241; 1.40.2 – AD 328.

14

LOOSE ENDS

Writing a book like this drives home to the author how uneven our information is, how many questions we cannot answer, how many problems we wish we could solve, how many loose ends remain. For example, were there litters or chairs for hire as taxis? If only . . . I have mentioned the problems raised concerning the organisation of construction work, the enforcement of legal restrictions on traffic, the location of the harbour-master's office, the disposal of excrement and other refuse, the disposal of human corpses, the distribution of bread rather than grain, the back-stage organisation at shows and spectacles, the policing role of the Urban cohorts, to name the most obvious. There are, however, some particular areas of importance in Rome's public law which have not been touched upon, but should be mentioned briefly here.

The role of religion in Roman life is unclear, as is the extent to which it influenced official attitudes. One suspects that it was more important than the legal texts allow, due partly to their having been edited in a thoroughly Christian world. The literary evidence is both limited and fragmentary, which explains why there is a relative paucity of modern literature, and what there is seems mostly anthropological.[1] Epigraphic evidence suggests that it was more pervasive, but to what depth and how far it affected behaviour, is very difficult to tell. Certainly the observances of religion were important in Roman public life, but it was the religion of the Roman *patria* and not a matter of local government.

Finance also is difficult to comprehend. There are some studies

1 On religion generally see still Wissowa (1912), and also Latte (1967).

on Roman taxation and finance, helpful as far as they go, but their limitations highlight the enormous areas of our ignorance. This may partly be because the emperors paid out so much from their own resources; unlike medieval and early modern kings, they never had a problem of 'living of their own'. It is hard for us to imagine a society where such wealth is concentrated in so few hands – perhaps Saudi Arabia would be our nearest model. Our understanding of Rome's economy is being deepened every year, but relatively little springing from these advances falls strictly within the sphere of local government.

Defence is definitely not part of what we would regard as local government; we may consider in passing, as a modern analogue, the arguments over whether it is proper for local authorities to implement government policies on civil defence. So far as Rome is concerned, the practical need for it against outside enemies does not occur within the period covered by this book; Aurelian's Wall was not put to the test until the fifth century. Civil war raises different problems.

Jurisdiction poses serious difficulties. The law books, particularly Gaius' *Institutes*, imply a system where the praetor (by reason of his *imperium*) had always a residual jurisdiction, a *nobile officium*. He may indeed have had a more important role in local government matters than generally appears; the evidence of the interdicts supports this, as does our knowledge that the Peregrine Praetor heard cases when the *curator aquarum* had laid down the exercise of his office for the year.[2]

It is clear, however, that there were many competing jurisdictions in the Principate; in particular, the Urban Prefect's role was increasing. And what of aedilician jurisdiction? We hear of the curule aediles' edict concerning sales made in the markets and the streets of slaves and beasts of burden, and of the edict on the restraint of wild animals. But their *cura urbis* suggests that they dealt with a wider range of matters; this too may have passed away by the time the legal texts came to reflect the position of the Urban Prefect as head of all the City services. Yet matters like the renting of market stalls, the cleaning of the streets, the supervision of baths open to the public were long under the care of the aediles. Surely jurisdiction followed from their functions of policing bars and eating-houses, prostitution and gambling?

2 Frontinus *aq.*101.

And we know relatively little about the clerks[3], the office staffs, who were busy with the very large quantities of paperwork that the institutions of local government required, issuing licences, putting out jobs (which ranged from the tiny to the very large) to tender and keeping records.

Nevertheless, it is clear that Rome did function successfully over a long period as a populous and complex city. The death-rate[4] was appalling, but (as far as we can judge) not of a very different order from medieval Europe or the slums of some parts of the Third World even today. There were opportunities for recreation and leisure, freely or cheaply open to all inhabitants of the City; public health was an aim of public policy. The emperors may have seen the *plebs frumentaria* as a grateful *clientela*,[5] but basic food was provided regularly, again either freely or cheaply, for a significant proportion of the population – if not necessarily the neediest. Housing was probably the weakest feature of the Roman local government structure, but the picture of thousands sleeping rough seems somewhat unlikely, since surely the satirists or the Christian critics of society, such as Tertullian, would have called it to our attention. Rome could not have grown and survived as a city if social stability had not been normal. The aim of maintaining that stability, rather than philanthropy, seems to underlie and explain much that we know of the policies of local government.

3 See Purcell (1983).
4 E.g. Frier (1982); Hopkins (1983); Scobie (1986).
5 Sirks (1984): 4.

ADDENDA AND CORRIGENDA
FOR THE PAPERBACK EDITION

pp.100–1

While Frontinus says that the *procurator aquarum* was responsible for stamping the valves with their correct measurement, this is not confirmed by any archaeological evidence, and Frontinus' accuracy as a technical writer must not be taken for granted (Bruun (1991): 370–1). It also appears that pipes were often manufactured by private *plumbarii* working for the emperor (Bruun (1991): 355).

p.158

On the baking of bread for distribution see Sirks (1991b): Appendix 2; Tengström (1974): 82–8.

p.210

Addition to paragraph 2: e.g., the *lares compitales* mentioned in chapter 1; on which see Flambard (1981). Watson (1992) puts forward a convincing explanation for the secular nature of Roman private law.

BIBLIOGRAPHY

ABBREVIATIONS

For periodicals I have followed the conventions of *L'Année Philologique*, with the following exceptions where either they are not listed or I have kept the normal Roman law usage (*AP* version in brackets):

J.EcHist Journal of Economic History
LQR Law Quarterly Review
RHD Revue Historique de Droit Français et Étranger (RD)
TR Tijdschrift voor Rechtsgeschiedenis (TRG)
ZSS Zeitschrift Savigny-Stiftung für Rechtsgeschichte, romanistische Abteilung (ZRG)

Other abbreviations, excluding those for classical authors, where resort should be made to the *Oxford Classical Dictionary* (OCD) or the *Oxford Latin Dictionary* (OLD):

ACM Acts of the Christian Martyrs, ed. Musurillo
ANRW Aufstieg und Niedergang der römischen Welt, ed. Temporini
CIL Corpus Inscriptionum Latinarum
CJ Justinian's Code
CTh Theodosian Code
D-S Daremberg and Saglio
D. Digest
FIRA Fontes Iuris Romani Ante-Iustiniani, ed. Riccobono, Baviera, Arangio-Ruiz
G. Gaius' Institutes
ILS Inscriptiones Latinae Selectae, ed. Dessau
Inst. Institutes of Justinian
P&A Platner and Ashby
PS Pauli Sententiae
RE Pauly-Wissowa Real-Encyclopädie
RG Res Gestae, ed. Brunt and Moore

Adams, J. N. (1982) *The Latin Sexual Vocabulary*, London.

Alföldi, A. (1974) 'Les *praefecti urbi* de César' in *Mélanges d'histoire ancienne offerts à W. Seston*, Paris, 1–14.

Alzon, C. (1965) *Problèmes relatifs à la location des entrepôts en droit romain*, Paris.

Ammerman, A. J. (1990) 'On the origins of the Forum Romanum', *AJA* 94, 627–45.

Amulree, Lord (1973) 'Hygienic conditions in ancient Rome and modern London', *Medic. Hist.* 17, 244–55.

Anderson, J. C. jr (1982) 'Domitian, the Argiletum and the Temple of Peace', *AJA* 86, 101–10.

—— (1983) 'A topographical tradition in fourth century chronicles: Domitian's building program', *Historia* 32, 93–105.

—— (1984) *The Historical Topography of the Roman Imperial Fora*, Brussels.

Anderson, M. J. (ed.) (1965) *Classical Drama and its Influence. Essays for H. D. F. Kitto*, London.

Anderson, W. J. and Spiers, R. P. (1927) *The Architecture of Greece and Rome*; vol.II – Ashby, T. (ed.) *The Architecture of Ancient Rome*, London.

André, J. (1961) *L'alimentation et la cuisine à Rome*, Paris.

—— (1980) 'La notion de *Pestilentia* à Rome', *Latomus* 39, 3–16.

—— (1987) *Etre médecin à Rome*, Paris.

Angelis d'Ossat, G. de (1943) *Tecnica costruttiva e impianti delle terme*, Rome.

Ankum, H. (1980) 'Afrikan *Dig*.19.2.33: Haftung und Gefahr bei der *publicatio* eines verpachteten oder verkauften Grundstücks', *ZSS* 97, 157–80.

Antaya, R. (1980) 'The etymology of *pomerium*', *AJPh* 101, 184–9.

Arnheim, M. T. W. (1970) 'Vicars in the Later Roman Empire', *Historia* 19, 593–606.

Ashby, T. (1901) 'Recent excavations in Rome', *CR* 15, 136–42.

—— (1923) 'Rome', *Town Planning Review* 10, 43–52.

—— (1935) *The Aqueducts of Ancient Rome*, Oxford.

—— and Reynolds, P. K. B. (1923) 'The *castra peregrinorum*', *JRS* 13, 152–67.

Auguet, R. (1972) *Cruelty and Civilization: The Roman Games*, English tr., London.

Babled, H. (1892) *De la cura annonae chez les romains*, Paris.

Badian, E. (1974) 'The quaestorship of Tiberius Nero', *Mnemosyne* 27, 160–72.

Balsdon, J. P. V. D. (1969) *Life and Leisure in Ancient Rome*, London.

Balzarini, M. (1969) 'In tema di repressione *extra ordinem* del furto nel diritto classico', *BIDR* 11, 203–311.

Barnes, T. D. (1968) 'Legislation against the Christians', *JRS* 58, 32–50.

—— (1978) *The Sources of the Historia Augusta*, Brussels.

Barton, I. M. (ed.) (1989a) *Roman Public Buildings*, Exeter.

—— (1989b) 'Religious buildings,' in Barton, I. M. (ed.), *Roman Public Buildings*, Exeter, 67–96.

Basanoff, V. (1939) *Pomerium Palatinum*, Rome.

Baudot, A. (1973) *Musiciens romains dans l'antiquité*, Montreal.

Bauman, R. A. (1974) 'Criminal prosecution by the aediles', *Latomus* 33, 245–64.

—— (1990) 'The suppression of the Bacchanals: five questions', *Historia* 39, 334–48.

Beare, W. (1964) *The Roman Stage* 3rd edn, London.

—— (1965) 'Plautus, Terence and Seneca', in Anderson, M. J. (ed.) *Classical Drama and its Influence. Essays for H.D.F. Kitto*, London, 101–15.

Beaujeu, J. (1975) 'Les jeux sacerdotaux du Haut Empire', *BICS* 22, 109–24.

Béchard, F. (1860) *Droit municipal dans l'antiquité*, Paris.

Beloch, J. (1886) *Die Bevölkerung der griechisch-römischen Welt*, Leipzig.

Below, K.-H. (1953) *Der Arzt im römischen Recht*, Munich.

Benario, H. W. (1958) 'Rome of the Severi', *Latomus* 17, 712–22.

Berger, A. (1953) *Encyclopaedic Dictionary of Roman Law*, Philadelphia.

Bieber, M. (1939) *The History of the Greek and Roman Theatre*, Princeton.

Birley, E. (1969) 'Septimius Severus and the Roman army', *Epigraphische Studien* 8, 63–82.

Birt, T. (1918) *Aus dem Leben der Antike*, Leipzig.

Blackman, D. R. (1978) 'The volume of water delivered by the four great aqueducts of Rome', *PBSR* 46, 52–72.

—— (1979) 'The length of the four great aqueducts of Rome', *PBSR* 47, 12–18.

Blake, M. E. (1947) *Ancient Roman Construction in Italy*, I, Washington.

—— (1959) *Roman Construction in Italy from Tiberius through the Flavians*, Washington.

—— (1973) completed by Bishop, T. D., *Roman Construction in Italy from Nerva through the Antonines*, Philadelphia.

Bleicken, J. (1958) *'Vici magister'*, *RE* 8A.2, 2480–3.

Bloch, H. (1968) *I bolli laterizi e la storia edilizia romana*, repr. Rome.

Blum, W. (1969) *Curiosi und regendarii*, diss. Munich.

Blümner, H. (1911) *Die römischen Privataltertümer*, 3rd edn, Munich.

Boak, A. E. R. (1924) *The Master of the Offices*, New York.

—— (1955) *Manpower Shortage and the Fall of the Roman Empire in the West*, Ann Arbor.

Boatwright, M. T. (1984–5) 'Tacitus on Claudius and the *pomerium*', *CJ* 80, 36–44.

—— (1986) 'The pomerial extension of Augustus', *Historia* 35, 13–27.

—— (1987) *Hadrian and the City of Rome*, Princeton.

Bodei-Giglioni, G. (1974) *Lavori pubblici e occupazione nell'antichità classica*, Bologna.

Boethius, A. (1932) 'The Neronian *nova urbs*', *Acta Inst. Rom. Regn. Suec.* 2, 84ff.

—— (1934) 'Remarks on the development of domestic architecture in Rome', *AJA* 38, 158–70.

—— (1956) 'L'insula romana secondo Léon Homo', *L'Erma*, 1–12.

—— (1960) *The Golden House of Nero*, Ann Arbor.

—— and Ward-Perkins, J. B. (1970) *Etruscan and Roman Architecture*, Harmondsworth.

Bonfante, P. (1922) 'Il regime delle acque dal diritto romano al diritto odierno', *AG* 34, 3–16.

Bonner, S. F. (1977) *Education in Ancient Rome*, Berkeley.

Booth, A. D. (1979) 'The schooling of slaves in first century Rome', *TAPhA* 109, 11–19.

Bourne, F. C. (1946) *The public works of the Julio-Claudians and Flavians*, Princeton.

Boyd, C. E. (1916) *Public Libraries and Literary Culture in Ancient Rome*, Chicago.

Bradshaw, H. C. (1923) 'A note on housing conditions in ancient Rome', *Town Planning Review* 10, 53–5.

Brancher, M. (1909) *La juridiction civile du praefectus urbi*, Paris.

Braund, S. H. (ed.) (1989) *Satire and Society in Ancient Rome*, Exeter.

Breeze, D. J. (1974) 'The career structure below the centurionate during the Principate', *ANRW* II.1, 435–51.

Briau, R. (1877) *L'archiatre romaine ou la médecine officielle dans l'empire*, Paris.

Brödner, E. (1951) *Untersuchungen an den Caracallathermen*, Berlin.

—— (1983) *Die römischen Thermen und das antike Badewesen*, Darmstadt.

Brothers, A. J. (1989) 'Buildings for entertainment', in Barton, I. M. (ed.), *Roman Public Buildings*, Exeter, 97–125.

Brown, F. E. (1961) *Roman Architecture*, New York.

Brunt, P. A. (1965) 'Italian aims at the time of the Social War', *JRS* 55, 90–109.

—— (1966) 'The *fiscus* and its development', *JRS* 56, 75–91.

—— (1971) *Italian Manpower*, Oxford.

—— (1977) '*Lex de imperio Vespasiani*', *JRS* 67, 95–116.

—— (1980) 'Free labour and public works at Rome', *JRS* 70, 81–100.

—— (1981) 'The revenues of Rome', *JRS* 71, 161–72.

—— (1983) '*Princeps* and *equites*', *JRS* 73, 42–75.

—— (1984) 'The role of the Senate in the Augustan regime', *CQ* 34, 423–44.

—— and Moore, J. M. (eds) (1967) *Res Gestae Divi Augusti*, Oxford.

Buckland, W. W. (1963) *A Textbook of Roman Law, from Augustus to Justinian*, 3rd edn, Cambridge.

Busacca, C. (1977) '*Ne quid in loco sacro religioso sancto fiat*', *SDHI* 43, 265–92.

Cadoux, T. J. (1959) Review-discussion of G. Vitucci: Ricerche sulla praefectura urbi in età imperiale, *JRS* 49, 152–60.

Cagnat, R. (1882) *Etude historique sur les impôts indirects chez les romains*, Paris.

—— (1919a) '*Urbanae cohortes*' in D-S 5, 602–4.

—— (1919b) '*Vigiles*' in D-S 5, 867–89.

Callmer, C. (1944) 'Antike Bibliotheken', *Act. Inst. Rom. Reg. Suec.* 10, 145ff.

Calza, G. and Lugli, G. (1941) 'La popolazione di Roma antica', *Bull. Com.* 69, 142ff.

Cameron, A. (1976) *Circus Factions*, Oxford.

Campbell, J. B. (1984) *The Emperor and the Roman Army, 31* BC – AD *235*, Oxford.

Cancelli, F. (1956) 'A proposito dei *tresviri capitales', Studi in onore di P. de Francisci*, Milan, III, 15–35.

—— (1957) *Studi sui censores e sull' arbitratus della lex contractus*, Milan.

Carcopino, J. (1956) *Daily Life in Ancient Rome*, Harmondsworth.

Cardini, M. (1909) *L'igiene pubblica di Roma antica*, Prato.

Carettoni, G. (1960) 'Excavations and discoveries in the Forum Romanum and on the Palatine during the past fifty years', *JRS* 50, 197–203.

—— *et al.* (1966) *Forma Urbis Romae (Pianta marmorea di Roma)*, Rome.

Carter, J. M. (ed.) (1982) *Suetonius: Augustus*, Bristol.

—— (1989) 'Civic and other buildings' in Barton, I. M. (ed.), *Roman Public Buildings*, Exeter, 31–65.

Casson, L. (1965) 'Harbour and river boats of ancient Rome', *JRS* 55, 31–9.

—— (1971) *Ships and Seamanship in the Ancient World*, Princeton.

—— (1974) *Travel in the Ancient World*, London.

—— (1980) 'The role of the state in Rome's grain trade', in D'Arms, J. H. and Kopff, E. C. (eds), *The Seaborne Commerce of Ancient Rome*, Rome, pp. 21–33.

Castagnoli, F. (1980a) *Topografia e urbanistica di Roma antica*, 3rd edn, Turin.

—— (1980b) 'Installazioni portuali a Roma' in D'Arms, J. H. and Kopff, E. C. (eds), *The Seaborne Commerce of Ancient Rome*, Rome, 35–42.

Cavallaro, M. A. (1984) *Spese e spettacoli, Antiquitas*, Band 34, Bonn.

Cerati, A. (1975) *Caractère annonaire et assiette de l'impôt fonçier au Bas Empire*, Paris.

Cerutti, S. M. and Richardson, L. jnr (1989) '*The retiarius tunicatus* of Suetonius, Juvenal and Petronius', *AJPh* 110, 589–94.

Champlin, E. (1982) 'The *suburbium* of Rome', *AJAH* 7, 97–117.

Chandler, D. C. (1978) '*Quaestor Ostiensis', Historia* 27, 328–35.

Chastagnol, A. (1953) 'La ravitaillement de Rome en viande au Ve siècle' *RH* 210, 13–22.

—— (1960) *La préfecture urbaine à Rome sous le Bas-Empire*, Paris.

Cheesman, G. L. (1914) *The Auxilia of the Roman Imperial Army*, Oxford.

Chilver, G. E. F. (1949) '*Princeps* and *frumentationes', AJPh* 70, 7–21.

Clark, A. C. (ed.) (1907) *Asconius*, Oxford.

Clarke, M. L. (1971) *Higher Education in the Ancient World*, London.

Clementi, F. (1935) *Roma imperiale nelle XIV regioni augustee*, Rome.

Coarelli, P. (1977) 'Public building in Rome between the Second Punic War and Sulla', *PBSR* 45, 1–19.

—— (1980) *Roma*, Rome/Bari.

Cohen, B. (1972) *The Roman ordines*, diss. Tel Aviv.

Coleman, K.M. (1990) 'Fatal charades: Roman executions staged as mythological enactments', *JRS* 80, 44–73.

Colini, A. M. (1941) 'Pozzi e cisterne', *Bull. Comm*, 71–99.

—— (1980) 'Il porto fluviale del foro boario a Roma', in D'Arms, J. H. and Kopff E. C. (eds), *The Seaborne Commerce of Ancient Rome*, Rome, 43–53.

Costa, E. (1919) *Le acque nel diritto romano*, Bologna.

Cramer, F. H. (1954) *Astrology in Roman Law and Politics*, Philadelphia.

Crawford, M. (ed.) (1983) *Sources for Ancient History*, Cambridge.

Crook, J. A. (1967) *Law and Life of Rome*, London.

Culham, P. (1989) 'Archives and alternatives in Republican Rome', *CPh* 84, 100–15.

Dagron, G. (1974) *Naissance d'une capitale*, Paris.

Daremberg, C. and Saglio, E. (eds) (1877–1919) *Dictionnaire des Antiquités Grecques et Romaines*, Paris.

D'Arms, J. H. and Kopff, E. C. (eds) (1980) *The Seaborne Commerce of Ancient Rome*, Rome.

Davies, R. W. (1989) *Service in the Roman Army*, Edinburgh.

Degrassi, D. (1987) 'Interventi edilizi sull' Isola Tiberina nel I secolo a.C.', *Athenaeum* 65, 521–7.

Dessau, H. (ed.) (1892–1906) *Inscriptiones Latinae Selectae*, Berlin.

Diepgen, P. (1949) *Geschichte der Medizin* I, Berlin.

Dignös, G. (1962) *Die Stellung der Ädilen im römischen Strafrecht*, diss. Munich.

Dilke, O. A. W. (1971) *The Roman Land Surveyors*, Newton Abbot.

—— (1985) *Greek and Roman Maps*, London.

Dill, S. (1911) *Roman Society from Nero to Marcus Aurelius*, London.

Dobson, B. (1978) *Die Primipilares*, Cologne/Bonn.

Domaszewski, A. von (1967), Dobson, B. (ed.) *Die Rangordnung des römischen Heeres*, Cologne/Graz.

Dudley, D. R. (1967) *Urbs Roma*, London.

Duncan-Jones, R. P. (1964) 'Human numbers in towns and town organisations of the Roman Empire: the evidence of gifts', *Historia* 13, 199–208.

—— (1982) *Economy of the Roman Empire: Quantitative Studies*, 2nd edn, Cambridge.

Dunn, F. S. (1914–15) 'Rome, the unfinished and unkempt', *CJ* 10, 312–22.

Duret, L. and Néraudeau, J.-P. (1983) *Urbanisme et métamorphoses de la Rome antique*, Paris.

Durry, M. (1938) *Les cohortes prétoriennes*, Paris.

Echols, E. J. (1958) 'The Roman city police: origin and development', *CJ* 53, 377–85.

Eck, W. (1979) *Die staatliche Organisation Italiens in der hohen Kaiserzeit*, Munich.

—— (1983) 'Die Wässer im römischen Reich: sozio-politische Bedingungen, Recht und Administration', in Frontinus-Gesellschaft: *Geschichte der Wasserversorgung*, I, Munich/Vienna.

Eder, W. (1980) *Servitus publica*, Wiesbaden.

Eisenhut, W. (1972) 'Die römische Gefängnisstrafe', *ANRW* I.2, 268–82.

Ertman, P. C. (1980) *Curatores viarum: a study of the superintendents of highways in ancient Rome*, diss. Ann Arbor.

Evans, H. B. (1980) 'The Romulean gates of the Palatine', *AJA* 84, 93–6.

Flambard, J.-M. (1977) 'Clodius, les collèges, la plèbe et les esclaves', *MEFR* 89, 115–56.

Fowler, W. Warde (1908) *Social Life at Rome in the Age of Cicero*, London.

Frank, R. I. (1969) *Scholae Palatinae*, Rome.

Frank, T. (1924) 'The Tullianum and Sallust's *Catiline*', *CJ* 19, 495–8.

—— (1930) 'Roman census statistics from 508 to 225 BC', *AJPh* 51, 313–24.

—— (ed.) (1933, 1940) *Economic Survey of Ancient Rome*, vol.I, vol.V, Baltimore.

Frederiksen, M. W. (1965) 'The Republican municipal laws: errors and drafts' *JRS* 55, 183–98.

—— (1984), Purcell, N. (ed.) *Campania*, Rome.

Freis, H. (1965) '*Urbanae cohortes*', *RE* Supp.10, 1125–40.

—— (1967) *Die cohortes urbanae*, Cologne.

Friedländer, L. (1919–21) *Darstellungen aus der Sittengeschichte Roms*, Leipzig.

Frier, B. (1977) 'The rental market in early imperial Rome', *JRS* 67, 27–37.

—— (1980) *Landlords and Tenants in Imperial Rome*, Princeton.

—— (1982) 'Roman life expectancy: Ulpian's evidence', *HSPh* 86, 213–51.

Frontinus-Gesellschaft (1982) *Wasserversorgung im Antiken Rom*, Munich/Vienna.

—— (1983; 1987) *Geschichte der Wasserversorgung* I, Munich/Vienna, II and III, Mainz.

Gaheis, A. (1927) *Gaukler im Altertum*, Munich.

Galsterer, H. (1981) 'Spiele und "Spiele": Die Organisation der *ludi juvenales* in der Kaiserzeit', *Athenaeum* 59, 410–38.

—— (1987) 'La loi municipale des Romains: chimère ou réalité?' *RHD* 65, 181–203.

Garnsey, P. (1976) 'Urban property investment' in Finley, M. I. (ed.), *Studies in Roman Property*, Cambridge, 123–36 (with Appendix, 133f, on demolition of houses and the law).

—— (ed.) (1980) *Non-slave Labour in the Greco-Roman World*, Cambridge Phil. Soc.

—— (1988) *Famine and Food Supply in the Graeco-Roman World*, Cambridge.

—— and Hopkins, K. and Whittaker, C. R. (eds) (1983) *Trade in the Ancient Economy*, London.

—— and Rathbone, D. (1985) 'The background to the grain law of C. Gracchus', *JRS* 75, 20–5.

Garrison, F. H. (1929) 'The history of drainage, irrigation, sewage disposal and water supply', *Bull. N.Y. Academy of Medicine* 5, 887–938.

Gärtner, H. and Wünsch, A. (1980) *Register zum PW RE*, Munich.

Garzetti, A. (1956) 'Le basi amministrative del Principato romano', *Aevum* 30, 97–114.

Gaudemet, J. (1967) *Institutions de l'Antiquité*, Paris.

Gerkan, A. von (1949) 'Grenzen und Grössen der 14 Regionen Roms', *BJ* 149, 5–65.

Giardina, A. (1977) *Aspetti della burocrazia nel Basso Impero*, Rome.

Gibbon, E. (1776/88) *The History of the Decline and Fall of the Roman Empire*, London.

Gilliam, J. F. (1961) 'The plague under Marcus Aurelius', *AJPh* 82, 225–51.

González, J. (1986) 'The *lex Irnitana*: a new copy of the Flavian municipal law', *JRS* 76, 147–243.

Graffunder, P. (1914) '*Regiones*', *RE* 1A.1, 480–6.

Grant, M. (1971) *Gladiators*, Harmondsworth.

Griffin, J. (1976) 'Augustan poetry and the life of luxury', *JRS* 66, 87–105.

Griffin, M. T. (1962) '*De brevitate vitae*', *JRS* 52, 104–13.

Grimal, P. (ed.) (1944) *Frontinus*, Paris.

—— (1969) *Les jardins romains*, 2nd edn, Paris.

Grosso, F. (1966) '*Equites singulares Augusti*', *Latomus* 25, 900–9.

Guarino, A. (1985) 'Il leasing dei gladiatori', *Index* 13, 461–5.

Gummerus, H. (1932) *Der Ärztestand im römischen Reiche*, Helsingfors.

Hainzmann, M. (1975) *Untersuchungen zur Geschichte und Verwaltung der stadtrömischen Wasserleitungen*, Vienna.

Halphen, L. (1907) *L'administration de Rome, AD 751–1252*, Paris.

Hands, A.R. (1968) *Charities and Social Aid in Greece and Rome*, London.

Hardy, E.G. (1912) *Roman Laws and Charters*, Oxford.

Harris, H.A. (1972) *Sport in Greece and Rome*, London.

Hart, G.D. (ed.) (1983) *Disease in Ancient Man*, Toronto.

Haverfield, F. (1913) *Ancient Town Planning*, Oxford.

Heck, A. van (1977) *Breviarium urbis Romae antiquae*, Leiden.

Heinz, W. (1983) *Römische Thermen*, Munich.

Heres, T. L. (1982) *Paries*, Amsterdam.

Hermansen, G. (1970) 'The *medianum* and the Roman apartment', *Phoenix* 24, 342–7.

—— (1974) 'The Roman inns and the law: the inns of Ostia' in Evans, J. A. S. (ed.), *Polis and Imperium: Studies in honour of E. T. Salmon*, Toronto, 167–81.

—— (1978a) 'The population of imperial Rome: the Regionaries', *Historia* 27, 129–68.

—— (1978b) 'The bread line through Ostia to Rome', *PACA* 14, 21–6.

—— (1982a) 'The *stuppatores* and their guild in Ostia', *AJA* 86, 121–6.

—— (1982b) *Ostia: aspects of Roman city life*, Edmonton, Alberta.

Herschel, C. (1913) *Frontinus and the Water Supply of Rome*, London.

Herz, P. (1988) *Studien zur römischen Wirtschaftsgesetzgebung: die Lebensmittelversorgung*, Stuttgart.

Herzog, E. (1884–91) *Geschichte und System der römischen Staatsverfassung*, Leipzig.

Hill, D.R. (1984) *A History of Engineering in Classical and Medieval Times*, London.

Hirschfeld, O. (1870) 'Die Getreideverwaltung in der römischen Kaiserzeit', *Philologus* 29, 1–96.

—— (1905) *Die kaiserlichen Verwaltungsbeamten bis auf Diocletian*, 2nd edn, Berlin.

Hodge, A. Trevor (1983a) 'Siphons in Roman aqueducts', *PBSR* 51, 174–221.

—— (1983b) 'A plain man's guide to Roman plumbing', *EMC* 27, 311–28.

—— (1989) 'Aqueducts' in Barton, I. M. (ed.), *Roman Public Buildings*, Exeter, 127–49.

Homo, L. (1971) *Rome impériale et l'urbanisme dans l'antiquité*, 2nd edn, Paris.

Hönle, A. and Henze, A. (1981) *Römische Amphitheater und Stadien*, Feldmeilen.

Hopkins, K. (1978) *Conquerors and Slaves*, Cambridge.

—— (1980) 'Taxes and trade in the Roman Empire (200 BC – AD 400)', *JRS* 70, 101–25.

—— (1983) *Death and Renewal*, Cambridge.

Houston, G. W. (1980) 'The administration of Italian sea ports during the first three centuries of the Roman Empire' in D'Arms, J. H. and Kopff E. C. (eds), *The Seaborne Commerce of Ancient Rome*, Rome, 157–71.

Howe, L. L. (1942) *The Praetorian Prefect from Commodus to Diocletian*, Chicago.

Hülsen, C. (1897) 'Der Umfang der Stadt Rom zur Zeit des Plinius', *Röm. Mitt.* 12, 148–60.

—— (1909) 'The burning of Rome under Nero', *AJA* 13, 45–8.

Humphrey, J. H. (1986) *Roman Circuses*, London.

Hyde, J. K. (1973) *Society and Politics in Medieval Italy*, London.

Impallomeni, G. (1955) *L'editto degli edili curuli*, Padua.

Isidori Frasca, R. (1980) *Ludi nell'antica Roma*, Bologna.

Janvier, Y. (1969) *La législation du Bas-Empire romain sur les édifices publics*, Aix-en-Provence.

Jashemski, W. F. (1979) 'The Garden of Hercules at Pompeii (II viii.6): the discovery of a commercial flower garden', *AJA* 83, 403–11.

Jennison, G. (1937) *Animals for Show and Pleasure in Ancient Rome*, Manchester.

Johnson, A. C., Coleman-Norton, P. R. and Bourne, P. C. (1961) *Ancient Roman Statutes*, Austin, Texas.

Jolowicz, H. F. and Nicholas, B. (1972) *Historical Introduction to Roman Law*, 2nd edn, Cambridge.

Jones, A. H. M. (1941) '*In eo solo dominium populi romani est vel Caesaris*', *JRS* 31, 26–31.

—— (1949a) 'The *aerarium* and the *fiscus*', *JRS* 39, 22–37.

—— (1949b) 'The Roman Civil Service (clerical and sub-clerical grades)', *JRS* 39, 38–55.

—— (1972) *The Criminal Courts of the Roman Republic and Principate*, Oxford.

Jones, J. W. (1929) 'Expropriation in Roman Law', *LQR* 45, 512–27.

Jordan, H. (1871–1907) *Die Topographie der Stadt Rom im Altertum*, vol.I,1 and 2; vol.II; vol.II,3 revised by Hülsen, C., Berlin.

Jory, E. J. (1970) 'Associations of actors in Rome', *Hermes* 98, 224–53.

Kaser, M. (1963) 'Die Jurisdiktion der kurulischen Ädilen', in *Mélanges P. Meylan*, Lausanne, 173–91.

—— (1971) *Das römische Privatrecht* I, 2nd edn, Munich.

—— (1978) 'Zum römischen Grabrecht', *ZSS* 95, 15–92.

Kaster, R. A. (1983) 'Notes on "primary" and "secondary" schools in late antiquity', *TAPhA* 113, 323–46.

Kennedy, D. L. (1978) 'Some observations on the Praetorian Guard', *Anc. Soc.* 275–301.

Keppie, L. (1984) *The Making of the Roman Army*, London.

Kienast, D. (1980) 'Zur Baupolitik Hadrians in Rom', *Chiron* 10, 391–412.

Kitto, H. D. F., *Classical Drama and its Influence. Essays presented to* (1965), Anderson, M. J. (ed.), London.

Kléberg, T. (1957) *Hôtels, restaurants et cabarets dans l'Antiquité Romaine*, Uppsala.

Knapp, C. (1925) 'The care of city streets in ancient Rome', *CW* 19, 82, 98, 114, 159.

Kolb, F. (1984) *Die Stadt im Altertum*, Munich.

Krautheimer, R. (1983) *Three Christian Capitals*, Berkeley.

Krencker, D. (1929) *Die Trierer Kaiserthermen*, Augsburg.

Kudlien, F. (1986) *Die Stellung des Artzes in der römischen Gesellschaft*, Stuttgart.

Kühn, E. (1864–5) *Die städtische und bürgerliche Verfassung des römischen Reichs*, Leipzig.

Kunkel, W. (1973) *An Introduction to Roman Legal and Constitutional History*, 2nd edn Oxford.

Kurylowicz, M. (1985) 'Das Glückspiel im römischen Recht', *ZSS* 102, 185–219.

Labrousse, M. (1937) 'Le *pomerium* de la Rome impériale', *MEFR* 54, 165–99.

Laet, S. J. de (1944) *Aspects de la vie sociale et économique sous Auguste et Tibère*, *Coll.Lebègue* 44, Brussels.

—— (1946–7) 'Les pouvoirs militaires des prefêts du prêtoire et leur développement progressif', *RBPh* 25, 509–54.

—— (1949) *Portorium*, Bruges.

Lafaye, G. (1909) '*Stabulum*' D-S 4.2, 1448–9.

Lampe, P. (1987) *Die stadtrömischen Christen in den ersten beiden Jahrhunderten*, Tübingen.

Lanciani, R. (1888) *Ancient Rome in the Light of Recent Discoveries*, London.

—— (1892) 'Gli edificii della prefettura urbana fra la Tellure e le terme di Tito e di Traiano'; 'Le mura di Aureliano e di Probo', *Bull. Comm.*, 19–37; 87–111.

—— (1897) *The Ruins and Excavations of Ancient Rome*, London.

—— (1902–12) *Storia degli scavi di Roma*, Rome.

—— (1917) 'Segni di terremoti negli edifizi di Roma antica', *Bull. Comm*, 45, 3–28.

—— [n.d. – 1924?] *Ancient and Modern Rome*, London.

—— (1975) *Le acque e gli acquedotti di Roma antica*, repr. Rome.

Landels, J. G. (1978) *Engineering in the Ancient World*, London.

La Rosa, F. (1957) 'Note sui *tresviri capitales*', *Labeo* 3, 231–45.

Le Gall, J. (1939) 'Notes sur les prisons de Rome à l'époque républicaine', *MEFR* 56, 60–80.

—— (1953) *Le Tibre, fleuve de Rome dans l'antiquité*, Paris.

Lehmann-Hartleben, K. (1929) 'Städtebau', *RE* 3A.2, 2018–82, esp. 2052ff.

—— (1938) '*Maenianum* and *basilica*', *AJPh* 59, 280–96.

Levick, B. (1983) 'The *senatusconsultum* from Larinum', *JRS* 73, 97–115.

Lewis, A. D. E. (1989) 'Ne quis in oppido aedificium detegito', in Gonzalez, J. (ed.), *Estudios sobre Urso*, Seville, 41–56.

Liebenam, W. (1900) *Städteverwaltung im römischen Kaiserreiche*, Leipzig.

Liebeschütz, J. H. W. G. (1972) *Antioch, city and imperial administration in the Later Roman Empire*, Oxford.

Liebs, D. (1976) 'Rechtsschulen und Rechtsunterricht im Prinzipat', *ANRW* II.15, 197–286.

—— (1987) *Die Jurisprudenz im spätantiken Italien (260–640 n.Chr.)*, Berlin.

Liénard, E. (1939) 'Les dégâts matériels causés par l'incendie de 64', *Latomus* 3, 52–7.

Lintott, A. W. (1968) *Violence in Republican Rome*, Oxford.

Littman, R. J. and M. L. (1973) 'Galen and the Antonine plague', *AJPh* 94, 243–55.

Llewellyn, P. (1971) *Rome in the Dark Ages*, London.

Loane, H. J. (1938) *Industry and Commerce of the City of Rome, 50 BC – 200 AD*, Baltimore.

Longo, G. (1934) 'Sull' uso delle acque pubbliche in diritto romano', in Albertario, E. (ed.), *Studi in memoria di U. Ratti*, Milan, 55–93.

—— (1959) 'Il regime delle concessioni e le derivazioni di acque pubbliche nel diritto romano classico e giustinianeo', *AFLM* 23, 53–78.

Lopuszanski, G. (1951) 'La police romaine et les Chrétiens' *AC* 20, 5–46.

Lot, F. (1945) 'Du chiffre de la population de Rome à la fin du IIIe siècle', *AHS (Hommage Bloch II)*, 29–38.

Löwenstein, K. (1973) *The Governance of Rome*, The Hague.

Lloyd, R. B. (1979) 'The aqua Virgo, Euripus and pons Agrippae', *AJA* 83, 193–204.

Lugli, G. (1931–40) *I monumenti antichi di Roma e suburbio*, Rome.

—— (1947) 'La "vecchia città" incendiata da Nerone', *Capitolium* 22, 41–50.

—— (1950) *Roma nei suoi monumenti*, Rome.

Lugli, I. (1952–5) *Fontes ad topographiam veteris urbis pertinentes*, Rome.

MacDonald, W.L. (1965 and 1986) *The Architecture of the Roman Empire*, I and II, Yale.

McKay, A. G. (1975) *Houses, Villas and Palaces in the Roman World*, London.

MacMullen, R. (1959) 'Roman imperial building in the provinces', *HSPh* 64, 207–35.

—— (1966) *Enemies of the Roman Order*, Cambridge, Mass.

—— (1970) 'Market days in the Roman Empire', *Phoenix* 24, 333–41.

—— (1976) *The Roman Government's Response to Crisis*, Yale.

Magdelain, A. (1977) 'L'inauguration de l'*urbs* et *imperium*', *MEFR* 89, 11–29.

Magistris, E. de (1898) *La militia vigilum della Roma imperiale*, 2nd edn, Rome.

Maier, F. G. (1953–4) 'Römische Bevölkerungsgeschichte und Inschriftenstatistik', *Historia* 2, 318–51.

Marquardt, J. (1881) *Römische Staatsverwaltung*, Leipzig.

—— (1886) *Das Privatleben der Römer*, 2nd edn, Leipzig.

—— (1888) *L'organisation financière chez les romains*, French tr., Paris.

Marrou, H.-I. (1948) *Histoire de l'éducation dans l'Antiquité: le monde romain*, Paris.

Marshall, B. A. (1985) *A Historical Commentary on Asconius*, Columbia.

Martin, S. D. (1986) 'A reconsideration of *probatio operis*' *ZSS* 103, 321–37.

Martino, F. de (1954) 'Nota sulla *lex Julia municipalis*', in *Studi in onore di U. E. Paoli*, Florence, 225–38.

—— (1972–5) *Storia della costituzione romana*, 2nd edn, Naples.

Mattingly, H. B. (1960) 'Naevius and the Metelli', *Historia* 9, 414–39.

Mau, A. (1896) 'Bäder', *RE* 2, 2743–58.

Mayer-Maly, T. (1956) 'Der rechtsgeschichtliche Gehalt der "Christenbriefe" von Plinius und Trajan', *SDHI* 22, 311–28.

Mayor, J. E. B. (ed.) (1886; 1881) *Thirteen Satires of Juvenal*, Vol.I, 4th edn, London; Vol.II, 3rd edn, London.

Meiggs, R. (1973) *Roman Ostia*, 2nd edn, Oxford.

—— (1980) 'Sea-borne timber supplies to Rome', in D'Arms, J. H. and Kopff, E. C. (eds), *The Seaborne Commerce of Ancient Rome*, Rome, 185–96.

Meusel, H. (1960) *Die Verwaltung und Finanzierung der öffentlichen Bäder zur römischen Kaiserzeit*, diss. Cologne.

Meyer-Steineg, T. (1907) *Geschichte des römischen Ärztestandes*, diss. Kiel.

Middleton, J. H. (1892) *The Remains of Ancient Rome*, London.

Millar, F. (1963) 'The *fiscus* in the first two centuries', *JRS* 53, 28–42.

—— (1964) 'The *aerarium* and its officials under the Empire', *JRS* 54, 33–40.

—— (1967) 'Emperors at work', *JRS* 57, 9–19.

—— (1983) 'Empire and city, Augustus to Julian: obligations, excuses and status', *JRS* 73, 76–96.

Moeller, W. O. (1970) 'The riot of AD 59 at Pompeii', *Historia* 19, 84–95.

Mommsen, T. (1887) *Römisches Staatsrecht*, 3rd edn, Leipzig.

—— (1899) *Römisches Strafrecht*, Leipzig.

Monti, G. M. (1934) *Le corporazioni nell' evo antico e nell' alto medio evo*, Bari.

Morgan, M. H. (1902) 'Remarks on the water supply', *TAPhA* 33, 30–7.

Moritz, L. (1958) *Grain Mills and Flour in Classical Antiquity*, Oxford.

Morlino, R. (1984) 'Cicero e l'edilizia pubblica', *Athenaeum* 62, 620–34.

Murga, J. L. (1975) 'Sobre una nueva calificación del *aedificium* per obra de la legislación urbanística imperial', *Iura* 26, 41–78.

Müri, W. (1962) *Der Arzt im Altertum*, Munich.

Murphy, J. P. (1976) *Index to the Supplements and Suppl. volumes of PW's RE*, Chicago.

Musca, D. A. (1970) '*Lis fullonum de pensione non solvenda*', *Labeo* 16, 279–326.

Musumeci, F. (1978) '*Statuae in publico positae*', *SDHI* 44, 191–203.

Musurillo, H. (1972) *The Acts of the Christian Martyrs*, Oxford.

Muth, R. (1945) '*Forum suarium*', *MH* 2, 227–36.

Narducci, P. (1889) *Sulla fognatura della città di Roma*, Rome.

Nash, E. (1981) *Pictorial Dictionary of Ancient Rome*, Deutsche Arch. Inst in Rome, 1961–2, re-issued New York.

Needleman, L. and D. (1985) 'Lead poisoning and the decline of the Roman aristocracy', *EMC* 29, 63–94.

Neppi-Modona, A. (1961) *Gli edifici teatrali Greci e Romani*, Florence.

Nicolet, C. (1976) 'Le Temple des Nymphes et les distributions frumentaires à Rome', *CRAI*, 29–51.

—— (1980) *The World of the Citizen in Republican Rome*, English tr. Berkeley.

Nilsson, M. (1926) *Imperial Rome*, London.

Nippel, W. (1984) 'Policing Rome', *JRS* 74, 20–29.

Noethlichs, K. L. (1981) *Beamtentum und Dienstvergehen*, Wiesbaden.

Nordh, A. (1949) *Libellus de regionibus urbis Romae*, Lund.

Nriagu, N.J. (1983) *Lead and Lead-Poisoning in Antiquity*, New York.

Nutton, V. (1977) '*Archiatri* and the medical profession in antiquity', *PBSR* 45, 191–226.

Oates, W. J. (1934) 'The population of Rome', *CPh* 29, 101–16.

Ogilvie, R. M. (1965) *Commentary on Livy I-V*, Oxford.

—— (1969) *The Romans and their Gods*, London.

Oleson, J. P. (1976) 'A possible physiological basis for the term *urinator* – diver', *AJPh* 97, 22–9.

Oliver, J. H. (1932) 'The Augustan *pomerium*', *MAAR* 10, 145–82.

—— and Palmer, R. E. A. (1955) 'Minutes of an act of the Roman Senate', *Hesperia* 24, 320–49.

Owens, E. J. (1989) 'Roman town planning', in Barton, I. M. (ed.), *Roman Public Buildings*, Exeter, 7–30.

Packer, J. E. (1967) 'Housing and population in imperial Ostia and Rome', *JRS* 57, 80–95.

Pailler, J.-M. (1985) 'Rome au cinq régions?', *MEFR* 97, 785–97.

Palma, A. (1980) *Le curae pubbliche*, Naples.

—— (1987) 'Le derivazioni di acqua *ex castello*', *Index* 15, 439–57.

—— (1988) *Iura vicinitatis*, Turin.

Palmer, R. E. A. (1970) *The Archaic Community of the Romans*, Cambridge.

—— (1974 and 1975) 'The *excusatio magisteri* and the administration of Rome under Commodus', *Athenaeum* 52 and 53, 268–88 and 57–87.

—— (1980) 'Customs on market goods imported into the City of Rome' in D'Arms, J. H. and Kopff, E. C. (eds), *The Seaborne Commerce of Ancient Rome*, Rome, 217–33.

Panciera, S. (1980) *'Olearii'*, in D'Arms, J. H. and Kopff, E. C. (eds), *The Seaborne Commerce of Ancient Rome*, Rome, 235–50.

Panimolle, G. (1984) *Gli acquedotti di Roma antica*, Rome.

Paoli, U. E. (1955) *Vita romana*, 7th edn, Florence.

Parker, J. H. (1876) *The Archaeology of Rome: The Aqueducts*, Oxford/London.

Passerini, A. (1939) *Le coorti pretorie*, Rome.

Pauly-Wissowa (1894–) *Real-Encyclopädie der classischen Altertumswissenschaft*, Stuttgart.

Pavis d'Escurac, H. (1976) *La préfecture de l'annone*, Rome.

Pavolini, C. (1984) *Ostia*, Rome.

Penso, G. (1984) *La médecine romaine*, Paris.

Petit, P. (1955) *Libanius et la vie municipale à Antioche au IVe siècle après J.C.*, Paris.

Pfeffer, M.E. (1969) *Einrichtungen der sozialen Sicherung in der griechischen und römischen Antike*, Berlin.

Pflaum, H.-G. (1950) *Les procurateurs équestres*, Paris.

—— (1960–1) *Les carrières procuratoriennes équestres sous le Haut-Empire*, Paris.

Phillips, E. J. (1973) 'The Roman law on the demolition of buildings', *Latomus* 32, 86–95.

Pineles, S. (1903) 'Beiträge zum römischen und heutigen Wasserrechte', *Grünhuts ZS* 30, 421–526.

Platner, S. B. and Ashby, T. (1929) *A Topographical Dictionary of Rome*, Oxford.

Poe, J. P. (1984) 'The secular games, the Aventine, and the Pomerium in the Campus Martius', *CSCA* 3, 57–81.

Posner, E. (1972) *Archives in the Ancient World*, Harvard.

Premerstein, A. von (1922) 'Die Tafel von Heraclea und die *Acta Caesaris*', *ZSS* 43, 45–152.

—— (1937) *Vom Werden und Wesen des Prinzipats*, Munich.

Prichard, A. M. (1959) 'Sale and hire' in Daube, D. (ed.) *Studies in Memory of F. de Zulueta*, Oxford, 1–8.

Purcell, N. (1983) 'The *apparitores*: a study in social mobility', *PBSR* 51, 125–73.

Quilici, L. (1974) 'La campagna romana come suburbio di Roma antica', *PP* 29, 410–38.

Rainbird, J. S. (1976) *The Vigiles of Rome*, unpublished diss. Durham.
—— (1986) 'The fire stations of imperial Rome', *PBSR* 54, 147–69.
Rainer, J. M. (1987a) 'Zum *SC Hosidianum*', *TR* 55, 31–8.
—— (1987b) *Bau- und nachbarrechtliche Bestimmungen im klassischen römischen Recht*, Graz.
—— (1990) 'Bauen und Arbeit im klassischen römischen Recht', *ZSS* 107, 376–81.
Rawson, E. (1981) 'Chariot-racing in the Roman Republic', *PBSR* 49, 1–16.
—— (1985) 'Theatrical life in Republican Rome and Italy', *PBSR* 53, 97–113.
—— (1987) *'Discrimina ordinum:* the *lex Julia theatralis'*, *PBSR* 55, 83–114.
Reynolds, P. K. Baillie (1923) 'The troops quartered in the castra peregrinorum', *JRS* 13, 168–87.
—— (1926) *The vigiles of imperial Rome*, Oxford.
Richardson, L. jnr (1988) *Pompeii: an Architectural History*, Baltimore/London.
Richmond, I.A. (1930) *The City Wall of Imperial Rome*, Oxford.
Richter, O. (1901) *Topographie der Stadt Rome*, 2nd edn, Munich.
Rickman, G. (1971) *Roman Granaries and Store Buildings*, Cambridge.
—— (1980) *The Corn Supply of Ancient Rome*, Oxford.
—— (1983) *'Porticus Minucia'*, in *Città e Architettura nella Roma Imperiale*, AnalDan, Copenhagen, 105–8.
Robertis, F. M. de (1935) 'La *cura regionum urbis* nel periodo imperiale', *Athenaeum* 13, 171–86.
—— (1936) *L'espropriazione per pubblica utilità*, Bari.
—— (1937) *La repressione penale nella circoscrizione dell'urbe*, Bari.
—— (1938) *Diritto associativo romano*, Bari.
—— (1945–6) 'Emptio ab invito: sul problema della espropriazione nel diritto romano', *AFLB* 7–8, 153–224.
—— (1955) *Il fenomeno associativo nel mondo romano*, Naples.
—— (1963) *Lavoro e lavoratori nel mondo romano*, Bari.
—— (1982) *'Lis fullonum* (CIL VI 266): Oggetto della lite e causa petendi', *ANRW* II.14, 791–815.
Robinson, O. F. (1968) 'Private prisons', *RIDA* 15, 389–98.
—— (1975) 'The Roman law on burials and burial grounds', *IJ* 10, 175–86.
—— (1977) 'Fire prevention at Rome', *RIDA* 24, 377–88.
—— (1980) 'The water supply of Rome', *SDHI* 46, 44–86.
—— (1981) 'Slaves and the criminal law', *ZSS* 29, 213–54.
—— (1984) 'Baths', in *Sodalitas; Scritti in onore di A. Guarino*, Naples, 3, 1065–82.
Rodenwaldt, G. (1936) 'Art from Nero to the Antonines' in *Cambridge Ancient History*, Cambridge, vol.XI, 775–805.
Rodger, A. (1972) *Owners and Neighbours in Roman Law*, Oxford.
Rodgers, R. H. (1982) *'Curatores aquarum'* *HSPh* 86, 171–80.
—— (1986) *'Copia aquarum'*, *TAPhA* 116, 353–60.

Rodriguez-Almeida, E. (1977) 'Forma urbis marmorea: nuovi elementi di analisi e nuove ipotesi di lavoro', *MEFR* 89, 219–57.
—— (1980) 'Vicissitudini nella gestione del commercio dell'olio betico da Vespasiano a Severo Alessandro' in D'Arms, J. H. and Kopff, E. C. (eds), *The Seaborne Commerce of Ancient Rome*, Rome, 277–90.
—— (1981) *Forma urbis marmorea: aggiornamento generale 1980*, Rome.
Ronna, M. (1907) *Les égouts de Rome: cloaques, égouts, collecteurs*, Paris.
Rose, H. J. (1948) *Ancient Roman Religion*, London.
Rosen, G. (1958) *A History of Public Health*, New York.
Rostovtzeff, M. (1912) 'Frumentum', *RE* 7, 126–87.
—— (1957) *The Social and Economic History of the Roman Empire*, 2nd edn, Oxford.
Rotondi, G. (1922) *Leges publicae populi romani*, Milan.
Ruggiero, E. de (1895) *Dizionario epigrafico di antichità romana*, Rome.
—— (1925) *Lo stato e le opere pubbliche in Roma antica*, Turin.
Sachers, E. (1954) 'Praefectus urbi', *RE* 22.2, 2513–32.
Säflund, G. (1932) *Le mura di Roma repubblicana*, (Acta Inst. Rom. Reg. Suec. II) Lund.
Saletta, V. (1967) *Ludi circensi*, Rome.
Salmon, E. T. (1969) *Roman Colonization in the Republic*, London.
Salmon, P. (1974) *Population et dépopulation dans l'empire romaine*, Brussels.
Sargenti, M. (1983) 'La disciplina urbanistica a Roma nella normativa di età tardo-repubblicana e imperiale', in *La città antica come fatto di cultura: Atti del Convegno di Como e Bellagio, 16/19 giugno 1979*, Como, pp. 265–84.
—— (1984) 'Due senatoconsulti: Politica edilizia nel primo secolo dell'impero e tecnica normativa', in *Studi in onore di C. Sanfilippo*, Milan, 5, 637–55.
Scarborough, J. (1969) *Roman Medicine*, London.
Schiller, A. A. (1949) 'The jurists and the Prefects of Rome', *RIDA* 31, 319–59.
Schmitter, P. (1975) 'Compulsory schooling at Athens and Rome?', *AJPh* 96, 276–89.
Schneider, K. (1928) 'Macellum' *RE* 14.1, 129–33.
Schönhardt, C. (1885) *Alea: über die Bestrafung des Glücksspiels*, diss. Stuttgart.
Schulz, F. (1953) *History of Roman Legal Science*, revised edn, Oxford.
Scobie, A. (1986) 'Slums, sanitation and mortality in the Roman world', *Klio* 68, 399–433.
Seeck, O. (1876) *Notitia Dignitatum*, repr. Frankfurt.
Sémonin, A. (1895) *De l'expropriation pour cause d'utilité publique*, diss. Vesoul – en droit romain: 1–51.
Serrigny, D. (1862) *Droit public et administratif romain du IVe au VIe siècle*, Paris.
Sherwin-White, A. N. (1952) 'The early persecutions and Roman law again', *JThS* 3, 199–213.

Shipley, F. W. (1931) 'Chronology of the building operations in Rome from the death of Julius Caesar to the death of Augustus', *MAAR* 9, 7–60.

—— (1933) *Agrippa's Building Activities in Rome*, Washington.

Siber, H. (1952) *Römisches Verfassungsrecht*, Leipzig.

Sigerist, H. E. (1943) *Civilization and Disease*, Cornell.

Simshäuser, W. (1982) 'Sozialbindungen des spätrepublikanisch-klassischen römischen Privateigentums' in *Festschrift für H. Coing zum 70. Geburtstag*, Munich, I 329–61.

—— (1984) 'Sozialbindungen des Eigentums im römische Bauwesen der späteren Kaiserzeit' in *Sodalitas: Scritti in onore di A. Guarino*, Naples, 4, 1793–1814.

Singer, C., Holmyard, E. J., Hall, A. R. and Williams, T. I. (1956) *A History of Technology* II, Oxford.

Singer, C. and Underwood, E. A. (1962) *A Short History of Medicine*, Oxford.

Sinnigen, W. G. (1957) *The Officium of the Urban Prefecture during the Later Roman Empire*, Rome.

—— (1959) 'The *vicarius urbis Romae* and the Urban Prefecture', *Historia* 8, 97–112.

—— (1962) 'The origins of the *frumentarii*', *MAAR* 27, 211–24.

Sirks, A. J. B. (1984) *Qui annonae urbis serviunt*, diss. Amsterdam.

—— (1989) '*Munera publica* and exemptions (*vacatio, excusatio* and *immunitas*)', in Sobrequés, J. and Peláez, M. J. (eds), *Studies in Roman Law and Legal History in honour of R. d'Abadal i de Vinyals*, Barcelona, 79–111.

Skydsgaard, J. E. (1983) 'Public building and society', in *Città e Architettura nella Roma Imperiale*, AnalDan, Copenhagen, 223–7.

Speidel, M. (1965) *Die equites singulares Augusti*, Bonn.

—— (1978) *Guards of the Roman Empire*, Bonn.

Spruit, J. E. (1989) *Themis en de tuinen van Rome*, Deventer.

Stambaugh, J. E. (1988) *The Ancient Roman City*, Baltimore.

Stangl, T. (1912) *Ciceronis Orationum Scholiastae*, Vienna/Leipzig.

Steinby, M. (1983) 'L'edilizia come industria pubblica e privata', in *Città e Architettura nella Roma Imperiale*, AnalDan, Copenhagen, 219–21.

Stockton, D. (1975) 'Christianos *ad leonem*', in Levick, B. (ed.) *The Ancient Historian and his Materials: Essays to C. E. Stevens*, Farnborough, 199–212.

Strong, D. E. (1968) 'The administration of public buildings in Rome during the Late Republic and Early Empire', *BICS* 15, 97–109.

Talamanca, M. (ed.) (1979) *Lineamenti di Storia del Diritto Romano*, Milan.

Talbert, R. J. A. (1984) *The Senate of Imperial Rome*, Princeton.

Tchernia, A. (1986) *Le vin d'Italie romaine*, Rome.

Tellegen, J. W. (1989) '*Responsitare* and the early history of the *ius respondendi*' in Sobrequés, J. and Peláez, M. J. (eds), *Studies in Roman Law and Legal History in honour of R. d'Abadal i de Vinyals*, Barcelona, 59–77.

Temporini, H. (ed.) (1972–) *Aufstieg und Niedergang der römischen Welt*, Berlin.

Tengström, E. (1974) *Bread for the People*, Stockholm.

Thédénat, H. (1904a) *'Latrina'*, D-S 3.2, 987–91.

—— (1904b) *'Macellum'*, D-S 3.2, 1457–60.

Thornton, M. K. (1986) 'Julio-Claudian building programs: eat, drink and be merry', *Historia* 35, 28–44.

—— (1989) *Julio-Claudian Building Programs*, Bolchazy-Caducci, Wauconda.

—— and R. L. (1983) 'Manpower needs for the public works program of the Julio-Claudian emperors', *J.EcHist* 43, 373–8.

Thuillier, J. P. (1982) 'Le programme athlétique des *ludi circenses* dans la Rome républicaine', *REL* 60, 105–22.

—— (1987) 'Les cirques romaines', *EMC* 6, 93–111 (review article on Humphrey's *Circuses*).

Tomulescu, C. St. (1976) 'Sur la *sententia Senecionis de sepulcris*', *TR* 44, 147–52.

Toynbee, J. M. C. (1971) *Death and Burial in the Roman World*, London.

—— (1973) *Animals in Roman Life and Art*, London.

Tucker, T. G. (1924) *Life in the Roman World of Nero and St Paul*, New York.

Valentini, R. and Zucchetti, G. (1940–53) *Codice topografico della città di Roma*, Rome.

Van Berchem, D. (1939) *Les distributions de blé et d'argent à la plèbe romaine sous l'empire*, Geneva.

Van Buren, A. W. and Stevens, G. P. (1915–16) 'The *aqua Traiana* and the mills on the Janiculum', *MAAR* 1, 59–62.

—— (1933) 'Antiquities of the Janiculum', *MAAR*, 69–79.

Van Buren, A. W. (1952) *'Pons . . . Pontes'* RE 21.2, 2428–37; 2450–84.

—— (1955) 'Wasserleitungen' *RE* 8.A.1, 453–85.

—— (1956) *'Pinacotheca'* RE 8 Supp. 500–2.

Van Deman, E. B. (1912) 'Methods of determining the date of Roman concrete monuments', *AJA* 16, 230–51.

—— (1922) 'The Sullan Forum', *JRS* 12, 1–31.

—— (1923) 'The Neronian *sacra via*', *AJA* 27, 383–424.

—— (1925) 'The *sacra via* of Nero', *MAAR* 5, 115–26.

—— (1934) *The Building of the Roman Aqueducts*, Washington.

Veyne, P. (1976) *Le pain et le cirque*, Paris.

Viganò, R. (1969) 'Sull' *edictum de fluminibus retandis*', *Labeo* 15, 168–77.

—— (1972) 'Appunti sulla *cura riparum et alvei Tiberis*: gestione diretta o indiretta', in *Studi in onore di G. Scherillo*, Milan, 2, 803–8.

Vigneaux, P. E. (1896) *Essai sur l'histoire de la prefectura urbis à Rome*, Paris .

Ville, G. (1981) *La gladiature en occident des origines à la mort de Domitien*, Rome.

Virlouvet, C. (1985) *Famines et émeutes à Rome des origines de la République à la mort de Néron*, Rome.

Visscher, F. de (1963) *Le droit des tombeaux romains*, Milan.

Vitucci, G. (1956) *Ricerche sulla praefectura urbi in età imperiale*, Rome.

Voigt, M. (1903) 'Die römischen Baugesetze', *BSG* 12, 175–98.

Wacke, A. (1976) 'Dig. 19.2.33: Afrikans Verhältnis zu Julian und die Haftung für höhere Gewalt', *ANRW* II.15, 455–96.

—— (1980) Rechtsfragen der römischen Lagerhausvermietung', *Labeo* 26, 299–324.

Wall, B. (1932) 'Porticus Minuciae', *Acta Inst. Rom. Regni Sueciae* 2, 31–54.

Waltzing, J. P. (1895–1900) *Étude historique sur les corporations professionelles chez les romains*, Louvain.

Ward-Perkins, J. B. (1970) 'From Republic to Empire: reflections on the early provincial architecture of the Roman West' *JRS* 60, 1–19.

—— (1974) *Cities of Ancient Greece and Italy: planning in classical antiquity*, New York.

—— and Toynbee, J. M. C. (1949) 'The Hunting Baths at Lepcis Magna', *Archaeologia* 93, 165–95.

Watson, A. (1970) 'Drunkenness in Roman law', in Becker, W. G. and Schnorr von Carolsfeld, L. (eds) *Sein und Werden im Recht: Festgabe für U. von Lübtow*, Berlin, 381–7.

—— (1987) 'Sellers' liability for defects: aedilician edict and praetorian law', *Iura* 38, 167–75.

—— (1991) *The State, Law and Religion*, Athens, Georgia.

Watson, G. R. (1969) *The Roman Soldier*, London.

Weaver, P. R. C. (1972) *Familia Caesaris*, Cambridge.

Webster, G. (1979) *The Roman Imperial Army*, 2nd edn, London.

Weinstock, S. (1960) '*Pax* and the "ara Pacis"', *JRS* 50, 44–58.

Weiss, E. (1925) 'Der Rechtsschutz der römischen Wasserleitungen', *ZSS* 45, 87–116.

Werner, P. (1906) *De incendiis urbis Romae*, Leipzig.

Whittaker, C. R. (1964) 'The revolt of Papirius Dionysius in AD 190' *Historia* 13, 348–69.

Williams, W. (1976) 'Individuality in the imperial constitutions, Hadrian and the Antonines', *JRS* 66, 67–83.

Woodside, M. St. A. (1942) 'Vespasian's patronage of education and the arts', *TAPhA* 73, 123–9.

Yavetz, Z. (1958) 'The living conditions of the urban *plebs* in Republican Rome', *Latomus* 17, 500–17.

—— (1969) *Plebs and princeps*, Oxford.

—— (1975) '*Forte an dolo principis*', in Levick, B. (ed.) *The Ancient Historian and his Materials: Essays to C. E. Stevens*, Farnborough, 181–97.

ADDITIONAL BIBLIOGRAPHY

Bruun, C. (1991) *The Water Supply of Ancient Rome*, Helsinki.

Flambard, J. M. (1981) '*Collegia compitalicia*: phénomène associatif, cadres territoriaux et cadres civiques dans le monde romain à l'époque républicaine', *Ktema* 6, 143–67.

Latte, K. (1967) *Römische Religionsgeschichte*, 2nd edn, Munich.

Marquardt, J. (1889, 1890) (tr. M. Brissaud) *Le culte chez les romains*, I and II, Paris.

Purcell, N. (1994) 'The city of Rome and the *plebs urbana* in the later Roman Republic' in C.A.H. IX, 2nd edn, ch.xvii, pp.644–88.

Sirks, A. J. B. (1980) 'A favour to rich freed women (*libertinae*) in 51 AD', *RIDA* 27, 283–94.

—— (1991a) 'The size of the grain distributions in imperial Rome and Constantinople', *Athenaeum* 69, 215–38.

—— (1991b) *Food for Rome*, Amsterdam.

—— (1993) 'Did the late Roman government try to tie people to their profession or status?', *Tyche* 8, 159–75.

Tortorici, E. (1991) *Argiletum: commercio, speculazione, edilizia e lotta politica dall'analisi topografica di un quartiere di Roma di età repubblicana*, Rome.

Trevor-Hodge, A. (1992) *Roman Aqueducts and Water Supply*, London.

Watson, A. (1992) *The State, Law and Religion in Pagan Rome*, Athens, Georgia.

Wissowa, G. (1912) *Religion und Kultus der Römer*, 2nd edn, Munich.

INDEX OF SOURCES

EPIGRAPHIC SOURCES

LITERARY SOURCES

GENERAL INDEX